REASONABLY RADICAL

Reasonably Radical

DELIBERATIVE LIBERALISM
AND THE POLITICS OF IDENTITY

ANTHONY SIMON LADEN

Cornell University Press

Ithaca and London

First published 2001 by Cornell University Press

Printed in the United States of America

Library of Congress Cataloging-in-Publication Data

Laden, Anthony Simon, 1967–
    Reasonably radical : deliberative liberalism and the politics of
identity / Anthony Simon Laden.
        p. cm.
    Includes bibliographical references and index.
    ISBN 0-8014-3831-4 (alk. paper)
    1. Liberalism   2. Legitimacy of governments   3. Reason.   4. Group
identity—Political aspects.   5. Pluralism (Social sciences)   6.
Radicalism.   I. Title.
    JC574 .L33 2001
    320.51—dc21   00-012516

Cornell University Press strives to use environmentally responsible
suppliers and materials to the fullest extent possible in the publishing
of its books. Such materials include vegetable-based, low-VOC inks
and acid-free papers that are recycled, totally chlorine-free, or partly
composed of nonwood fibers. Books that bear the logo of the FSC
(Forest Stewardship Council) use paper taken from forests that have
been inspected and certified as meeting the highest standards for
environmental and social responsibility. For further information, visit
our website at www.cornellpress.cornell.edu.

Cloth printing   10 9 8 7 6 5 4 3 2 1

for Caroline

Contents

Preface

This book comes of trying to answer two questions at once. The first, rather practical question concerns the possibility of collective action. It first took shape for me in the following example: two friends with widely divergent tastes often rent movies together. Most of the time, each enters the video store with different lists of what she wants to see. On many occasions, they reach a compromise, selecting a movie that is number five for both of them rather than one that is the first choice of one but appears nowhere on the other's list. Sometimes they take turns picking their first choice with no regard to the other's preferences, or they rent two movies, each picking one. But once in a while, they emerge from the store having rented a movie they regard as their collective choice. When this happens, it is neither because their preferences coincided more than usual, nor that one of them has strong-armed the other into submission. Rather, they have come to an agreement instead of a compromise, and as a result are in a position to make a shared decision. The question is: what makes this possible, and how does it come about?

The second question arose for me through my engagement with the work of two philosophers: John Rawls and Catharine MacKinnon. I found each one's work extraordinarily compelling while I was reading it, and yet I found myself having trouble holding that impression while reading the other. In an effort to avoid falling into a kind of doctrinal schizophrenia, I started thinking about how their theories might be reconciled. You might say that I wanted to be able to go into a video store with Rawls and MacKinnon and find a movie on which we could all come to a shared decision.

ix

The initial spark that led to the present book came from the insight that solving the first problem would provide a means for addressing the second. With an understanding of how the process of reasoning together could yield shared decisions among people who differ in important respects without either ignoring or manipulating some people's interests, it would be possible to develop a liberal theory that, like Rawls's, rested political legitimacy on the process of reasonable political deliberation, and yet, like MacKinnon's, required a robust form of equality and sensitivity to group-based harms and oppression and the social construction of identity. Until someone picks up the film rights to this book, it might still not be possible for MacKinnon and Rawls to reach a shared decision about a movie to rent. My hope, however, is that they might now do better in a bookstore.

Between the initial spark of an idea and the finished book it set in motion, I have been lucky in my teachers, my readers, my friends, and my critics, and there are thus many people I wish to thank.

First and foremost of these debts is to John Rawls. The degree to which Rawls has influenced my own thinking about philosophy in general and liberalism in particular will be obvious to anyone who reads this book. I was lucky enough to be his student, and he continues to provide me with an ideal of what it is to be a philosopher and a teacher and a person. If, as a result of reading this book, some more radical thinkers are moved to return to Rawls's work and to see it in a new and more exciting light, then I will have begun to repay him the debt I owe.

Three other teachers—Amartya Sen, Christine Korsgaard, and Fred Neuhouser—have had faith in me and the possibility of this project, even when it seemed unbelievably ambitious and unwieldy. I have benefited from their wisdom, their patience, their encouragement, and their criticism. To Fred Neuhouser I owe special thanks for having read many subsequent drafts of chapters 2 and 3, even after any of his official responsibilities were long finished.

This book began in the Harvard philosophy department, where my fellow graduate students provided the kind of stimulating and supportive intellectual environment that made becoming a philosopher both possible and fun. Amongst that group, I owe particular thanks to Tamar Szabó Gendler, Talbot Brewer, and Tamar Schapiro, with whom I discussed (and continue to discuss) much of this material and much else besides.

Much of the original writing was done in Montréal, where I was warmly welcomed as an unofficial member of the philosophical community. For that welcome, I am most grateful to Ravi Chimni, Sarah Stroud, Jim Tully, and Daniel Weinstock. Jim, in particular, has gone beyond every duty of both mentor and friend. He has read every word of at least three separate versions of this project and has always shown incredible faith in its promise. I cannot imagine what this project would have looked like without his input. Daniel, too, provided valuable advice and extensive comments on an early draft, as did David Kahane. Sue Dwyer and Charles Taylor also provided helpful comments on portions of those early drafts.

Since moving to Chicago, I have been lucky enough to be a member of the Philosophy Department at the University of Illinois at Chicago, which must be the best place in the world to be a junior faculty member. It is hard to conceive of a more welcoming and nurturing place to begin a career and I am grateful to all of my colleagues for creating and sustaining such an atmosphere. I owe special thanks to Sam Fleischacker, who gave me extensive feedback on an earlier draft at a crucial point; to Peter Hylton and Charles Mills, who read large portions of the book; and especially to Bill Hart, who read over the final version on short notice and with exemplary speed and care. Sandra Bartky also gave me valuable feedback on chapter 6. Charles Chastain, Josh Gert, and Avner Baz read and commented on various versions of chapter 4. Charlotte Jackson and Valerie Brown provided administrative help at every turn. In the wider Chicago philosophical community, I owe special thanks to John Deigh, Martha Nussbaum, and Daniel Brudney for their comments on various chapters and their general support and encouragement, and to Lori Watson for proofreading.

Most of the revisions that led to the final version of the book were completed during a year I spent at the Institute for the Humanities in 1998–99. Mary Beth Rose and Linda Vavra and my fellow Fellows helped make that year astoundingly productive as well as intellectually stimulating. I am particularly grateful to Ike Balbus, who read over each chapter as it emerged from the printer and helped me to see the error of my ways on any number of issues. I am also grateful to three anonymous readers for Cornell for their comments; to Roger Haydon, for his faith, interest, advice, and help in making this book a reality; to my sister, Jennifer Laden, for the artwork on the jacket; and to Ange Romeo-Hall, Evan Young, Susan Barnett, and everyone else at Cornell who helped with editing and production.

Though this book is the product of who I am as a philosopher and has been shaped in deep and important ways by all those who have contributed to shaping me as a philosopher, it is, in less obvious but no less important ways, a product of who I am in all of my other identities and of the ways in which those identities leave me room to be a philosopher as well. I thus want to thank all those who have helped me become all those other things, from my parents, Richard Laden and Caroline Simon, on down. Maria Corral, Liana Giannoni, Janet Holzman, Ramie Graf Koch, and Sophie Pasek have been particularly important in helping me to structure my life as a

father and spouse and teacher and friend so that it also left room for thinking and writing. Jacob and Raphaël Laden-Guindon made me into a father
by coming into the world, and they make that identity a particularly joyous
one by their very different ways of being in the world. My most important
debts, however, are to Caroline Guindon. She has made me, at various times,
a husband, a father, a better man, a better person, a better philosopher, a
francophone, a Quebecker and sometime nationalist, and at all times, very
happy. She has shared in every moment and every struggle and triumph in
the writing of this book and the life that continued when the books were
closed and the computer turned off. None of it, neither the book nor the
life, would have happened without her, and it is in gratitude and admiration
and with great love that I dedicate the pages that follow to her.

Tony Laden

Chicago

REASONABLY RADICAL

1

Legitimacy and Deep Diversity

If you are reading this sentence, you live in a diverse society. If you live in a diverse society, then the question this book seeks to answer is one that concerns you. It asks how (and whether) people who live together but who otherwise may have nothing important in common can nevertheless agree to a shared form of political organization and political principles and thus legitimately structure and regulate their interactions and their lives.

Although this question is by no means new, it has taken on a new urgency in recent decades. As both political activity and political theorizing have become more inclusive of the full panoply of human diversity, older answers to this question have been found wanting, charged with relying on exclusion and assimilation to achieve their purported legitimating agreement. One theme that emerges from this critical literature is that human diversity is deep: it is not a surface phenomenon that covers over a common human core. Robust accounts of our common human nature have always erased or excluded some people. Forging legitimate political principles that neither exclude nor assimilate thus requires coming to terms with the fact of deep diversity.[1]

This coming to terms requires overcoming a pair of oppositions that recent debates, both political and philosophical, have generated. The first is between

---

1. The term "deep diversity" is Charles Taylor's. I use it to capture a view of human diversity that is not thought to stop at some common core of human nature. It is diversity that goes all the way down, as it were. Taylor introduces the term in his "Shared and Divergent Values," in *Reconciling the Solitudes*, ed. Guy LaForest (Montréal: McGill-Queen's University Press, 1993). See also Charles Taylor et al., *Multiculturalism and the Politics of Recognition*, ed. Amy Guttman (Princeton, N.J.: Princeton University Press, 1992).

"the reasonable" and "the radical." The second is between liberalism and the politics of identity. Reasonable, in these contexts, often means moderate, practical, what can be easily accomplished. It is often taken as well to be synonymous with rational where this implies unemotional, objective, distant, and universal. Liberals, at least as distinct from advocates of the politics of identity, are reasonable: they value reason, they go in for reform over revolution, and they are seen basically as defenders of the status quo modulo some tinkering around the edges. Radical, by contrast, suggests fundamental change, but also a kind of starry-eyed and thus unrealistic idealism accompanied by a failure to respect the value of existing structures. Radicals are critics and destroyers, not builders and defenders. The politics of identity is radical.

Radicals are suspicious of calls to reasonableness, seeing in them the hidden force of the authority of the status quo and a means of ruling out serious change from the beginning. Take, for example, the following passage from William Greider's indictment of contemporary U.S. politics, *Who Will Tell the People:*

> "If I represent an industry, I can always get into the argument in the Executive Branch or Congress by nature of the fact that I have money," Curtis Moore, former Republican counsel for the Senate environmental affairs committee, explained. "But if you're an environmental group, you can't get into the argument unless they want to let you in. And they're not going to let you in if they think you're crazy, if you don't think in the same terms they do. So you have to sound reasonable or you won't even get in the room. And you don't find many people in the major environmental groups who are willing to be seen as unreasonable."
>
> Moore's point is crucial to understanding the compromised performance of citizen politics. The admission ticket to the debate is: "You have to sound reasonable." The broad ranks of citizens whose own views have become "radicalized" by experience . . . will always sound "unreasonable" to the government elites. They not only won't get a seat at the table, but may conclude that the Big Ten environmentalists are in collusion too, bargaining settlements with government and business behind closed doors.[2]

Advocates of a politics of identity are similarly suspicious of and critical of liberalism, seeing the theory as fully responsible for the exclusion and assimilation that have been done in its name. They claim that liberal theories tacitly rely on strategies of exclusion and assimilation to bring about the unanimous consent both sides regard as necessary for legitimacy, often by hiding such

2. William Greider, *Who Will Tell the People* (New York: Simon and Schuster, 1992), 216.

strategies under the banner of norms of reasonableness. Many of the flash-point issues for identity politics involve matters where liberal policies fail to notice how the application of uniform standards harms particular groups.

French notions of secular, republican citizenship were charged with failing to accommodate the religious and cultural practices of Muslim citizens in what is known as *l'affaire du foulard*, in which three French schoolgirls were expelled from a public school for wearing headscarves in class in violation of French laws that prohibit the ostentatious display of religion in the classroom. Some of the girls' defenders argue that the restrictions placed on religious observance by French law are not in fact neutral but reflect an assumption that all religions resemble Christianity.[3]

Feminists who support legal regulation of pornography charge that laws guaranteeing freedom of speech fail to take account of the way in which, in certain social climates, certain forms of speech have the effect of constructing sexual roles that subjugate women. In such cases, they argue, uniform governmental noninterference in the name of freedom and equality turns out to leave women subjugated and thus neither free nor equal. Furthermore, they argue, the harm that pornography inflicts on women cannot be understood adequately unless it is seen in connection with the way women's identity is constructed in a sexist society.[4]

Quebec nationalists and some native tribes demand a greater degree of autonomy within the Canadian federation. They claim that for the federal government to treat them the same as it treats anglophone residents of Ontario in the name of liberal equality prevents them from fully participating in Canadian politics as both Canadians and members of a given tribe or a distinct province in ways their Ontarian neighbors are not prevented from participating.[5]

3. See, for instance, Anna Elisabetta Galeotti, "Citizenship and Equality: The Place for Toleration," *Political Theory* 21 (1993): 585–605; and Norma Claire Moruzzi, "A Problem with Headscarves: Contemporary Complexities of Political and Social Identity," *Political Theory* 22 (1994): 653–672. Although Moruzzi is highly critical of Galeotti, they agree on this general point.

4. The classic feminist arguments for the regulation of pornography are found in Andrea Dworkin, *Pornography: Men Possessing Women* (New York: Perigee, 1981); and Catharine MacKinnon, *Only Words* (Cambridge: Harvard University Press, 1992). See also *In Harm's Way: The Pornography Civil Rights Hearings*, eds. Catharine MacKinnon and Andrea Dworkin (Cambridge: Harvard University Press, 1997); Susan Dwyer, ed., *The Problem of Pornography* (Belmont, Calif.: Wadsworth, 1995).

5. See, among others, *Constitutional Predicament: Canada after the 1992 Referendum*, ed. Curtis Cook (Montréal: McGill-Queen's University Press, 1994), especially James Tully's "Diversity's Gambit Declined"; Taylor, "Shared and Divergent Values"; and most recently, Tully, "The Unattained Yet Attainable Democracy: Canada and Quebec Face the New Century," © Programme d'études sur le Québec, Université McGill, 2000. Tully also discusses these matters in *Strange Multiplicity: Constitutionalism in an Age of Diversity* (Cambridge: Cambridge University Press, 1995). Both issues play a substantial role in the development of Will Kymlicka's diversity-sensitive liberalism. See Kymlicka, *Liberalism, Community, and Culture* (Oxford: Clarendon Press, 1989) and *Multicultural Citizenship* (Oxford: Oxford University Press, 1995).

Things look no better for reconciliation from the other side of the divide. Champions of the reasonable see radicalism as irresponsible and ill-considered, as more likely to be dangerous and oppressive than constructive and emancipatory. Liberals, similarly, have been critical of the politics of identity, claiming that its emphasis on group identities (and ascriptive ones such as race, gender, and ethnicity at that) fails to respect sufficiently the value of individual self-determination that all liberals hold dear. Giving a place to such identities within a political theory, they worry, will threaten individual liberties by assigning people to groups without the assignees' consent. Liberals thus conclude that policies favored by advocates of a politics of identity could not meet with universal consent or be legitimate.

Perhaps the most prominent form of this criticism comes in the form of liberal complaints about the rise of political correctness. Concern with identity and the radical transformation of society is blamed for encouraging violations of individual rights and for the circumventing of due process on university campuses and in workplaces.[6] The three examples I gave of policies favored by advocates of the politics of identity are generally opposed by liberals. Displays of religion in public institutions are challenged as violating liberal neutrality and the separation of church and state.[7] The regulation of pornography is dismissed as censorship and state enforcement of a particular morality.[8] Diverse federalism and native rights are criticized as giving special privileges to some citizens over others, and thus threatening to undermine liberal commitments to equality.[9] In this context, it should come as no surprise that the staunchest Canadian defenders of the status quo on matters of federalism are in the Liberal party.

6. For a particularly strident indictment of the effects of identity politics on American campuses, see Allan Charles Kors and Harvey A. Silverglate, *The Shadow University* (New York: The Free Press, 1998). The authors describe themselves as "staunch civil libertarians" and seem to take as a premise of their argument that engaging in a politics of identity requires abandoning liberal principles. Thus, they constantly regard the incidents they catalogue and rightly find disturbing as natural outgrowths of identity politics, rather than as distortions or abuses of its claims.

7. The most famous example of this in the French case was an open letter published in *Le Nouvel Observateur* in November 1989 by five prominent leftist intellectuals, bearing the title *"Profs, ne capitulons pas"* (Teachers, don't capitulate), which began by drawing a comparison between allowing the girls to continue attending school while wearing the headscarves and the capitulation to Hitler at Munich.

8. See, for instance, Ronald Dworkin, "Liberty and Pornography," *New York Review of Books*, 21 October 1993, 12–15.

9. See, for instance, Janet Ajzenstadt, "Decline of Procedural Liberalism: The Slippery Slope to Secession," in *Is Quebec Nationalism Just?* ed. Joseph Carens (Montréal: McGill-Queen's University Press, 1995).

In this book I develop a theory I call deliberative liberalism, a form of liberalism that includes an important place for, and in fact relies on, a politics of identity. Deliberative liberalism provides a strategy for thinking about political legitimacy in the face of deep diversity. It lays out a framework in which we, as citizens, can deliberate together about the nature of the political society we inhabit together, and within which that deliberation can generate legitimate political principles without thereby requiring that we abandon our differences. The theory makes three central claims: (1) our political deliberation will confer legitimacy if it is reasonable; (2) it can only be reasonable if we can all identify ourselves and each other as fellow democratic citizens and deliberate on that basis; and (3) we can only identify ourselves in this manner if two conditions are satisfied: (a) no one has an aspect of their nonpolitical identity imposed on them, and (b) full and active participation in political deliberation as a citizen does not unduly burden the occupation of nonpolitical identities. Deliberative liberalism is reasonably radical: its commitment to radical politics develops out of its commitment to reasonable politics.

1.1. Philosophy as Defense

Philosophical projects of reconciliation tend to be overly ambitious, aiming to resolve all conflicts in the blinding glare of philosophical illumination. In the realm of liberal democratic political philosophy, this sort of ambition is a serious mistake, for two reasons. The first is that liberal democratic political philosophy oversteps its bounds if it leaves no room for politics. A society is only democratic if it is up to citizens to determine the precise nature of their political institutions. Liberal theories are sometimes charged with being antidemocratic or antipolitical because they leave too little explicit room for such self-determination.[10] This charge often assumes that philosophy or philosophers have a kind of extrapolitical authority by which they imagine their proposals taking on the force of law merely on the basis of their having affirmed them—an assumption that is plainly unwarranted. Philosophy has, at most, the authority of reason, which as Kant insisted is "no dictatorial authority; its verdict is always simply the agreement of free citizens, of whom each one must be permitted to express, without let or hindrance, his objections or even his veto."[11] Thus, the authority of philosophy

10. See, for instance, Bonnie Honig, *Political Theory and the Displacement of Politics* (Ithaca, N.Y.: Cornell University Press, 1993).
11. Immanuel Kant, *Critique of Pure Reason*, trans. Norman Kemp Smith (New York: St. Martin's Press, 1929), 593 (A738–39/B766–7).

is simply the authority of democratic politics. In this book, I approach the division of labor by distinguishing the conditions under which political deliberation can be legitimacy-conferring from the results of political deliberation, and I suggest that philosophy's role lies primarily in helping us to see clearly the former category.

The second, related reason is that political philosophers are generally not well placed to provide compelling solutions to the difficult political problems that face any complex modern society. One unavoidable lesson of the criticism launched at liberal political theory by advocates of a politics of identity is that liberal philosophers are generally blind to at least some of the ways in which their particular perspective biases their account of what neutrality and impartiality require. Leaving room for actual politics helps address the second worry as well, since particular perspectives and biases can be challenged and corrected by those who do not share them.[12]

In this book, I limit my ambitions to providing a form of what John Rawls has called a "philosophy as defense." In *Political Liberalism*, Rawls describes his own project this way and says that it shares with Kant's philosophy a sense of its mission: to provide a "defense of the possibility of a just constitutional democratic regime."[13] I also see the articulation of deliberative liberalism as engaging in philosophy as defense. Casting it in this light will help to clarify my aims in what follows.

Philosophy as defense starts from a set of assumptions that are taken to be uncontroversial and yet threatening to some possibility (the realization of the Highest Good, a just constitutional democratic regime) and aims to show that these conditions do in fact leave conceptual room for the possibility that the entity in question could exist.[14] So, for instance, what Rawls calls the fact of reasonable pluralism appears to pose a threat to certain principles of political legitimacy. If political legitimacy requires the consent of the governed, and people will only consent to principles that derive from their comprehensive conceptions of the good, then the fact that people hold an

---

12. Seyla Benhabib makes a similar point in "The Generalized and Concrete Other," in Benhabib, *Situating the Self* (New York: Routledge, 1992), though I would take issue with her reading of Rawls.

13. John Rawls, *Political Liberalism*, (New York: Columbia University Press, 1993; paperback edition, 1996) 101.

14. Kant aimed to defend both our political faith in the possibility of a just constitutional democratic regime and our ethical faith in the realizability of the highest good. Kant's strategy for defending our political faith rested on his account of the cunning of history and nature in setting out our collective path towards that goal. Rawls's defense eschews such metaphysical claims and follows more closely the approach I outline below. I am grateful to Tamar Schapiro for discussion about Kant's position.

irreconcilable and irreducible plurality of different conceptions of the good appears to threaten the possibility that a pluralistic society could ever be governed by a legitimate regime. Rawls defends the possibility of a just constitutional democratic regime by showing how the principle of legitimacy can be satisfied by a political conception of justice that does not rely on any particular comprehensive doctrine.

Rawls focuses on pluralism among comprehensive conceptions of the good. As he explicitly acknowledges, this form of pluralism is a close and direct descendant of the religious pluralism that in Europe became a significant political issue only after the Reformation and the wars of religion in the sixteenth and seventeenth centuries. He regards it as an open question whether his strategy can be extended to more contemporary problems involving race, ethnicity, and gender, although he expresses his hope and expectation that it can.[15] Deep diversity includes these differences as well as others, such as language, which I will group under the heading of differences in identity.

The worry that Rawls's question about difference of identity cannot be answered rests on the thought that the conclusions reached by the advocates of a politics of identity on the one hand and their liberal critics on the other represent the only options. The development of deliberative liberalism in this book serves to defend our reasonable faith in the possibility of a legitimate constitutional democratic regime in the face of deep diversity. Understood in this manner, that development does not claim to lay out a kind of *a priori* blueprint for an ideal society, but rather bolsters our confidence that such a society is both possible and worth pursuing. In the current philosophical and political climate, I take that to be neither a trivial nor a pointless task.

1.2. Grounds for Doubt

Consider the following four propositions:

(1) *A regime's power over one of its subjects is legitimate only if the subject consents to the principles on which the regime rests.* This democratic principle of legitimacy lies at the heart of the idea of a government by the people. I have purposely stated it in a rather vague fashion. As will become clear below, much turns on just how consent is understood.

(2) *In the utter absence of justice, there can be no legitimacy.* Legitimacy concerns the origins of political authority. Principles of legitimacy spell out the

15. Rawls, *Political Liberalism*, xxx–xxxi.

conditions under which a duly formed political authority has the proper sort of mandate to exercise its power. Justice asks rather about the content of political action or the principles on which it is based. Principles of justice tell us what a duly constituted government should do with its power, independent of whether it has the authority to do it. As a result, full justice is not a necessary condition for legitimacy. Legitimate regimes can act unjustly without thereby calling their legitimacy into question. We are no doubt all too familiar with legitimate but unjust governments. Nevertheless, at some level of injustice, legitimacy starts to waver. Thus, if it turns out that a principle of legitimacy is not only compatible with but has no tendency to prevent certain forms of injustice, then we have reason to doubt that it is in fact an adequate principle of legitimacy.[16]

(3) *Consent that relies on exclusion or assimilation does not secure legitimacy.* Exclusion involves denying a certain group of persons within a political society a voice in the shaping of that society. It thus has the effect of denying the importance of the consent of certain individuals. A political system can exclude people without explicitly disenfranchising them. Even such tacit forms of exclusion systematically deny certain groups of people an effective voice, often by creating conditions under which their voices are not heeded. Thus, for instance, many feminists argue that although women are formally granted equal status by the law in the United States and other Western democracies, they are nonetheless not treated as full persons.[17]

Assimilation can be seen as the flip side of exclusion; it involves the exclusion of behaviors or beliefs rather than of people. When assimilation is a condition of inclusion, then people who are subject to the laws of a political regime are only given a voice in the shaping of that regime if they conform themselves to certain norms of behavior, belief, or argumentation. When these norms are those of only a particular segment of the society, then other groups in the society must change in order to be included. Such people are not exactly excluded, as their voices are heeded, but they are not fully included in that they are not able to speak in what might be thought of as their "authentic" voices. As a result, when assimilation is a condition of entry, the ability of assimilated people to govern themselves in accordance with their own customs and ways is undermined.[18]

The claim that both exclusion and assimilation undermine legitimacy can

16. Rawls discusses and defends this premise in his "Reply to Habermas," reprinted in the paperback edition of *Political Liberalism*, 427–431.

17. See, for instance, Catharine MacKinnon, *Towards a Feminist Theory of the State* (Cambridge: Harvard University Press, 1989); and Carole Pateman, *Sexual Contract* (Oxford: Polity Press, 1988).

18. The phrase comes from Tully's *Strange Multiplicity*.

be further specified in a number of ways. To some degree, all regimes will rely on both of these methods in determining who has a rightful voice and what sorts of things can be said. Thus, for instance, most political theories deny a full political voice to infants and tourists, but they might differ on how to treat noncitizen immigrants and older children. Similarly, no political theory can allow all forms of utterance to carry political weight. Perhaps all theories will rule out clear gibberish, but there might be more contention about the role of narrative or myth in political debate.[19] Liberal legitimacy is threatened when exclusion and assimilation are based on distinctions that are arbitrary—and not just from the point of view of the theory being formulated. Where exactly we draw the line between arbitrary and acceptable forms of assimilation and exclusion will depend on many aspects of our political theory, however. For now it is enough to note that the claim that a regime rests on an arbitrary form of exclusion or assimilation is a charge that it has failed to meet the condition of legitimacy laid out in the first proposition.

(4) *Human societies are all characterized by deep diversity.* This diversity includes not only diversity among comprehensive conceptions of the good, but diversity of identity. I do not here claim that all aspects of identity should be considered politically relevant; I merely open the possibility that they might be.[20]

If all four of these propositions are true, then together they support doubt about the possibility of a legitimate democratic regime in the face of deep diversity. Such doubt arises because the combination of these four propositions undermines a common strategy for arguing that political principles will meet with universal consent and thus be legitimate. According to the first premise, the legitimacy of a regime requires that each of its subjects consent to at least its basic principles and procedures. From this premise, it follows that in order for the regime to be legitimate, it must secure the consent of all its subjects. According to the second proposition, the regime must also be sufficiently just. The effect of this condition is to require that the principles to which everyone must consent have more than minimal content. Mere procedural neutrality or fairness, for instance, will not be a sufficient basis for the legitimacy of a regime.

19. Iris Marion Young argues that these forms should be regarded as appropriate methods of political deliberation in "Communication and the Other: Beyond Deliberative Democracy," in *Democracy and Difference*, ed. Seyla Benhabib (Princeton, N.J.: Princeton University Press, 1996). For some criticisms of such inclusion, see Benhabib's "Towards a Deliberative Model of Democratic Legitimacy" in the same volume, 82–83.

20. In chapters 4–7 I discuss in more detail how such identity-based political claims can be formulated within deliberative liberalism.

On what basis could we conclude that a group of people would agree to the same set of substantive political principles? One popular route is to find a path to those principles from properties or beliefs that everyone is thought to have already. Unanimity thus follows from uniformity.[21] Take, for example, what is generally regarded as the Hobbesian strategy for generating unanimous consent to the authority of the government: everyone has an overwhelming interest in survival and the powers of rationality that allow them to realize that unless they all submit to the absolute authority of a political sovereign, their survival will be threatened. Since everyone starts from the same interests, the same situation, and the same knowledge and reasoning power, if one person's reasoning leads him to consent to the conditions of the absolutist state, then we can conclude that everyone will likewise consent.[22]

Establishing unanimity on the basis of uniformity allows a theorist to derive an expectation of consent to a set of political principles on the basis of the attributes that all people are held to have in common. Armed with such a derivation, the theorist then concludes that these principles satisfy the unanimous consent condition, because no matter what other attributes or capacities people have, they all have those characteristics that lead to the expectation of consent. We might then describe this strategy as taking a theoretical approach to the legitimation of political principles.

The problem is that a theoretical approach runs headlong into the fact of deep diversity, which denies that there is any sufficiently thick set of common attributes. Not only do we not share a full-blown comprehensive world view on which justification of a political system might rest, but we do not even share fundamental interests or desires or beliefs. In fact, we may not even agree about which reasons are authoritative. The fact of deep diversity presents a particularly serious obstacle in virtue of the need for political principles to be substantive. This requirement raises the standard of what kind of agreement will be sufficient to ground political legitimacy, while deep diversity lowers the starting point from which to

21. Although in what follows I discuss the version of this strategy that is employed in social contract theory, it also forms the basis of arguments for the standard rivals of social contract theory, such as utilitarianism, natural law theory, and Marxism, all of which start from certain claims about human nature.

22. Such a strategy is commonly attributed to Rawls (although on the basis of different interests and thus with a different outcome than Hobbes), most often by his critics. See, for instance, Seyla Benhabib, "The Generalized and Concrete Other" and Michael Sandel, *Liberalism and the Limits of Justice* (Cambridge: Cambridge University Press, 1982). I think this reading is deeply mistaken. I try to show why at various points throughout the book.

forge such consensus. Thus, even if it is claimed that very basic facts about us, such as our mortality and our dependence on one another and on certain materials to provide food and shelter, are universal even given the fact of deep diversity, these will turn out to be insufficient to generate compelling reasons to adopt a particular set of substantive political principles on their own. They will not, for instance, help us to choose between the very different political systems of Hobbes, Locke, Rousseau, Marx, and Mill, even if they would tell us to choose any of these over Hobbes's state of nature.

If, however, uniformity is necessary for unanimity and deep diversity denies the necessary uniformity, then the only route to unanimity is to construct the necessary uniformity in spite of deep diversity. It is at this point that the strategies of exclusion and assimilation enter the picture. [23] There are roughly two ways to find uniformity in heterogeneity: remove the non-conforming elements or alter them. Such strategies need not be done explicitly and overtly. We might, for instance, claim legitimacy for a particular political system on the basis of an argument that derives consent from certain beliefs or interests or capacities or positions incorrectly thought to be universal. In assuming that this argument meets the unanimity requirement, we are, in essence, denying the importance of the consent of those who do not share the necessary premises and thus cannot be assumed to consent as a result of these calculations. That is to say, we exclude them from the class whose consent is necessary to secure legitimacy or require them to change such that they adopt the necessary attitudes or beliefs to accept the argument. If exclusion and assimilation are necessary to the project of deriving unanimity from uniformity in the face of deep diversity, then, given the third proposition, this strategy will fail to secure legitimacy after all.[24] If we are to uphold our reasonable faith in the possibility of democratic

23. For a sample of the vast critical literature that discusses the ways in which such exclusion and assimilation take place, see Susan Okin, *Women in Western Political Thought* (Princeton, N.J.: Princeton University Press, 1979); MacKinnon, *Towards a Feminist Theory of the State*; Pateman, *The Sexual Contract*; Iris Marion Young, *Justice and the Politics of Difference* (Princeton, N.J.: Princeton University Press, 1990); Charles Mills, *The Racial Contract* (Ithaca, N.Y.: Cornell University Press, 1997); and Tully, *Strange Multiplicity*. Although all these thinkers criticize the exclusive and assimilationist tendencies of purportedly universalist and tolerant theories like liberalism, they disagree on their final diagnosis of such theories, and thus on their views of what a liberal theory would have to do to avoid these problems, and whether that would render it unrecognizable.

24. For a statement of this position along with an embrace of its conclusions (though not in these terms), see Stanley Fish, "Boutique Multiculturalism," in Arthur M. Melzer, Jerry Weinberger, and M. Richard Zinman, eds., *Multiculturalism and American Democracy* (Lawrence: The University Press of Kansas, 1998).

legitimacy in the face of deep diversity, we will need a different strategy by which to secure legitimacy. [25]

1.3. The Promise of Deliberation

Theoretical approaches to political legitimation start from within individuals and work up to political principles. Deliberative liberalism proceeds in the opposite direction: it starts with an ideal, and then asks what conditions are necessary to realize that ideal. In doing so, it adopts what I will call a political approach to legitimation. The ideal from which deliberative liberalism starts is that of political principles supported by practices and institutions that embody the shared will of citizens. If a society can be structured around political principles so grounded, then it will realize a key component of justice: the political autonomy of all citizens.[26] It will also meet the consent condition for legitimacy. The roots of deliberative liberalism lie in the political thought of Rousseau and Hegel, both of whom (as I argue in chapters 2 and 3) conceived of political legitimacy in terms of the shared will of citizens.

The question, then, is: what can serve to embody the shared will of otherwise diverse citizens? Deliberative liberalism argues that a truly shared will can only be embodied in and maintained by reasonable political deliberation. Through what I call reasonable deliberation, people who do not have any identity in common can come to share an identity and thus a will. Grounding legitimacy in deliberative endorsement thus provides a means for establishing legitimate political principles without assuming uniformity.[27] In chapter 4, I lay out a theory of reasonable deliberation that can serve this function. One of its key components is that it regards partic-

25. John Rawls's *Political Liberalism* is, I think, best read as developing such a strategy. For a sampling of other recent work on this question, see *Democracy and Difference*, ed. Seyla Benhabib; Tully, *Strange Multiplicity*; and Amy Guttman and Dennis Thompson, *Democracy and Disagreement* (Cambridge: Harvard University Press, 1996). In a somewhat different area of political philosophy, the work of Amartya Sen on the importance of thinking about inequality in terms of capabilities is in large measure motivated by a concern for respecting diversity. See Sen, *Inequality Reexamined* (Cambridge: Harvard University Press, 1992).

26. Rawls distinguishes political from ethical autonomy in *Political Liberalism*, 77–81. Citizens realize their political autonomy when they act from principles of justice they would give to themselves under appropriate conditions.

27. In this sense, deliberative liberalism agrees in large measure with Henry Richardson's account of deliberative democracy. See, for instance, his "Democratic Intentions," in *Deliberative Democracy*, eds. James Bohman and William Rehg (Cambridge: MIT Press, 1997).

ular aspects of our practical identities as the ground for the authority of reasons.[28]

With a general theory of reasonable deliberation in place, we can focus on the special case of political deliberation. Deliberative liberalism conceives of political deliberation as the deliberation of citizens and claims that in order for such deliberation to be reasonable, its participants must exchange only public reasons, those reasons that are authoritative for us insofar as we are citizens. At the heart of deliberative liberalism, then, is a picture of reasonable political deliberation among citizens. Chapter 5 discusses political deliberation and sets out a conception of citizenship that follows from the role citizens play in legitimating political principles by engaging in reasonable political deliberation across diverse nonpolitical identities.

We can then take another step backward, and ask whether there are other conditions that must be met if political deliberation is to be reasonable. If it is the reasonableness of deliberation that generates legitimacy, then such deliberation must be fully open to all citizens. In other words, exclusion and assimilation undermine the legitimacy of political principles precisely because they undermine the reasonableness of political deliberation. It must be possible, then, for citizens to object to policies or practices that exclude or assimilate them, and for that objection to make a difference in the further deliberation of their fellow citizens. Chapters 6 and 7 investigate the ways in which exclusion and assimilation undermine the reasonableness of deliberation and suggest how citizens can formulate public reason arguments that resist policies and practices that foster exclusion and assimilation.

Chapter 6 investigates various forms of exclusion and argues that they rely on the way certain forms of power, when distributed asymmetrically, allow some people to impose particular practical identities on others. As a result of such identity imposition, some people cannot relate to other members of their society as fellow citizens. They are thus excluded from political deliberation, and consequently that deliberation cannot be reasonable. Reciprocal levels of constructive power give groups the wherewithal to resist identity imposition effectively. Thus, deliberative liberalism avoids exclusion by recognizing arguments in favor of reciprocal levels of social power and against the conditions that permit exclusion as invoking valid public reasons.

Chapter 7 investigates pressures to assimilate and argues that reasonable political deliberation requires that the identity we share as citizen not place

28. I borrow the term "practical identity" from Christine Korsgaard. See her *Sources of Normativity* (Cambridge: Cambridge University Press, 1996), 100–113. Korsgaard also connects the authority of reasons to practical identities, and I have learned a great deal from her on these topics. For some differences in our accounts, see chapter 4.

undue burdens on our ability to occupy our nonpolitical identities. Taking part in political deliberation requires exchanging public reasons, and obeying this requirement is tantamount to taking up the identity of a citizen. If, then, the identity of citizen sits ill with some other aspect of my identity, then in order to take part in political deliberation I may have to abandon that aspect of who I am or what I value, or at least keep it fenced off. Such a demand is, however, nothing less than the demand that I assimilate nonpolitical aspects of my identity to a given range in order to participate in political deliberation. By requiring that citizenship remain nonburdensome, deliberative liberalism avoids reliance on assimilation to achieve a shared will. Once again, it does so by recognizing a set of reasons (here reasons of burdensomeness) as valid public reasons. Recognizing the reasonableness of arguments against exclusion and assimilation means that deliberative liberalism includes space for the radical demands of a politics of identity.

One consequence of this backwards derivation is that much is left theoretically open. Deliberative liberalism can generate real democratic legitimacy without exclusion or assimilation, but only if citizens are motivated to act reasonably and in good faith in political deliberation. We cannot, however, presume ahead of time that people will be so moved, and their failure to be so moved cannot serve as grounds for excluding or assimilating them. A full defense of our reasonable faith in the possibility of a legitimate democratic regime requires providing grounds for thinking it likely that a deliberatively liberal regime could generate its own support. We must thus address what I call the problem of stability. Doing so adds an extra dimension to the defense of our reasonable faith. The argument that develops in chapters 4 through 7 shows that a legitimate democratic regime is a theoretical possibility. Addressing the problem of stability shows that it is more than a mere theoretical possibility, that in a world like ours one of the effects of reasonable political deliberation is that citizens become more, and not less, reasonable. If deliberative liberalism is stable, then we have good reason not only to have a kind of abstract faith in the possibility of a certain kind of desirable political society, but to work to bring about such a society by taking here and now the first steps toward its realization. I take up the stability of deliberative liberalism in chapter 8.

1.4. Defining Terms: Liberalism and the Politics of Identity

Having set out the sweep of the argument of the book, and having indicated how the strategy I pursue can overcome the grounds for doubt I rehearsed above, I want to return to the conflict between liberalism and the politics of identity, to set out more clearly how I am understanding each of these terms and the precise sense in which deliberative liberalism can be understood as being both liberal and an appropriate home for the politics of identity.

1.4.1. Liberalism

For a theory to be liberal, it must, of course, provide grounds for the strong protection of a familiar set of basic individual rights and liberties for all. However, I take the fundamental commitment of liberal theory to be the claim that political authority derives from reason. It is the combination of these two commitments that has made liberalism a prime opponent of the advocates of a politics of identity. Nevertheless, there are many ways of making good on these commitments, and it will be helpful to distinguish them at the outset so as to mark out more clearly where deliberative liberalism fits into the liberal landscape. Deliberative liberalism is a form of political liberalism in two different but related senses: it is political in scope and in approach. The sense of being political in scope is the more familiar of the two, as it is central to Rawls's characterization of his own account of political liberalism.[29] A liberal theory is political in scope if it is not comprehensive, if instead of providing an overarching theory of human nature or the human good it merely sets out an account of a legitimate liberal regime that draws on only political values for its inputs, and generates only political principles as its output. The central motivation for adopting such a restriction in scope is to address the fact of reasonable pluralism. Whereas the liberalisms of Kant, Mill, Dworkin, Raz, and Kymlicka are comprehensive in scope, Rawls's political liberalism, along with many other variations on its general themes, is political in scope.[30] Deliberative liberalism is political in this sense, but no less liberal for being so.

But it is important to note that there is another way in which a liberal theory can be political: in what I called above its approach.[31] Liberal theories that take a theoretical approach to legitimation derive political principles

29. Rawls, *Political Liberalism*, xx–xxx, xxxvii–xlii.
30. See, for instance, Immanuel Kant, *The Metaphysics of Morals*, trans. Mary Gregor (Cambridge: Cambridge University Press, 1991); John Stuart Mill, *On Liberty*, ed. Currin V. Shields (New York: Liberal Arts Press, 1956); Ronald Dworkin, *Taking Rights Seriously* (Cambridge: Harvard University Press, 1977); Joseph Raz, *The Morality of Freedom* (Oxford: Clarendon Press, 1986); and Kymlicka, *Liberalism, Community, and Culture*.
31. Fred D'Agostino makes something like this distinction in his *Free Public Reason: Making It Up as We Go* (New York: Oxford University Press, 1996), arguing that only a political conception of public justification could be adequate to a plural society. While I do not agree with the details of his account of public reason, I do agree with his general point.

from theoretical considerations about the nature of human beings (if they are also comprehensive) or about the nature of democratic citizenship or political relations (if they are political in the first sense). What distinguishes such approaches is that the reasoning of the theorist serves to determine the shape of the political principles the theory defends. What ultimately justifies such principles, according to the theory's own self-understanding, then, is the soundness of the theorist's reasoning.

In contrast, political theories that take a political approach argue that what justifies political principles is ultimately the endorsement (in some suitably defined sense) of actual people acting politically in actual societies. Such an approach must, therefore, leave a great deal open to the activity of politics itself. Nevertheless, such theories need not be completely formal or procedural. Even when taking a political approach, we need to work out what sort of endorsement could serve to justify political principles, and perhaps whether there are any structural features a society must have if its citizens are to be capable of (individually and collectively) providing that sort of endorsement.

A liberal theory that takes a political approach claims that among the preconditions necessary for people to confer legitimacy on political principles through their endorsement are the standard bundle of liberal protections of basic rights and liberties. Whereas theoretical liberalism attempts to justify the basic liberties as what suitably theorized citizens would endorse, political liberalism justifies the basic liberties as being among the necessary conditions for real citizens to be capable of conferring legitimacy through their actual endorsement. Much criticism of liberals from radically democratic quarters gains its plausibility, it seems to me, from a failure to recognize the possibility of a liberal theory that is political in approach.[32]

While theoretical approaches are much more common in political philosophy (some might even argue that such an approach is constitutive of a theory being a work of political philosophy), there are both historical and contemporary examples of political approaches to political theory, some of which are recognizably liberal. As I argue in chapters 2 and 3, there is a way of understanding Rousseau and Hegel as having adopted something like a political approach. Among contemporary theorists, perhaps James Tully is the most explicit exemplar of the political approach.[33] Rawls's

32. D'Agostino makes this point in *Free Public Reason*, 121–130. For an example of such criticism, see Jürgen Habermas, "Reconciliation through the Public Use of Reason: Some Remarks on John Rawls's Political Liberalism," *Journal of Philosophy* 92 (March 1995): 109–131.

33. See Tully, *Strange Multiplicity*. Though in that work Tully takes himself to be a critic of liberalism, he has in more recent writings come to articulate his position as a form of liberalism. See, for instance, "Democratic Constitutionalism in a Diverse Federation," in *Ideas in Action: Essays in Politics and Law in Honor of Peter Russell*, eds. Joseph Fletcher and Jennifer Nedelsky

political liberalism is also best understood as taking such an approach.[34] Deliberative liberalism too is political in this second sense. It thus justifies the protection of basic liberties in a somewhat indirect way, as among the necessary preconditions for the possibility of reasonable political deliberation.

Insofar as it takes a political approach, deliberative liberalism aims to set out the framework in which political deliberation can fruitfully and justly take place, rather than to argue for one or another set of specific policy proposals. In this sense, it is not best thought of as a competitor with either comprehensive liberalism on the one hand or theories of identity politics on the other. Rather, it is aimed at the prior question of whether there is a framework in which the questions of both sides in this debate can be taken up in terms that each side could accept. The answer it provides is that there is such a framework: the framework that makes possible reasonable political deliberation among democratic citizens.

This has important consequences for the status of the examples I use throughout the book to illustrate the kinds of arguments that could find a foothold in the principles of deliberative liberalism. They are not meant to serve as policy recommendations or even predictions of what policies would emerge from reasonable political deliberation. They are meant merely to illustrate how certain kinds of arguments commonly made by liberals and advocates of a politics of identity, and commonly dismissed by their opponents, could find a foothold in deliberative liberalism. Of course, between finding such a foothold and making a suitably convincing case before one's fellow citizens there is a lot of work to be done, both conceptual and empirical. I do not even pretend to do such work in this book.

1.4.2. The Politics of Identity

I take the politics of identity to claim that aspects of a person's identity (and in particular her identity as a member of some group or other) not reducible to such standard political categories as interest, preference, income, or class are nonetheless of political significance, and that justice thus demands that arguments for political policies that rest on claims about such identity

---

(Toronto: University of Toronto Press, 1999); "Multicultural and Multinational Citizenship," in *The Demands of Citizenship*, eds. Iain Hampsher-Monk and Catriona McKinnon (London: Continuum International, 2000); "Struggles over Recognition and Distribution," *Constellations* 7 (2000): 469–482.

34. Although I do not explicitly argue for such a claim here or anywhere else in the book, one could read my frequent use of Rawls's work to set out my own account as the basis for such an argument.

aspects be taken seriously within political debate and political theorizing. I understand the politics of identity in much the same way that Iris Marion Young describes the politics of difference, which she distinguishes from the politics of identity.[35]

Young argues that what she calls the politics of identity gets into trouble with its characterization of groups by a set of essential characteristics. Among other things, this approach obscures the diversity within groups, makes groups appear to be the result of natural or inevitable facts about humans, leaves the politics of identity in the position of seeming to deny human freedom and agency, and leads to a politics of division and mutual antagonism, with everyone vying for special rights and privileges on the basis of membership in one group or another. In contrast, what she describes as the politics of difference characterizes groups relationally, in terms of the social positions their members occupy in virtue of their membership in the group. Since people can differ in all sorts of ways and yet occupy similar social positions, this approach need not deny intragroup diversity. Since it ties groups to social structures rather than to essential characteristics, it makes clear their socially constructed nature. And since a person's social position can shape her alternatives without fully determining her actions, it leaves room for human agency.

Furthermore, the politics of identity attempts to locate the political significance of social group membership in the fact of common interests among group members, whereas Young's politics of difference argues that the political relevance of social groups consists in their providing members with a shared perspective on the social system. How one forms interests from a particular perspective is also a matter of individual agency and self-constitution. Nevertheless, people who share a perspective are likely to share a sense of what is politically alienating, what harmful, what beneficial, and so forth, and are in some cases not likely to be able to see things from opposed perspectives without some work.[36] That work, however, involves listening to others with humility and respect. As a result, for the politics of difference, difference becomes a resource for fostering democratic communication and unity rather than an obstacle to it.

35. Young discusses the "politics of difference" at great length in her *Justice and the Politics of Difference*. She distinguishes the politics of identity from the politics of difference most clearly in "Difference as a Resource for Democratic Communication," in *Deliberative Democracy*.

36. The ways in which social structures can shape perspectives has been a long-running theme in feminist scholarship, particularly in work in feminist epistemology. It is also beginning to find expression with regard to other forms of difference, such as race. See, for instance, Charles Mills, "Alternative Epistemologies," in *Blackness Visible* (Ithaca, N.Y.: Cornell University Press, 1997).

I follow Young in conceiving of social identities relationally, and in understanding their importance in a manner that does not deny the importance of individual agency and self-constitution. In particular, I will argue that the political significance of ascriptive social aspects of our identities is that they constrain our ability to form reciprocal political relationships with people in other groups, and thus undermine the possibility that all citizens can deliberate reasonably together. That is, certain social structures (including, for instance, those in current U.S. society that set out racial and gender identities) stand in the way of reasonable political deliberation because they prevent some members of a political society from relating to other members of the society as citizen to citizen. In saying this, I claim neither that these aspects of our social identity determine our interests or behaviors, nor that they are politically relevant only when taken up as important by individual group members. When members of social groups object to the social structure that determines their group membership, then, they are making a first personal claim (they are being prevented from forming relationships they have reasons to form) on the basis of their ascribed identity (it is in virtue of this identity and the social position that comes with it that they are so prevented). I argue both that this claim is recognizably liberal and that it recognizably invokes the politics of identity.

Though I follow Young's understanding of groups and their relation to identity, I do not follow her shift of terminology. Partially, this is a matter of taste. The term "politics of identity" has a certain resonance that I want to hold onto. It expresses the sense that aspects of our identity are of political significance whether or not they can be reduced to categories like interest and preference. In addition, "difference" calls to mind (at least to my mind) structural features, rather than qualities of individuals. I may be different from others in a whole host of ways, but I am not, on my own, different. Thus, to talk of a politics of difference has the rhetorical effect of leaving individuals behind (even if it is designed explicitly to do the opposite). On the other hand, I do have an identity all on my own (even if, as I argue in chapter 4, my identity is in large part constituted by the relationships I form and those in which I stand). Talking of the politics of identity, then, serves to highlight individuals in their particularity rather than to submerge them, if only rhetorically, under the weight of social structures. I thus stick with the older, albeit more abused, term.

1.5. In Defense of Philosophy

The problems the fact of deep diversity presents to a society that grounds the legitimacy of its political authority on the consent of its citizens are both profound and very concrete. As the examples at the beginning of this chapter and throughout this book remind us, the question of how to understand ourselves as coequal members of society without thereby erasing the variety of ways in which we differ from one another lies at the center of some of the most hotly contested and difficult political issues of this, or any, day. Political philosophy cannot on its own offer definitive solutions to these problems: these issues must be addressed in the course of actual political deliberation and activity in which philosophers and others participate as equal citizens, not as authoritative experts. This conclusion thus raises a question about the point of engaging in the philosophical project that occupies the rest of the book. If philosophy cannot, on its own, answer these questions, then what can it do? What is the point of engaging in abstract reasoning about the structure of justification and deliberation and identity if, in the end, we must still turn to politics and hash things out with our fellow citizens?

Philosophy as defense heads off doubts that can serve to undermine our faith in legitimate liberal democracy. Why, we may ask, should it matter that we have such faith, or that it have firm and reasonable grounds? There are two related answers to that question, and together they help to provide a clear picture of the value of the kind of abstract political philosophy in which this book engages. First of all, a society where the fact of deep diversity erodes people's faith in the possibility of legitimate liberal democratic government is not likely to have a liberal democratic government for long, if at all. In the absence of such reasonable faith, citizens will at best pay lip service to the ideals of liberal democracy, and will not be willing to make the sacrifices that are often necessary to make democracy work. A society where such faith is lacking will be increasingly a society marked by political disillusionment and alienation, and will thus be ripe pickings for demagogues of all sorts. Furthermore, if deep diversity is seen as the source of this problem for liberal democracy, then those who are seen as different, as visible representatives of the diversity of the society, are more likely to be blamed for the increasing fragmentation and alienation of society. The chances that such people will be treated with due respect as equals will become ever smaller. No doubt some people will recognize their own societies in these descriptions, as I too often recognize mine. Those who are more sanguine about the current status of political faith in their societies can think of historical examples where lack of political faith was widespread, such as Weimar Germany, to see the potential value of a philosophy that bolsters reasonable faith in the possibility of legitimate liberal democratic government.[37]

There is a second reason for engaging in philosophy as defense. While having reasonable faith is necessary, it may not help us figure out how to act politically here and now. For instance, we may not doubt that liberal democracy is possible under conditions of deep diversity, yet still be unsure of how to support particular policies we favor, or of how to enter properly into political debate. We might not realize that certain types of interventions serve to weaken the very basis of legitimate liberal democracy. Faced with fellow citizens who do not share our habits and ways of thought, or our deepest interests and concerns, we may not know how to begin deliberating with them as citizens. We may be tempted to gather up as much power as possible and push through as much of our agenda as we can, or to rely only on reasons that rest on aspects of our identities we do not share with our fellow citizens.[38]

In articulating deliberative liberalism even at this abstract level, I hope to provide some general guidance in these questions. Whether or not we think that our own society is a legitimate liberal democratic one, having faith in the possibility of such a regime and seeing it as an ideal to pursue can guide the ways we enter into political debate. So, for instance, understanding the point of public reason can help us to refrain from urging what we see as the whole truth on matters of fundamental political importance if doing so would violate the ideal of public reason. Seeing the role played by arguments in favor of reciprocal levels of power or against the burdensomeness of citizenship gives us a way to argue against certain policies in public reason terms and can help us to take more seriously arguments others make on the basis of these concerns.

Marx famously complained that philosophers had only interpreted the world, and that the task now was to change it. Philosophy on its own merely interprets the world. Political philosophy is no different in this regard: it can help us to understand the political world we make together through political action, but to change that world requires political action. Nevertheless, political philosophy helps to remake the political world

37. Rawls makes a similar point in *Political Liberalism*, lxi–lxii.
38. These seem to be the strategies Fish suggests in his "Boutique Multiculturalism." He argues that all forms of multiculturalism must draw a line of exclusion at the differences that really matter. Acknowledging this fact leads him to the conclusion that we should be more honest about what we are doing, and should openly describe those who fall on the other side of our line as our enemies, against whom all available means should be used to limit their numbers and influence.

when it guides us in action, by helping us to see more clearly what possibilities exist, and perhaps in general terms what the path toward them looks like. Deliberative liberalism, conceived as a form of philosophy as defense, aims to provide such guidance by providing an interpretation of liberal legitimacy that puts it back on the map of possibilities, even in the face of deep diversity.

2

Rousseau

The problems to which deliberative liberalism responds are not new. Deep diversity has characterized all human societies. In many times and places, to be sure, it has been met with attempts at homogenization via repression, exclusion, or assimilation. The accommodation of diversity is not, however, an invention of the late twentieth century, even if real success at such accommodation will have to wait for the twenty-first.

Nor is the question of how to bring unity out of plurality without imposing uniformity a new problem for political philosophy. It goes back at least to Plato's *Republic*, arguably the founding text of political philosophy. In recent centuries, as what James Tully describes as the language of "modern constitutionalism" has become dominant, much of political philosophy, including much liberal thought, has assumed or imposed uniformity in an attempt to promote unity.[1] Nevertheless, the tradition includes figures who have argued against these homogenizing assumptions and their resulting programs. Two of these figures in particular, Jean-Jacques Rousseau and G.W.F. Hegel, address questions very similar to those that motivate the development of deliberative liberalism, and their theories mirror deliberative liberalism in important ways. Rousseau worried about the possibility of legitimate government given modern conditions. Although he did not explicitly address issues of diversity, he did, for other reasons, develop a method of arguing for political principles that did not rely exclusively on

---

1. James Tully, *Strange Multiplicity: Constitutionalism in an Age of Diversity* (Cambridge: Cambridge University Press, 1995), esp. chap. 3.

23

either a theory of human nature or fundamental interests. His work thus develops many of the resources on which deliberative liberalism relies, including a conception of human reason that stresses reasonableness as well as rationality, a conception of consent based on reason rather than interest, and the idea of a shared will along with attention to the conditions necessary for its formation and maintenance.

Hegel was more explicitly concerned with questions of forging unity out of plurality. He took up many of Rousseau's ideas and developed them further. Hegel provides a more detailed articulation of the idea of reasonableness and its connection to human freedom and the legitimacy of political principles. His justification of political principles is more thoroughly freed from a theory of fundamental human interests or human nature than Rousseau's. In addition, Hegel brings questions of identity to the foreground of his discussion, and thus points out a path by which a politics of identity can find expression in a politics of reason, such as liberalism.

This chapter and the next can be thought of as rehearsals for the arguments that occupy the rest of the book.[2] By beginning my development of deliberative liberalism with an exploration of the political thought of Rousseau and Hegel, I hope to ease the reader into a conceptual landscape that may not be familiar. Although I regard deliberative liberalism as a clearly recognizable form of liberalism, it does not share many of its conceptual foundations with much of contemporary liberal theory. Unless its foundations are clearly laid out, much that is of interest in the view will be misunderstood. The contrast between deliberative liberalism and more familiar forms of liberal theory is most easily brought out by focusing on their respective historical roots.

Contemporary liberal thought generally conceives of itself as historically rooted in the thought of Locke, Kant, and Mill. On this view of the history of liberal thought, Rousseau and Hegel, if they are discussed at all, are viewed as somewhat contrarian figures whose politics are at best not reliably liberal, and at worst thoroughly antiliberal.[3] Deliberative liberalism, in contrast, traces its roots back to Rousseau and Hegel. Surveying their thought

2. As with any rehearsals, these chapters involve repetition. Readers impatient with such repetition can skip directly to chapter 4 without missing any of the plot. Readers who think of reading a work of philosophy as more like acting in a play than watching one may find that these rehearsals help prepare them for the later chapters.

3. Although few contemporary liberals see themselves as heirs to Rousseau and Hegel, there is an older liberal tradition, represented by figures like T. H. Green, that traces its roots back to Hegel. Such a connection is also still commonplace in much Hegel scholarship. See, for instance, Kenneth Westphal, "The Structure and Context of Hegel's Philosophy of Right," in *The Cambridge Companion to Hegel*, ed. Fred Beiser (Cambridge: Cambridge University Press, 1993).

prior to setting out the details of deliberative liberalism will help to bring out its distinctive features more clearly. In addition, in these relatively abbreviated discussions it will be easier to keep large structural issues in view in a way that will be more difficult when we move to the details of deliberative liberalism in subsequent chapters.

In this chapter, I examine Rousseau's theory, focusing primarily on his account of political legitimacy. I lay out the importance of his conception of humans as reasonable and how this provides him with a new way of understanding consent-based legitimacy. I then distinguish two argumentative strands within his theory and show how they intertwine and what is at stake in the adoption of each.

2.1. Rousseau's Project

Of the Social Contract, Rousseau's central work of political philosophy, begins with a question about the possibility of legitimate government: "I want to inquire whether in the civil order there can be some legitimate and sure rule of administration, taking men as they are, and the laws as they can be."[4] His project is related to mine on two fundamental tracks. First, Rousseau sets himself the task of establishing the possibility of a legitimate political regime. He asks whether there *can* be such a regime. In this sense, he is engaged in a project of philosophy as defense: giving us grounds for faith by demonstrating that a legitimate regime is possible. Philosophy as defense, I suggested in chapter 1, involves a defense against particular grounds for doubt. Rousseau suggests the nature of those grounds in the passage above. A legitimate administration must take "men as they are, and laws as they might be." In order to understand Rousseau's defense, then, we will have to understand why our current characteristics raise doubts about the possibility of our forming a legitimate government.

Doing so leads us to the second connection, which is less strong. A central tenet of Rousseau's philosophy is that we are no longer fully natural

4. Jean-Jacques Rousseau, *Of the Social Contract*, in *The Social Contract and Other Later Political Writings*, trans. and ed. Victor Gourevitch (Cambridge: Cambridge University Press, 1997), Book I, Introduction, ¶1; *Oeuvres complètes*, eds. B. Gagnebin and M. Raymond (Paris: Pléiade, 1959–1995), 3.351; LW, 41. In what follows, I will refer to passages from this work by SC followed by book, chapter, and paragraph number; then by OC (for *Oeuvres complètes*), volume and page number; and finally by LW (for Later Writings) and page number. Passages from Rousseau's *Discourse on Inequality*, published in *The Discourses and Other Early Political Writings*, trans. and ed. Victor Gourevitch (Cambridge: Cambridge University Press, 1997), will be referred to by DI, followed by section and paragraph number; then OC and page number; and finally EW (for early Writings) and page number.

creatures—the differences between us and the inhabitants of the state of nature he describes in the *Discourse on Inequality* are so great as to amount to a difference in kind. By denying that human nature comprises a constant and unchanging set of capacities and interests, Rousseau thus raises questions about the possibility of deriving norms of justice from human nature, as Locke and Hobbes and indeed the whole modern natural law tradition had tried to do.[5] Although Rousseau ultimately relies on a theory of fundamental human interests to do some of the work in justifying the system he defends, the problems he raises with such a strategy bear important resemblances to the problems posed by the fact of deep diversity.

2.2. Reasonableness and the Capacity for Self-Rule

In the *Discourse on Inequality*, Rousseau discusses a number of ways in which we differ from the inhabitants of the state of nature: we have a variety of capacities and needs that they do not. We live in society, use language, have reason and they do not. We depend on others to satisfy both physical and psychological needs and they do not. To a large degree, all of these differences can be traced to our being creatures of reason whereas the inhabitants of the state of nature are not.[6] For our purposes, the important element of Rousseau's view of reason is the way reason makes possible forms of social organization by altering our capacity for willing. This aspect of reason is related to what Kant called pure practical reason; I will describe it here as that which makes us "reasonable."[7] It allows us to act on the basis of considerations that do not ultimately connect to our desires.

5. Thomas Hobbes, *Leviathan*, ed. Richard Tuck (Cambridge: Cambridge University Press, 1991); John Locke, *Second Treatise of Government*, ed. C. B. MacPherson (Indianapolis: Hackett, 1980). For other figures in the modern natural law tradition, see Hugo Grotius, *On the Law of War and Peace*, trans. Francis W. Kelsey (Oxford: Oxford University Press, 1925), esp. the "Prolegomena"; and Samuel Pufendorf, *On the Duty of Man and Citizen*, trans. Michael Silverthorne, ed. James Tully (Cambridge: Cambridge University Press, 1991).

6. For instance, at DI, 1.21; OC, 3.144; EW, 143. Rousseau, of course, does not claim that the inhabitants of the state of nature lack all abilities that might be thought to require reason. They have, for instance, the ability to imitate others. Nevertheless, it is crucial to Rousseau's account that reason in the sense I articulate in this section is something that develops in us through social interaction and is thus not a natural endowment of human beings.

7. Note, however, that Rousseau's conception of reason does not involve the element of "purity" that is so important to Kant. Practical reason, for Rousseau, while it allows us to rule our desires is nevertheless intimately and intricately related to them. The central point of comparison with Kant is the way reason for Rousseau, and pure practical reason for Kant, demonstrate that we have what I call below a two-level psychic structure, with a reason-guided will ruling over our otherwise unorganized desires.

In most of the passages where Rousseau discusses the development of reason, he complains of it, and endeavors to show what a detrimental effect it
has. It is important, however, to look beyond his rhetoric to see what reason
does and thus what he takes reason to be. In the *Discourse on Inequality*, for
example, he claims that pity is the source of all the social virtues, and adds
that the identification on which pity rests "must, clearly, have been infinitely
closer in the state of Nature than in the state of reasoning." Reason, he goes
on to say, "separates [social man] from everything that troubles and afflicts
him." As a result, the philosopher can stifle pity: "he only has to put his
hands over his ears and to argue with himself a little in order to prevent
Nature which rebels within him, from letting him identify with the man
being assassinated."[8]

Pity, being a natural sentiment, works more or less automatically: it is
produced by our sense of similarity with the one suffering and the apparent
extent of her suffering. Reason, Rousseau here claims, gets in the way of the
automatic functioning of pity, its ability to produce action (or at least emo-
tion) directly. This point suggests that in a creature of reason no natural
sentiments automatically and directly lead to action. If we take the will as
the source of action, the consequence of becoming reasonable can then be
put in terms of a separation between will and desire. It is the separation
between will and desire that accounts for reason's ability to "separate" us
from "everything that troubles and afflicts" us. Such a separation is also
essential to the capacity to form shared wills and thus to secure political
legitimacy.

The separation reason effects is not the whole story, however. In distinguishing the will from our desires, the acquisition of reason also deeply
changes our psychic structure. In fact, it provides us with a coherent psychic
structure for the first time. Reason not only distances us from our natural
desires, but, Rousseau claims, "turns man back upon himself."[9] Elsewhere,
he concludes that it is reason that "eventually makes him his own and
Nature's tyrant."[10] Note, however, that being a tyrant requires being a ruler,
and being a ruler requires that there be a structure that admits of having a
ruler and being ruled. I cannot become the tyrant of the weather patterns
because I cannot exert any authority over them. The problem is not that the
weather will rebel against arbitrary rule, but that it is not capable of submit-
ting to any rule whatsoever.

The inhabitants of the state of nature, prior to the development of reason,

8. DI, 1.37; OC, 3.155–156; EW, 153.
9. Ibid.
10. DI, 1.17; OC, 3.142; EW, 141.

are like the weather. They are not capable of being ruled by others (Rousseau makes much of this point), but this is less a result of their fiercely independent spirit than because they are not capable of being ruled at all, or of being organized by some authoritative principle. The inhabitants of the state of nature have a set of natural desires, each of which corresponds to an easily satisfiable need. When these desires arise, they lead to action. As we saw in the case of pity, these desires and sentiments yield action more or less directly. Since the connection between desire and action is direct, since there is no separation between desire and will, the inhabitants of the state of nature are capable of neither concerted collective action, nor organized long-term planning.[11] To put the point in strong terms, the inhabitants of the state of nature are not really selves at all, but merely loci of desires, sentiments, and other natural impulses.

Reason creates the conditions for self-rule by making us into proper selves to begin with, and thus shapes what it is to be a self. At the end of his essay on *The State of War*, Rousseau writes that the "body politic, since it is only a moral person, is only a being of reason." He goes on to say that as a result, there is a sense in which all the constituent parts of the state—the land, the people, the goods—do not really belong to it, and that the state can be destroyed by destroying the "public convention" without the "least change for the worse in anything which makes it up."[12] Notice two things about these claims. First, the reason that constitutes the state is something over and above its constituent parts. This claim fits together with my conclusions about reason in the individual. Reason is something over and above our desires, an extra psychic layer, as it were. Nevertheless, it is in virtue of reason, whether in the state or the individual, that the lower level (the desires in the individual, the people, land, and goods in the state) are somehow part of the whole. In the case of the individual, reason constitutes a self out of the mêlée of our desires; it is in virtue of my having reason that these desires come to be truly mine, even when I choose not to act on them.[13]

11. On the incapacity for collective action, see DI, 2.9; OC, 3.166–167; EW, 163 where Rousseau claims that were a group of these creatures to organize a collective effort to catch a deer, any one of them would abandon his post were a rabbit to wander by. On the incapacity for foresight, see DI, 1.21; OC, 3.144; EW, 143, where Rousseau cites the Carib who sells his bed in the morning unaware that he will need it again that night.

12. Rousseau, "The State of War," ¶57; OC, 3.608; LW, 176.

13. Although Rousseau offers an account in the *Discourse on Inequality* of the development of human agency through the development of reason, I do not mean to be pointing toward or endorsing that story here. My interest is limited to the structure of human agency once it has developed and the place reason occupies in that structure. I use the verb "constitute" in this connection despite this ambiguity because of its clear and, to my mind, important political resonances.

Rousseau is here making the same point about the state: what makes the things "included within the confines of the state [belong] to it without reservation"[14] is what constitutes the state as a moral person: its reason.

The second point takes us further. In this passage Rousseau identifies reason with the public convention, the social contract. This identification points toward an understanding of reason as something akin to pure practical reason, the set of claims that have the authority to determine a will, whether individual or general. The public convention lays out the structure and content of legitimate authority within the state. It tells us what claims are valid and when. We might say that it serves to set out what constitutes reasons before the state. If the public convention is identified with reason, then it suggests that reason must perform these roles in the individual. Reason, that is, tells us what claims are legitimate—what claims we ought to regard as reasons, as having some claim to authority over our actions.[15]

In establishing both a united self and a structure of legitimate authority, reason makes it possible for us to be ruled and for us to rule ourselves, both individually and collectively. Reasonable creatures have a distinctive psychic structure. They need not act on their desires. They can act on the basis of reasons, of claims made by others or by other parts of themselves that they regard as authoritative. On top of the layer of desires, characterized by the interplay of force, is the layer of will, characterized by the interplay of reasons. The action of reasonable creatures is a result of their will, which is determined at the level of reasons. If we identify ourselves both with our will and with our desires, then we can see how this psychic structure will make it possible for us to rule over ourselves: our will governs the satisfaction of our desires.

Since reason both establishes our psychic structure and determines our actions, it can be both essential to our humanity (and what Kant called our dignity) and the source of our degradation. As creatures of reason, we are endowed with a psychology that makes us capable of both self-rule and rule by others, but such rule can be just or not, good for us or not. Rousseau heaps scorn on reason because he thinks our reason develops in contexts that lead us to misuse its authority. If some of our desires, at least our natural desires, are good for us, and have a legitimate claim to satisfaction, then when reason remains deaf to their claims, its rule descends into tyranny.

14. Rousseau, "The State of War," ¶57; OC, 3.608; LW, 176.

15. For a more detailed discussion of the connection between Rousseau's conception of reason and that of Kant, and the role reason plays for both thinkers in "legislation" and "constitution," see Andrews Reath, "Legislating the Moral Law," *Noûs* 27 (1994): 435–464.

But—and this is the point I want to emphasize—reason can only lead us to tyrannize ourselves because it makes it possible for us to rule ourselves.[16]

2.3. Legitimacy and Consent

Rousseau's conception of reason provides the resources for a new way of conceiving of consent-based legitimacy. Rousseau's discussion of legitimacy is at best complicated and at worst ambiguous. While Rousseau shares with his predecessors in the social contract tradition a conception of legitimacy as resting on consent, he relies on two quite different conceptions of consent itself. He takes the first, interest-based conception from the natural law strand of the social contract tradition as espoused by Hobbes and Locke. The second, reason-based conception, however, represents one of Rousseau's key innovations in political thought. This second conception of consent and the theory of legitimacy that follows from it provide the foundations for deliberative liberalism.

According to the interest-based conception of consent, we can presume consent as long as someone's fundamental interests will be advanced. Such consent can thus be derived. If, for example, we know that the move from the state of nature to a particular type of civil society will advance fundamental interests, then we can conclude that this move will meet with consent. If the interests in question are general enough, and the advantages of leaving the state of nature large enough, we can conclude that everyone would consent to the new society. On the interest-based conception, then, we ask whether the change of state is rational. The reasons someone has for consenting to the principles in question are limited to those that can find support in her preexisting interests.

In addition, conceiving of consent on the interest model leads us to think of consent as a one-time action. The relevant question is whether a change of state will advance individuals' fundamental interests. Once it is determined that the change will in fact advance these interests, the question can be taken as more or less settled. Whether it is entirely settled will depend on the interests at stake and the size of the gain brought about by leaving the state of nature. Thus Hobbes, who takes our interest to be in preserving our life and the gain in this regard to be absolute, thinks that once a state is set

16. Note that this reading makes sense of the explicitly political language in which he describes the stifling of pity, which causes Nature to rebel within the philosopher. Rebellion is a calling into question of an established authority. In the absence of such authority, one cannot rebel.

up, it cannot be dissolved. Locke, on the other hand, takes our interests to include the secure use of our property and the protection of our liberty, and he therefore sees the advantages to be gained as less total. He claims that under certain conditions, as when the government begins to interfere arbitrarily with our property, a state may leave us worse off. As a result, his theory leaves room for citizens to withdraw their consent.

In the *Discourse on Inequality*, Rousseau lays out a theory of fundamental human interests. Chief among our interests is the preservation and protection of our lives and our freedom. In *Of the Social Contract*, Rousseau states the fundamental problem to which the social contract provides a solution in a manner that suggests that the legitimacy of the social contract will derive from an interest-based conception of consent: "to find a form of association that will defend and protect the person and goods of each associate with the full common force, and by means of which each, uniting with all, nevertheless obey only himself and *remain as free as before.*"[17]

In contrast, a reason-based conception of consent regards consent as an act of will in the sense laid out in section 2.2. We consent to political principles only if we find the reasons for living under such principles to be sufficient, to impose genuinely authoritative claims on us. Reasons, as we saw above, include a broader range of claims than those that flow from our prior individual interests. As a result, we may not always be able to read off what a given person will be able to regard as a reason. Furthermore, the emphasis here is on the capacity to agree oneself, to be the source of the authority of the laws that govern us. Thus, adopting the reason-based theory of consent leads us away from arguments that attempt to derive consent. Instead of merely showing the gain to fundamental interests, the defender of political principles must explain why the reasons supporting those principles should be generally compelling. Doing so, however, must be regarded as making an argument to other citizens, rather than as deriving the truth of a proposition.

Where the interest-based conception of consent leads to a view of consent as a one-time act, the reason-based conception leads to a view of consent as an ongoing process. Consent, on this view, is an act of will. Acts of will, however, are momentary. In order to serve as the ground of stable, legitimate government, consent must be ongoing, continually repeated. It is thus not enough for there to be one initial set of reasons that serve to justify the formation of the state. Rather, even an established state must constantly

17. SC, I.6.4; OC, 3.360; LW, 49–50, emphasis added. What exactly is entailed by the requirement that we are left as free as before plays a large role in determining just how heavily Rousseau relies on the interest-based conception of consent. I discuss this question below.

be able to justify its actions in terms of reasons that can garner support from citizens. As we will see below, this aspect of the reason-based conception of consent winds up radically shifting the role the social contract plays in political theory.

Rousseau discusses the need for the state's actions to receive continuous consent in a number of contexts.[18] One of the clearest comes in his discussion of the "death of the body politic," where he insists that the state continues to exist as a result of continued willed endorsement by the people: "It is not by laws that the State subsists, it is by the legislative power. Yesterday's law does not obligate today, but tacit consent is presumed from silence, and the Sovereign is assumed to be constantly confirming the laws which it does not abrogate when it can do so. Everything which it has once declared it wills it continues to will, unless it revokes it."[19] Earlier he remarks that the body politic, just like the bodies of individuals, "begins to die as soon as it is born."[20] Were he to have thought of the original consent as a one-time event that established political society for all subsequent eternity, it is hard to understand how he could have thought of it as destined for decay and death. If, however, consent is a momentary act of will that has to be continuously (if only tacitly) renewed, then it is easier to see how even the most perfect of constitutions would be destined to erode and finally dissolve, as various and sundry forces led people to find the reasons for consent less compelling.

The reason-based conception of consent is also in evidence in Rousseau's discussion of the limits of sovereign power. He begins by setting out these limits in conventional social contract terms. Sovereign power extends only over those aspects of their lives that individuals give up in joining the society. Unlike Locke, however, Rousseau defines this limit primarily in terms of the needs of the society, rather than in terms of some original natural endowment we form society to protect: "It is agreed that each man alienates by the social pact only that portion of his power, his goods, his freedom, which it is important for the community to be able to use, but it should also be agreed to that the Sovereign is alone judge of that importance."[21] He goes on to say, and it is this point I want to highlight, that the sovereign is constrained in its demands on citizens because it must offer sufficient reasons tied to the good of the community: "the

18. Steven Affeldt ("The Force of Freedom," *Political Theory* 27 [1999]: 299–333) provides a compelling discussion of the importance to Rousseau's theory of the insistence that citizens constantly reconstitute the general will.

19. SC, III.11.4; OC, 3.424; LW, 109.

20. Ibid., III.11.2.

21. SC, II.4.3; OC, 3.373; LW, 61.

Sovereign, for its part, cannot burden the subjects with any shackles that are useless to the community; it cannot even will to do so: for under the law of reason nothing is done without a cause, any more than under the law of nature."[22]

Taken alone, this remark might not seem fully to support my claim that Rousseau here relies on a reason-based theory of consent. After all, Rousseau says that the Sovereign must *offer* reasons why some sacrifice would be useful to the community. It is certainly conceivable that such reasons, even if granted, would not on their own be sufficient to garner the consent of the citizen of whom the sacrifice is demanded. Rousseau's remark must be read in light of his whole political theory, which includes the sovereign being animated by a general will that is the shared will of citizens. Because it is the general will that is making the demand, and because the citizen shares in that general will, it turns out that reasons offered as compelling will be seen as such by any citizen who genuinely shares in the general will. The possibility that the Sovereign's reasons will not garner consent, then, turns out to arise not because the Sovereign's reasons do not meet with the consent of citizens, but because some subjects are not full citizens, because they do not share in the general will. While this latter possibility ought to be a worrisome one for any political theory centered around a shared will, it does not undermine the connection I am arguing Rousseau makes here between the reasons of the Sovereign and the consent of citizens.[23]

Finally, it is also the reason-based conception of consent that leads Rousseau to identify legitimate and republican forms of government.[24] He explains in a footnote to this identification that his claim is about the relationship of the government (that part of the state charged with executing the laws) and the sovereign people, on whose authority laws are passed. Republican governments are guided by the general will, and thus are in service to the sovereign. Nevertheless, claiming that governments must be republican in order to be legitimate can be seen as placing limits on sovereign authority: it can be delegated but not alienated. In light of what I have been arguing above, it makes sense to see this remark as following from Rousseau's conception of consent. If consent is reason-based and momentary, then in order to be legitimate a government must garner the continuing consent of the people. But that is merely to say that the people must remain sovereign, that it is their collective will that must lay down the laws

22. Ibid., II.4.4.

23. I take up the difficulties for Rousseau's theory which arise from the possibility that not all subjects will be full citizens at the end of this chapter where I discuss the problem of stability and Rousseau's attempt to address it.

24. SC II.6.9; OC, 3.380; LW, 67: "Every legitimate Government is republican."

and always be regarded as the ultimate ground of their authority.[25] Thus, it is the reason-based conception of consent that supports one of Rousseau's central themes: the idea that a people is free if and only if they make their own laws.

Rousseau's remarks on republican government also suggest a means of separating out the places in his theory where he relies on an interest-based conception of consent from those where he relies on a reason-based conception. To do so, I make a distinction that is sometimes lost in discussions of Rousseau, between the social contract and the general will.[26] It is the social contract that constitutes a people as a people, that makes them a political unit, capable of having a general will. The general will is the will of that people. The social contract, then, sets out the terms and conditions under which a group of people can and do form a general will. These include not only a set of legitimate procedures but also substantive constitutional constraints, which help to ensure that the will the people collectively form is in fact general. But these do not completely determine the content of the general will. The determination of the content of the general will is a task left to the citizens in their political deliberations, actions, and voting. The general will is the source of legitimate law and the final authority for legitimate government. The terms of the social contract, however, determine whether or not a group of people are legitimately constituted as citizens. Note that this structure is reminiscent of the psychic structure reason creates in individuals. An individual with reason is a self because his will has the authority to organize his desires and other psychic forces into a unity. Likewise, the social contract establishes the psychic structure of a political society. Our psychic structure makes it possible for us to will, and in particular, to act for reasons, but it alone does not determine what we will or how we act. That requires that we reason and will. Similarly, the social contract makes possible the particular political actions of society, but does not itself determine them. That is the job of the general will.

Having distinguished the social contract from the general will, we can then distinguish two strands of argument in Rousseau's theory. The first, which is reminiscent of the strategy found in earlier social contract theories, relies on an interest-based conception of consent. It argues that the inhabitants of the state of nature would consent to the terms of the social contract

25. See also SC II.1.3; OC, 3.369; LW, 57: "If, then, the people promises simply to obey, it dissolves itself by this very act, it loses its quality of being a people."

26. Rousseau makes something like this distinction when he distinguishes "the social Pact" that gives "the body politic existence and life" from giving that body "motion and will by legislation" (SC, II.6.1; OC, 3.378; LW, 66). I am grateful to Frederick Neuhouser for calling this passage to my attention.

if these turned out to advance their fundamental interests. We then argue from the terms of the social contract to the structure of the general will. That is, the general will is justified because it enables a society to advance the fundamental interests of its citizens and thus to fulfill the promise of the social contract. I will call this line of argument the natural law strand of Rousseau's theory.

Focusing on the reason-based conception of consent, however, leads to a very different argument, which I will call the deliberative strand. According to this line of argument, what renders political principles legitimate is that they are supported by the general will. We then justify the terms of the social contract not by appeal to a theory of fundamental human interests, but by showing how it establishes the social conditions that are necessary if people are to form and be governed by a general will. These, in Rousseau's terms, are the conditions under which the people can be sovereign.

2.4. Shared Wills, Dependence, and Fundamental Interests

Although these two argumentative strands are rather distinct, they are hard to tease apart in the context of Rousseau's presentation. Rousseau regards as legitimate only those societies that would meet the criteria laid out by both strands, and it has no doubt been one of the enduring attractions of Rousseau's theory that it derives support from both strands. In untangling these strands, I hope to show that the natural law strand runs headlong into the fact of deep diversity while the deliberative strand provides some of the resources we will need to address that fact adequately. In this section, I examine the ways in which each strand gives rise to a similar set of substantive requirements for a legitimate state. By focusing on the areas of overlap and yet distinguishing the ways in which the elements of that overlap appear from the perspective of the different argumentative strands, we will also be able to see the ways in which familiar notions in political philosophy work in perhaps unfamiliar ways within the landscape of deliberative liberalism. Once we have seen how each strand functions in Rousseau's argument, we will then be in a position to isolate and evaluate them.

According to the reason-based criterion of consent, laws are legitimate if they are supported by reasons all citizens can take as authoritative. In my discussion of Rousseau's account of the development of reason, I suggested that reasons should be understood as claims that have the authority to determine our wills, and thus to guide our actions. We might say, in line with this thought, that the shape of a given person's will is given by the reasons that are authoritative for it, or could be under the right circumstances. If there are to be reasons that all citizens can recognize as authoritative, then the shapes of their wills must overlap. In the case of such an overlap, the overlapping aspects of their wills will authorize the same set of reasons. If these reasons serve to support the actions of the government, then the government will be legitimate.

Such overlap is part of what I have in mind in talking of shared wills. Sharing a will involves more than just that the shapes of our wills coincide. A group of people shares a will when they come to agreement about the authority of a set of reasons in some domain. Such agreement may rest on the prior constitution of the individuals' interests, desires, and so forth, but it need not. As we have seen, the fact that we are reasonable creatures means that we are susceptible to reasons offered by others; such reasons can have the effect of changing which interests we pursue and which desires we endeavor to satisfy. We can also further determine the shape of our wills through the exchange of reasons with others, through what I call in later chapters reasonable deliberation.[27] Being reasonable thus gives us the capacity not only to share wills with others but to form such shared wills. That capacity in turn means that we can come to agree on the authority of a set of reasons, including political reasons, even when our wills do not initially overlap in the right way. According to Rousseau's deliberative strand, then, the possibility of legitimate government turns on the possibility of citizens forming a shared will that authorizes the reasons that justify the actions of the government.[28] Since citizens can form a shared will without having a prior alignment of interests, needs, and desires, we can establish the possibility of legitimate political principles without recourse to a theory of fundamental human interests or of human nature, and thus, at least conceivably, in the face of deep diversity.

This, however, is not the only criterion that legitimate political principles must meet. The sentence in which Rousseau asks about the possibility of legitimate government goes on to ask whether such government could serve to satisfy our fundamental needs. It appears at first glance that we cannot

27. I discuss how reasonable deliberation can serve to form our identities in chapter 4. Whether or not Rousseau thought that something like a process of reasonable political deliberation could serve to shape citizens' wills in the proper way is somewhat unclear. For a discussion of Rousseau that claims that he did not think this happened, see Bernard Manin, "On Legitimacy and Political Deliberation," *Political Theory* 15 (1987): 338–368. I suggest below that Rousseau has the resources in his theory for such an argument, even if he doesn't make use of them in that way.

28. That Rousseau thought of the general will as the shared will of citizens is suggested, for instance, by his discussion of the general will as being constituted by what citizens' different interests have in common. See, for instance, SC, II.1.1; OC, 3.368; LW, 57.

know if a political system will meet people's needs unless we have a prior means of establishing what those needs are, and that suggests that we will need a theory of fundamental interests after all. It is over the matter of needs that the two strands of Rousseau's argument intertwine most thoroughly. It turns out that there are several ways to conceive of meeting the needs of citizens, and how we conceive of this will depend on which argumentative strand we are following.

We can distinguish two requirements built into the general idea that a legitimate government must meet its citizens' needs. First, it must advance any fundamental interests we have. These are needs that are natural in the sense of stemming from characteristics we share with the inhabitants of the state of nature, such as our interest in our own preservation and our freedom. But, as I pointed out above, Rousseau stresses the radical nature of human development, and the degree to which very few of our most deeply human characteristics are natural. As a result, in addition to whatever natural needs we have, according to his theory of fundamental interests, we also have a host of social needs, and these are in large part the result of living in a particular society. Since these needs are the product of our living in a given society, they can be met either by satisfying them or by organizing society so that they do not arise in the first place. For a legitimate government, resting on the shared will of citizens, to meet these two kinds of needs—natural and social—constraints will have to be placed on the content of the shared will, so that the actions of the government it authorizes serve to satisfy all our natural needs and those social needs it generates while not fostering new needs that it cannot satisfy.

In addition, we can distinguish two grounds for insisting on this criterion for legitimacy. First, it is clear that a government that did not meet its citizens' needs would not leave them better off than they were in the state of nature, which Rousseau thought did meet all of its inhabitants' needs. Thus, from the point of view of an interest-based conception of consent, only such a political system will meet with the consent of its citizens. Second, citizens can only form a truly shared will in a society in which all of their needs are reliably met. Our dependence on others for the satisfaction of our needs can give rise to relations of domination and subjection, and such relations undermine the possibility of forming a truly shared will. Since it is only when citizens form a shared will that their reason-based consent is forthcoming, a legitimate state must meet basic needs from the point of view of a reason-based conception of consent as well.

Notice, however, that these two reasons for insisting that a state meet its citizens' needs in order to be legitimate need not agree on which needs are to be met or how. Nothing in the account as I have described it to this point requires that the needs whose satisfaction makes possible the formation of a shared will among citizens are also the needs whose satisfaction advances our fundamental interests. It turns out, however, that these demands are both jointly satisfiable and rather intricately linked. Both the advancement of our fundamental interests and the establishment of conditions under which the formation of a shared will are possible involve the careful negotiation and restructuring of our dependence on one another. To see just what is required for the social contract and the general will to give rise to legitimate government, we need to turn our attention to the various forms of dependence that reason engenders, and ask how they can be managed politically.

We need to start by distinguishing between physical dependence, where we depend on others to help us satisfy our desire for physical objects we cannot acquire on our own, and psychological dependence, where we depend on others to recognize our worth.[29] Our psychological dependence is a result of particular desires for recognition that we develop along with reason. Physical dependence, however, results from our limited capacities.[30] It turns out that the means of meeting our needs as conceived of on the reason-based strand also meet the criteria of need-satisfaction as it arises on the interest-based strand. In each case, needs are met by eliminating forms of dependence that interfere with the satisfaction of those needs.

Starting with the deliberative strand, we can ask if there are conditions of dependence under which the formation of a shared will is rendered impossible. To see what these amount to, I consider each form of dependence in turn. Psychological dependence arises, according to Rousseau, because in reflecting on our place first in the natural world and then among our fellow humans, we develop a consciousness of our status and a desire for others to recognize that status. This desire he calls *amour-propre*.[31] There is an important sense in which the mere formation of a shared will with others can serve to satisfy our *amour-propre* without generating a freedom-threatening

29. Frederick Neuhouser insists on the importance of this distinction in "Freedom, Dependence, and the General Will," *Philosophical Review* 102 (1993): 363–395, esp. 377, although he describes what I am calling "physical dependence" as "economic dependence." My discussion below basically follows his.

30. Here I take capacities to include not only brute physical abilities, but what might be called social capacities. Thus, for instance, in a society with a modern economy, I am physically dependent on others for the food I eat, not because I am physically incapable of growing it myself, but because within the context of a modern market economy I acquire my food, as I do other commodities, through exchange in the market.

31. For a very helpful discussion of *amour-propre* and its role in Rousseau's theory, see N.J.H. Dent, *Rousseau* (Oxford: Basil Blackwell, 1988), esp. chap. 2. For the development of *amour-propre* and the dependence that develops from it, see DI, II.15–18; OC, 3.169–171; EW, 165–167.

dependence on others. If, in response to our desires being in conflict, we reason together about what to do and this leads us to adopt a shared will, then whether or not this will serves to satisfy my desire, the process by which we form a shared will confirms to me that others regard me as an equal moral being whose desires count for something and to whom reasons are owed. Our psychological dependence will interfere with our ability to form a shared will only if our *amour-propre* becomes inflamed, becomes a desire to be recognized as superior rather than as an equal.[32] A legitimate political society must thus protect against social institutions and arrangements that inflame *amour-propre*. Rousseau is, of course, deeply concerned with this matter, and many of his polemics against the decadent luxuries of Parisian life and his praise of the simple life of Geneva revolve around this worry.[33] One of the main ways inflamed *amour-propre* is kept in check is through restraints on material inequality. Since such restraints are also a means of solving concerns about physical dependence, I treat them further below.

Although the presence of certain unmet psychological needs can undermine the possibility of forming a shared will, there are ways of organizing a society so that this does not happen. Attending to questions of psychological dependence and the generation of inflamed *amour-propre* will thus be required from the point of view of the deliberative strand of argument. But we achieve the same result if we start from the natural law strand. *Amour-propre* is not a natural desire, and the need for recognition not a natural need. As such, it can be met either by preventing its development or by satisfying it. Ordinary *amour-propre* is satisfiable, in large part by organizing a society via the constitution of a general will. Inflamed *amour-propre*, on the other hand, generates psychological needs that can be neither generally nor stably met, and so a society can only "meet" these needs by preventing the desires that lead to them from developing. If, then, we are concerned to set up a society that will meet its citizens' psychological needs in order to fulfill the promise of the social contract, the society will have to be organized in such a way that *amour-propre* does not become inflamed and citizens participate in determining the laws that govern them through their constitution of a general will. Thus, whether we start from the demand that our psychological needs be met or from the demand that conditions be established in which we can form a truly shared will, we end up with the same requirements.

32. "Inflamed" is Dent's adjective. He makes a convincing case for the importance of distinguishing ordinary from inflamed *amour-propre* in *Rousseau*, 52–58.

33. See for instance his *Letter to D'Alembert*, trans. Allan Bloom (Glencoe, Ill.: The Free Press, 1960).

Moving on to physical dependence, we can ask whether certain forms of physical dependence undermine the possibility of forming a shared will. Here, as well, we need to distinguish a troublesome from an acceptable form of dependence: what I will call "one-way physical dependence" from "physical interdependence." Our relationship is characterized by one-way physical dependence when I am physically dependent on you but you are not physically dependent on me.[34] In such a situation my dependence on you for the satisfaction of my basic needs will lead me to subject my will to yours, if that is what is necessary for me to satisfy my needs. Thus, one-way physical dependence can lead the dependent party to subjugate his will to the person on whom he is dependent.

Because the presence of one-way physical dependence can lead one person to subject his will to that of another, it can prevent the formation of a truly shared will. As I argue in later chapters, a truly shared will must be the product of a true exchange of reasons, where this involves all parties giving due weight and consideration to the reasons offered by others. If I can effectively demand that you subject your will to mine, then I do not have to take your reasons seriously in determining the shape of our joint will: its shape is the shape of my will regardless of what reasons you offer to change it. In that sense, although our wills coincide, we do not share a will. If the exchange of reasons is to lead to a shared will, then one-way physical dependence must be sharply curtailed or eliminated. Furthermore, in a society characterized by one-way physical dependence, at least some people will not remain as free as before. Their fundamental interest in freedom will not have been protected. Such one-way dependence is likely to have a deleterious effect on the dependent parties' ability to satisfy their other needs. Thus, such dependence turns out to undermine the legitimacy of the social contract from the point of view of the interest-based conception as well.

Physical interdependence, however, has neither of these consequences. Physical interdependence involves a relationship where both parties depend on each other for the satisfaction of some of their physical needs. Such a situation, especially if fully reciprocal, will not lead to a loss of freedom. If I try to subject your will to mine by refusing to satisfy your needs unless you act as I wish you to, you can retaliate by refusing to satisfy my

34. In an argument later made famous by Hegel, Rousseau points out that even in cases of one-way physical dependence, both parties' freedom will be compromised. See, for instance, SC, I.1.1; OC, 3.351; LW, 41. The idea, roughly, is that such relationships create an unsustainable form of psychological dependence that goes both ways. The master is dependent not merely for recognition from his servant, but for recognition that he is superior. The servant's acknowledgment of his master's superiority, however, turns out to be insufficient, coming as it does from a mere servant. See Dent, *Rousseau*, 56–64, for a particularly clear discussion of this argument and its role in Rousseau's thought.

needs. Since physical interdependence does not relieve either party of the need to take seriously the reasons offered by the other, it need not threaten the formation of a shared will. Furthermore, it will be possible for a shared will to will the mutual satisfaction of our physical needs if we are physically interdependent.

If we can restrict the sort of physical dependence people face to reciprocal forms of physical interdependence, then our physical dependence does not prevent the formation of a truly shared will that wills the satisfaction of our needs, and thus it does not prevent the possibility of a legitimate political society, whether the criteria of that legitimacy are interest-based or reason-based. Rousseau's frequent insistence on the importance of equality points to the solution I have sketched above. Note that his emphasis on equality, where this includes limits on wealth as well as attempts to eliminate poverty, is explained by the need to reduce one-way physical dependence rather than by a mere concern with ensuring that the state provide for the physical needs of its citizens, and the need to prevent the inflammation of *amour-propre* rather than merely assuring everyone a basic minimum of self-respect.[35]

One important consequence of this intertwining of arguments is that it suggests that what is at stake in choosing an argumentative strategy is not necessarily the content of the view being defended. A common concern with eschewing a theory of fundamental interests or human nature in justifying political principles is that doing so will hamper our ability to offer a strong defense of a robust set of individual rights or claims. Liberals may be wary of arguing without recourse to a theory of human nature that stresses the importance of liberty or autonomy to human life, because they think that no other argumentative strategy would provide the uncompromising commitment to individual liberty and value that is the hallmark of liberalism. The above analysis suggests that this may be mistaken. At least with regard to Rousseau's theory, both the natural law strand and the deliberative strand lead to equally strong requirements on the maintenance of equality and the protection of liberty. The deliberative strand provides constraints on what can be legitimately consented to because it places substantive constraints on the conditions under which actual consent can be legitimacy-conferring. In the arguments above, these constraints arose through the requirements that the general will be truly shared. In deliberative liberalism similar constraints will develop out of the requirement that deliberation be reasonable. Abandoning the natural law strand does come at a price, however. We lose a kind of direct and prior guarantee that the results of actual political deliber-

---

35. Rousseau's most important remark on equality can be found at SC, II.11.2; OC, 3.391–392; LW, 78.

ation will not stray too far from our considered judgments about justice. In the face of deep diversity, however, that guarantee has perhaps done more harm than good. It is in part the aim of this book as a whole to provide a suitable alternative.

2.5. Justification and the Problem of Stability: Two Approaches

Having seen more fully how each strand works to justify the substance of Rousseau's view, we are now in a position to isolate them and evaluate their strengths and weaknesses separately. When Rousseau talks about the social contract from the point of view of the natural law strand, as protecting our interest in freedom, he describes it as a sort of exchange: we give up our natural state for a civil one. The essence of this exchange, he maintains, is that we exchange forms of freedom: we give up natural freedom for civil and moral freedom.[36] It is important, he maintains, that we distinguish between these different sorts of freedom: "one has to distinguish clearly between natural freedom which has no other bounds than the individual's forces, and civil freedom which is limited by the general will. . . . To the preceding one might add to the credit of the civil state moral freedom, which alone makes man truly the master of himself; for the impulsion of mere appetite is slavery, and obedience to the law one has prescribed to oneself is freedom."[37]

In the state of nature, you are free because there is no one else who can make you act in a certain way, while in civil society the only "one" who can make you act a certain way is the general will. This latter situation is a form of freedom, however, because the general will is not foreign to the individual, but rather a will in which he shares (which is why it realizes our moral freedom). What makes the social contract legitimate on this line of thought is that it protects us and leaves us as free as before. Thus, what justifies our adoption of the social contract is that it secures our civil freedom. The general will secures our civil freedom by realizing our moral freedom (by being a shared will), but realizing our moral freedom is not conceptually necessary for the social contract to be legitimate. (Of course, Rousseau thinks that realizing our moral freedom is the only way political principles could truly secure our civil freedom.)

36. We also exchange a form of possession guaranteed only by force for property, a form of possession guaranteed by law. For my purposes, however, discussing the exchange of forms of freedom will be sufficient.
37. SC, I.8.2–3; OC, 3.365; LW, 54.

This form of justification rests on a theory of fundamental interests. The ultimate reason why the social contract is legitimate on this view is that it advances the interests that people have even in the state of nature by protecting their freedom and property. Thus, we can only know what particular articles of the social contract are justified if we know which interests are universally advanced by the terms of the contract. That, in turn, requires that we know which interests are universal, and so we need a theory of fundamental interests. The point here is not that Rousseau does not have such a theory; he clearly does. The point rather is that insofar as deliberative liberalism is to avoid relying on a theory of fundamental interests in order to address the fact of deep diversity, it finds no help in this strand of Rousseau's thought.

Following the deliberative strand of Rousseau's argument involves coming at the justification of the terms of the social contract from the other end. We know that the product of political activity must be a shared will if there is to be a legitimate government. That, in turn, requires that certain conditions be met. Thus, the justification for the social contract will be that it realizes those conditions. In terms of the distinction between civil and moral freedom, we could say that insofar as the realization of our moral freedom is equivalent to the formation of a shared will that guides the government, then the social contract will be justified because it realizes our moral freedom. Since one condition of forming a truly shared will is that everyone is free to endorse or reject the reasons that shape that will, it will be necessary that the social contract preserve civil freedom. Nevertheless, it is the realization of moral freedom that plays the justifying role in the theory on this approach.

There are a number of places where Rousseau seems to be relying on such a strategy in determining the content of the social contract. These are most apparent when he is defending its creation and maintenance of equality. As we saw above, the elimination of one-way physical dependence, in part through the establishment of rough equality, is a necessary condition for citizens to be able to form a shared will. It is not, however, a natural outgrowth of our natural condition. In fact, Rousseau claims, the social contract has the effect of substituting "a moral and legitimate equality for whatever physical inequality nature may have placed between men."[38]

Elsewhere, in maintaining that freedom and equality are the "greatest

---

38. SC, I.9.8; OC, 3.376; LW, 56. See also SC, II.4.8; OC, 3.374–375; LW, 62–63, where Rousseau claims that the social pact establishes equality, a conclusion one arrives at "from whatever side one traces one's way back" rather than because it is a conclusion derived from premises about our natural and fundamental interests or status.

good . . . which ought to be the end of every system of legislation," he offers what might be called structural reasons for his position: "Freedom, because any individual dependence is that much force taken away from the State; equality, because freedom cannot subsist without it."[39] Freedom is here defended as the appropriate end of every system of legislation not because we have a fundamental interest in it, but because its absence, in the form of dependence on particular individuals, takes force away from the general will, presumably because it undermines the degree to which it is truly shared. Similarly, equality is defended as instrumental in making it possible for the necessary freedom to exist.

Although the two strands give rise to similar substantive proposals, there are two considerations that, at least from the perspective of the project of deliberative liberalism, recommend the deliberative strand over the natural law strand. The first, which I have already discussed, is the reliance of the natural law strand on a theory of fundamental human interests or human nature. Beyond this consideration, there is the matter of how each conceives of and addresses what I will call the problem of stability.

No matter how we justify the social contract, it cannot adequately serve the role it plays within Rousseau's political system if its terms are not endorsed by the general will. Were the general will to reject the terms of the social contract, one of two unacceptable states of affairs would result. Either we would have to say that the terms of the social contract are inviolable, and that they thus place an external constraint on the range of options over which the general will can will; or we would have to accept that the general will has the power to alter the terms of the social contract, in which case it will be possible for a legitimate government to thwart our fundamental interests (according to the natural law strand) or undermine the conditions of its own successful functioning (according to the deliberative strand).

We might think of the problem in terms of the content of the general will itself. For the whole system to be self-supporting and thus stable, it will have to be the case that part of the content of the general will is an affirmation of the terms of the social contract. The question, then, is: on what basis can we ensure that the general will is going to have that content? Given the form of the general will as the shared will of citizens, its content will have to be a function of what individual citizens can come to will. Solving this problem thus requires figuring out what would lead citizens to endorse a general will with the right sort of content. What would serve to construct their wills in the proper manner? Rousseau's answer to that question appears to arise out

39. SC, II.11.1; OC, 3.391; LW, 78.

of the natural law strand of his argument. He asks how we can be sure that the people will collectively will the satisfaction of their fundamental needs. He claims that such a guarantee must come from outside. It is, he thinks, up to the Legislator, who is in charge of originally designing the laws the people adopt, also to attend to the constitution of their individual wills by attending to their sources in opinions and morals:

> To these three sorts of laws must be added a fourth, the most important of all; which is graven not in marble or in bronze, but in the hearts of the Citizens; which is the State's genuine constitution; which daily gathers new force; which, when the other laws age or die out, revives or replaces them, and imperceptibly substitutes the force of habit for that of authority. I speak of morals, customs, and above all of opinion; a part [of the laws] unknown to our politicians, but on which the success of all the others depends: a part to which the great Lawgiver attends in secret, while he appears to restrict himself to particular regulations which are but the ribs of the arch of which morals, slower to arise, in the end form the immovable Keystone.[40]

From the point of view of the natural law strand, this seems like the only available solution. Our fundamental interests are fixed by nature. They are not the products of society, and so if society tends to alter us so that we are not moved to protect those interests, then this problem can only be fixed from the outside. The legislator provides such an external solution by shaping the citizens' individual wills so that they form the right sort of general will. In this way, he ensures the stability of the laws he writes.

We might, however, hope to find a solution that is less external to the problem of stability. Coming at the problem from the perspective of the deliberative strand can help us to do that. As I suggested above, from that perspective, the problem of stability is the problem of ensuring that the general will wills the conditions of its continued formation. We might hope that the very process of coming to form a general will served to transform us in such a way that we could be expected also to endorse the conditions of that will's proper functioning.

Although Rousseau often talks of the social contract in the language of exchange, he also famously speaks of it as effecting a transformation:

> This transition from the state of nature to the civil state produces a most remarkable change in man by substituting justice for instinct in his con-

40. SC, II.12.5; OC, 3.394; LW, 81.

duct and endowing his actions with the morality they previously lacked. Only then, when the voice of duty succeeds physical impulsion and right succeeds appetite, does man, who until then had looked only to himself, see himself forced to act on other principles, and to consult his reason before listening to his inclinations. Although in this state he deprives himself of several advantages he has from nature, he gains such great advantages in return, his faculties are exercised and developed, his ideas enlarged, his sentiments ennobled, his entire soul is elevated to such an extent, that if the abuses of this new condition did not often degrade him to beneath the condition he has left, he should ceaselessly bless the happy moment which wrested him from it forever, and out of a stupid and bounded animal made an intelligent being and a man.[41]

It is in thinking of the transition from the natural to the civil state as a transformation that I think we can find a different route to the solution of the problem of stability. What produces all these changes is the creation of a social order in which people are able to make claims on others and acknowledge the claims of others on them. Although Rousseau never develops the mechanism of the transformation he describes, I think it is not too far-fetched to imagine it coming about not as a result of some legendary figure toying with our psychology but through the very process of reasoning together about our common interest and the lives we must necessarily lead together. The thought, then, is that it is through the participation in the institutions that embody the general will that we are led to constitute our own wills in such a manner that we freely endorse a general will whose content includes the terms of the social contract. This thought is made even more plausible when we think of the terms of the social contract not as growing out of a philosophical account of our fundamental interests, but as establishing the conditions under which we might form a truly shared will at all.

Building on this line of thought would involve making the realization of our moral freedom the source of political legitimacy and not merely the means for securing it. It would thus give pride of place to Rousseau's republicanism: the idea that a people's freedom is secured not by a government that protects individual liberties, but by a government guided by laws of which the people together are authors, and that political legitimacy rests not in conformity with natural law or some other external standard of justice,

41. SC, I.8.1; OC, 3.364; LW, 53.

but in a people's collective, ongoing, self-determination.[42] Rousseau, however, never disentangled this idea from the natural law strand of justification
that rests on an account of fundamental interests. Whether we regard this as
a shortcoming of Rousseau's theory will depend on whether we have reason
to eschew dependence on a theory of fundamental human interests, and
whether we think it is ultimately possible to rely entirely on the other, trans-
formational line of justification.

42. For discussion of republican conceptions of liberty, see Quentin Skinner, "The republican ideal of political liberty," in *Machiavelli and Republicanism*, eds. Gisela Bock, Quentin Skinner, and Maurizio Viroli (Cambridge: Cambridge University Press, 1990), 293–309; Skinner,
Liberty before Liberalism (Cambridge: Cambridge University Press, 1998); and Philip Pettit,
Republicanism: A Theory of Freedom and Government (Oxford: Oxford University Press, 1999). I
discuss the republican conception of liberty and its connection to those found in Rawls's political liberalism in "Republican Moments in Political Liberalism" *Croatian Journal of Philosophy* 3
(Fall 2001).

3

Hegel

Hegel is a great admirer of Rousseau, crediting him with putting political philosophy on the right track for the first time by making the free will the principle for the justification of the state.[1] At the same time, he is a forceful critic of the social contract tradition, and explicitly of Rousseau as a member of that tradition. In light of the discussion in chapter 2, we can see these two attitudes as perfectly consistent. What Hegel admires in Rousseau is the deliberative strand of his argument; what he criticizes is the natural law strand.

In an effort to avoid the problems he saw with the natural law strand of Rousseau's argument, Hegel attempts to set out a political theory that rests entirely on a version of the deliberative strand. He grounds the legitimacy of political principles and institutions on their capacity to allow people living together to share a will about the institutions that mediate and regulate their interactions. In doing so, he provides much of the framework within which I go on to articulate deliberative liberalism. He sets out in greater detail what is involved in sharing a will, and how sharing a will need not require us to give up our differences. He emphasizes the importance of our identification with social institutions as central to their ability to unite us while respecting our diversity, and shows how that identification supports rather than competes with a conception of legitimacy that rests on the

---

1. G.W.F. Hegel, *Lectures on the History of Philosophy*, trans. E. S. Haldane and Frances H. Simson (Lincoln: University of Nebraska Press, 1995), 3.401.

requirement that institutions provide members adequate reasons for their actions. He also provides a more internal solution to the problem of stability, showing how legitimacy requires stability and why legitimate institutions must generate their own support.

Of course, it should be said at the outset that even if Hegel is a forerunner of deliberative liberalism and there is much in his work on which a deliberative liberal can draw, Hegel is certainly not a *deliberative* liberal. To the extent that it plays any role in politics at all for Hegel, deliberation is not done among citizens but by members of legislative bodies in front of citizens. Nevertheless, the central role Hegel gives to shared wills and the way they figure in his account of political legitimacy make his work a suitable place to continue to develop the ingredients of deliberative liberalism.

One final note before beginning: much of Hegel's political philosophy, like much of his work generally, is couched in deeply metaphysical language and appears to rest for its support on a comprehensive metaphysics. Insofar as my ultimate interest in Hegel is to find inspiration for a manner of doing political philosophy that can find legitimacy in the face of deep diversity, and that therefore rests neither on robust accounts of what we are like nor on robust metaphysical systems, it might seem that his own metaphysical project would constitute an enormous obstacle.

The points I want to make about Hegel's theory and the lessons I want to take from it can be separated out from his metaphysical arguments, however. In fact, two separate lines of justification can be found running through at least the *Philosophy of Right*. Call them the metaphysical freedom argument and the social freedom argument. The metaphysical freedom argument appeals to his larger metaphysical project and the conception of freedom formed there. It thus argues for certain institutions on the grounds that they have "the structure of the Concept," or they constitute the "actuality of the ethical Idea." The social freedom argument, in contrast, appeals to the ways in which certain institutions serve to realize particular forms of human freedom. In my discussion of Hegel, I will be concerned exclusively with those parts of his view that can be supported by the social freedom argument alone. Within Hegel's theory, the social freedom argument ultimately rests on the metaphysical freedom argument, insofar as Hegel defines social freedom in terms of the metaphysical freedom argument. We can nevertheless recognize the value and the nature of the kind of freedom Hegel discusses on its own. Insofar as Hegel's social freedom is something we can recognize as freedom even in the absence of the metaphysical support Hegel gives it, we can adopt the interpretive strategy I set out here.

3.1. Will, Freedom, and Stability

Rousseau conceived of the will of reasonable creatures as a reason-guided source of actions that is separate from the flux of their interests and desires. In large part as a result of that conception, he is able to develop the resources of the deliberative strand of his argument and thus to offer a version of social contract theory that is in many ways radically different from that of his predecessors. Similarly, it is in large part because of the ways Hegel further develops the idea of the will and its relation to reason and freedom that he is able to develop a political theory that completely abandons the natural law strand of Rousseau's argument. I thus begin this discussion of Hegel's political theory by looking at his conception of the free will.

According to a rather standard approach to the nature of free will, the will is more or less a faculty, which may or may not have the property of being free. Think, for instance, of Rousseau's conception of the will. For Rousseau the will is a faculty that yields action and is somehow responsive to reason rather than to the mere force of desires and interests. This faculty is free if it is not dominated by the will of another. Hegel rejects both the idea that the will is a faculty, and the conclusion that freedom is an accidental property of the will. I start with the second of these claims and then move on to the first.

Hegel draws rather close connections between the will, freedom, and thought. First of all, "freedom is just as much a basic determination of the will as weight is a basic determination of bodies . . . that which is free is the will. Will without freedom is an empty word, just as freedom is actual only as will or as subject."[2] Since the will is precisely that which is free, freedom is no mere accidental property of the will. Rather, the will is the embodiment or realization of freedom. Thus, understanding our conception of the will and how it functions will tell us what we mean by freedom as well. Unlike on the standard view mentioned above, these are not two separable questions.

Because the will is essentially free, Hegel claims that it must be thoroughly self-determining in a way that a faculty of choice cannot be. A faculty of choice determines itself by choosing one option over others. In so doing, however, it determines itself in a manner that is ultimately tied to the range of choices given. In this regard, a faculty of choice is still dependent on its antecedent desires and interests. It can choose among these, but since

2. G.W.F. Hegel, *Elements of the Philosophy of Right*, trans. H. B. Nisbet (Cambridge: Cambridge University Press, 1991), §4A. This work will hereafter be cited as PhR, followed by section number. Where I am citing Hegel's remarks the section number will be followed by an R; when I am citing the additions taken from his student's lecture notes, the section number will be followed by an A.

these options are antecedent and external to it, not its own products, it is nevertheless dependent on things outside itself even in its freedom.[3]

The problem here is that nothing that a mere faculty of choice chooses makes it truly free, truly self-determining. As a result, in the very act of choosing that is supposed to realize its freedom, such a faculty becomes dependent on the object of its choice. Hegel suggests that we think of the problem as follows: the will understood as a faculty of choice gets into trouble because of its ends. In adopting a particular end, it identifies itself with that end. Because the end is some given, determinate thing, the will in choosing an end makes itself into a determinate, predetermined thing, into less than a will. The will avoids this trap by adopting itself as its end.

It will seem obscure at this point how the truly free will could adopt itself as its end. If we think of the will as a faculty, then it appears that the will cannot do this: ends and faculties are different sorts of things. The key, Hegel argues, is to think of the will as a form of activity. That is, if we must think of the truly free will as adopting itself as its end, then we must think of it as the kind of thing that could be the end of a will. The end of a will is activity, so we have to think of the will itself as a form of activity.[4]

To think of the will as a form of activity is to think of it as coming into existence through the act of willing itself. On such a view, the natural question to ask is, "what does the will constitute itself as, in various sorts of willing?" With respect to the freedom of the will, then, we need to ask not "which property of the will constitutes its freedom and how do we protect that?" but rather, "what sorts of willing must the will engage in so that the product of its willing is the constitution of a free will?" The answer to this question will bring us to the problem of stability.

The idea that the will is a form of self-actualizing activity can appear circular, and in some sense it is. What makes the circle virtuous rather than vicious is what lies along its path. In particular, Hegel thinks that the sorts of willing that can constitute us as creatures of free will involve willing our participation in certain kinds of social institutions. Institutions are constituted through the activity of their members. A family, for instance, is nothing over and above its members, and what makes a group of people into a family is precisely that they act as members of a family. They act in this manner when they occupy particular roles (parent, child) in their interactions with each other as well as in their interactions with others (where the identity in question may be their collective identity as the Smiths or the Joneses). At the same time, individuals are formed through their participation in institu-

3. PhR, §15A.
4. PhR, §7R.

tions. My understanding of myself is shaped by having grown up in a certain kind of family, and by playing certain roles in the family I form through marriage and through having and raising children.

I thus constitute myself as free through my actions when my actions are those of a member of an institution that forms me as a free being. In such a case, my activity serves to constitute the institution in question, and consequently to constitute me as a member of it. So, for instance, I help to constitute the family of which I am a part by acting as a parent and spouse within it, and as a member of this particular family in my dealings with others. But it is only because I act as I do within the structure of the institution of the family that I am a parent and spouse. Absent the institution of the family, my care for my offspring or my love for a particular sexual partner would not make me either a parent or a spouse. To show that my willing participation in my family constitutes me as free, all that is left to show is that being a family member is a way of being free. I have not yet said why that might be true (I will turn to that question in section 3.3). For now, we need only note the connection between the shape of institutions and the realization of freedom. By conceiving of the will as an activity, then, Hegel leads us to see that our freedom lies precisely in acting according to the norms set out by the social roles that make up particular institutions. It is as a result of this connection that he can offer an internal solution to the stability problem.

Institutions are just for Hegel insofar as they realize forms of human freedom. An institution is stable if its members, through their activity in the institution, serve to endorse the conditions under which the institution is possible. Thus, for instance, what makes the Rousseauvian state stable is the free willing by its citizens of the content of the social contract, because its terms are what makes possible the formation of a general will. According to Hegel, an institution realizes the freedom of its members only when they constitute themselves as members of the institution by willingly acting as members of the institution. This, however, requires that they will in such a way as to produce the conditions under which the institution (and their continued participation in it) is possible. Thus, on this account, institutions can only realize their members' freedom (and thus be just) if they are stable. Hegel's conception of the will thus leads to an internal connection between justice and stability. It also gives us the basis for determining the legitimacy of social institutions by looking at their structure rather than evaluating them in terms of their promotion of some list of fundamental human interests. It thus fulfills the potential suggested by Rousseau's deliberative strand. Furthermore, Hegel provides a much more detailed picture of the structural requirements legitimate institutions must meet.

3.2. The Criteria of Legitimacy

The structural features I discuss in this section can be thought of as criteria of legitimacy because a political order that satisfies them can offer its members reasons they can regard as authoritative, and so can garner their consent. I should note at the outset that the criteria of legitimacy I propose are reconstructed out of Hegel's theory rather than set out by him as criteria. My claim is thus that these criteria capture the central aspects of the institutions of modern social life in virtue of which Hegel concludes that these institutions collectively serve to realize our freedom. Whether or not Hegel relied on these criteria, they are implicit in his project, and thus thinking about his theory in terms of these criteria can yield insight into it. Because these criteria are reconstructed out of Hegel's remarks about particular institutions, my later discussion of Hegel's description of these institutions will not constitute an argument that these institutions meet these criteria (that is something of a foregone conclusion), but rather an illustration of what, in more concrete terms, these criteria amount to, and why we might think that they are adequate criteria for legitimacy.[5]

I offer three criteria. First, institutions must embody (or at least include) shared wills. Second, they must provide room for individual choice and self-determination. Third, they must reproduce themselves in a manner that is both accessible to and stable in the face of rational insight. All three criteria can be seen as flowing from Hegel's understanding of just what needs to be shown in order to show that a particular institution realizes our freedom. Although they can be distinguished, they are also related to one another.

If an institution embodies a shared will, then as a member of the institution I participate in that shared will. Acting out my role in that institution, then, can be seen as following the demands of the shared will that the institution embodies. Since a shared will is also my own will, in acting out the demands of the shared will I follow the demands of my own will, and so determine myself. Since in determining myself in this manner I determine myself as someone who shares in this will, I determine myself as self-determining, which is to say that I actualize my will as free.

To see this point in more concrete terms, contrast the institution of slavery with the institution of private property (what Hegel calls Abstract Right). The institution of slavery does not embody a shared will (at least not

---

5. My project in this chapter is thus similar to, if far less exhaustive than, that of Frederick Neuhouser in *Foundations of Hegel's Social Theory: Actualizing Freedom* (Cambridge: Harvard University Press, 2000). Although he lays out his reading of Hegel in different terms, I do not see any significant differences in content between my picture and his.

one that includes both masters and slaves). I willingly occupy my role as slave if I willingly act as that role demands that I act. Acting as a slave involves subordinating my own will to that of my master. In doing so, I constitute myself as a slave, as someone whose will is wholly determined by a master. If I really do this willingly, as opposed to under force, we can say that I determine myself, because I give myself the identity of a slave. But I do not thereby constitute myself as free, for what I determine myself to be is a creature who is determined by another, and not one who is self-determining. The problem arises because the will I adopt as my own in willing my participation in this institution is not a will in which I share.

The case of private property is different. I willingly adopt the role of property owner in a system of property rights by acting as a property owner.[6] I do that when I respect the rules of property, in particular the property of others, and the rules governing the formation of contracts. It is in virtue of these rules that my connection to my possessions is raised to the level of ownership and that I can properly view myself as a property owner. Property owners in such a system can be said to share a will authorizing the rules governing private property and contract. Thus, when I willingly act as a property owner in such a system and thereby constitute myself as a property owner, I am not only determining myself, but determining myself as someone guided by his own will: the shared will that supports the system of property rights. The system of property rights, at least insofar as it embodies a shared will, realizes a form of freedom.

According to the second criterion of legitimacy, it is not enough for an institution to embody a shared will. It must also provide room for individual subjectivity, individual freedom. It is in virtue of this second criterion of legitimacy that Hegel's theory requires the protection of property and what Rousseau called civil freedom.[7] As I understand it, this criterion has two

6. Note here that a system of property rights is to be distinguished from what Marx calls an economic mode of production. The sort of property owners I have in mind here are neither feudal lords nor industrial capitalists, but people who have some personal property—stuff that is theirs in virtue of the system of property rights. Property ownership in this sense is thus a potentially universal status, unlike that of slave or master (or capitalist or proletariat).

7. In Hegel's theory, there are actually two distinct types of freedom at stake: personal freedom and moral freedom. Personal freedom is the freedom particular to Abstract Right; moral freedom is the freedom of moral subjects discussed in the section on *Moralität*, the freedom to act only according to one's own conception of the good. Since I am ultimately interested in drawing general lessons about Hegel's general strategy of justification and am not trying to provide a comprehensive account of all the details of Hegel's view, I do not distinguish them carefully here. For a clear discussion of the difference between them and how the institutions of *Sittlichkeit* serve to realize both, see Neuhouser, *Foundations of Hegel's Social Theory*, esp. chaps. 1, 4, and 7.

interrelated aspects. First, the institutions of a just political order must provide room for us to occupy a number of different roles. Second, at least some of those roles must offer room for a robust form of self-fashioning. If none of the roles we occupied, and through which we realized our freedom, allowed for significant choice of ends, then it would be hard to imagine how we could think of them as realizing a kind of freedom we care about. Having a choice of significant ends within a particular institutional structure and having that structure dictate all of my significant ends are quite different, and for Hegel only the first could truly realize our freedom. Thus, at least some of the institutions of a just political order will have to provide room for individual subjectivity and choice to find expression.

That said, Hegel thinks that certain institutions, most particularly the state, cannot appropriately leave completely open to their members what role they play.[8] One of his criticisms of the social contract tradition is that it regards membership in the state as optional.[9] In order to make room for individual freedom within a political order where citizenship is unchosen and irrevocable, our membership in the political realm cannot be the only form of shared will in which we take part. As a result, a legitimate social order will comprise a multiplicity of essential institutions.[10] The idea is that while a legitimate Hegelian state will have to provide room for the protection and expression of individual freedom, it can do that by providing room for *other* institutions whose ends are more closely tied to that protection. It is the presence of those other institutions that allows the state to have its end in something other than the protection of individual freedom and yet necessarily provide space for that protection. At the same time, the argument about the necessity of embodying shared wills will apply to all the legitimating institutions of a political order. Thus, even those institutions that contribute to the legitimacy of the social order by providing protection for individual freedom must do so through the embodiment of shared wills, so that our willing participation in them can realize our freedom.

The third criterion requires that the social order be stable. As we saw in the last section, a social order will be stable if its members come to identify

8. The qualification is necessary since according to Hegel's theory men do choose the role they play vis-à-vis the state insofar as that is determined by their role in civil society, which they choose freely. What is not chosen is whether or not to be a citizen. In this, the state differs from the family and civil society, both of which it is possible to opt out of even if doing so would lead to a relatively impoverished life.

9. PhR, §258R.

10. See, for instance, PhR, §75A, where Hegel says that the social contract theory is "the result of superficial thinking, which envisages only a *single* unity of different wills" (emphasis in original).

with their roles in it through their growing up and living their lives within its institutions. We can break down this third criterion into three parts as well. First, the institutions of a stable social order must play an educative role. Growing up under the institutions of a legitimate social order must form our interests, desires, and ends so that they are best met through taking up our roles in the institution. It is not necessary for each institution to play this educative role for itself, as long as the whole set of institutions offers this kind of education for each institution. Although the educative function can be delegated out in this manner, the second and third aspects of the stability criterion cannot.

The second aspect is that legitimate institutions be transparent to rational inquiry. Transparency requires that legitimate institutions bring about their ends in ways that can be made public. Violations of transparency occur when an institution requires that its members be ignorant as to its real function if it is to perform that function successfully. The transparency requirement is necessary in light of the education requirement and the requirement that the social order not trample on moral subjectivity. Although the education requirement goes a long way to making sure that legitimate institutions will reproduce themselves, it also has the potential to undermine moral subjectivity. The freedom associated with moral subjectivity is only realized when the institutions of which we are members offer us what we take to be adequate reasons for their action. One result of legitimate institutions forming us to find our ends in the roles they set out for us is that we come to see certain reasons as authoritative, but as a result of our education rather than our reflection.[11] The transparency requirement can be seen, then, as a way of blunting this worry. When an institution is transparent, there will be an explanation of why we not only do, but ought to, regard the reasons it offers us as authoritative, and that explanation will not rely on the institution's formative power.

The final aspect of the stability requirement can be seen as a consequence of the first two. It requires that we can be reconciled to the institution. The concept of reconciliation is central to Hegel's political philosophy, and more complicated than I can adequately capture here.[12] The basic idea, which will suffice for my purposes, is that reconciliation involves taking up an affirma-

---

11. The point is not that reflection and education will always be opposed, that education is always a form of brainwashing. Rather, the worry is that the unreflective absorption of my education might undermine the degree to which I can be said to reflectively adopt ends in keeping with my moral subjectivity.

12. For a clear and thorough account of the role of reconciliation in Hegel's thought, see Michael Hardimon, *Hegel's Social Philosophy: The Project of Reconciliation* (Cambridge: Cambridge University Press, 1994).

tive attitude toward the institutions of one's social world, wherein one finds that they can be a home. Reconciliation is the opposite of alienation, and reconciling oneself to the institutions of one's social world (assuming of course that they are worthy of reconciliation, that they do or can constitute a home) centrally involves overcoming alienation. An institution whose members can become reconciled to it is one in which they find, after critical reflection, that their fundamental ends and interests are met. Reconciliation is thus, in large part, a result of the institution having provided the educative role in a sufficiently transparent manner. In an important sense, no institution provides for all of our ends, and thus no institution by itself can be an adequate home for us, and thus we cannot become reconciled to any single institution in isolation. Rather, for Hegel, we become reconciled to the full array of institutions that make up the modern social world, which includes most importantly the sphere of *Sittlichkeit*: the family, civil society, and the state.

There is at least a derivative sense in which we can talk of being reconciled to any single institution, though, insofar as we come to see not only what ends it meets on its own, but what role it plays in the system of social institutions. Thus, for instance, I affirm the institutions of civil society insofar as they meet my material needs and provide me a means of self-expression. But if civil society were the only sphere of social institutions, I could not become reconciled to civil society, since it would fail to meet my needs for a stronger form of social membership and freedom from contingency, both of which are provided by the state, and for intimacy and love, which is provided by the family. Thus, civil society passes the reconciliation test, if it does, in large part because it fits into a larger arrangement of social institutions. The reconciliation test thus points toward the need for legitimate institutions both to meet certain substantial needs and to fit together with other legitimate institutions that can meet other needs.

Before turning to the institutions Hegel discusses in the *Philosophy of Right*, it is perhaps worth dwelling for a moment on how the three criteria of legitimacy outlined here work together. It is possible to think of each criterion as having certain shortcomings that are compensated for by the other two. In particular, each criterion on its own would allow as legitimate social institutions that would be neither stable nor just. It is thus only in combination that they serve as adequate criteria of legitimacy. Thus, for instance, institutions that embody shared wills may have a tendency to undermine diversity, especially if the formation of a shared will is taken to require a high degree of uniformity. The second criterion, which requires that legitimate institutions protect individual freedom and self-expression, serves to blunt this concern. Similarly, we have seen how institutions that embody shared wills can run into problems with stability. The third criterion serves to ensure that legitimate institutions will generate their own stability, so that there will be no need to call on external forces to ensure their stability.

The same kind of point can be made with regard to the second criterion: the protection of individual freedom. One potential drawback of fore-grounding the protection of individual freedom, as Hegel points out, is that it misconstrues as optional our relation to the state. It also has a tendency to see the state as playing a merely instrumental role in our lives, as indeed it is supposed to according to libertarian theories of the state. The second criterion alone, then, would count as legitimate institutions that fail to provide us with a strong form of social membership. The shared will criterion, however, protects against this worry. In addition, a state whose principal aim was the protection of individual freedom could create an alienating society, one in which citizens felt divided from one another and their state. The third criterion is meant to block this possibility.

Finally, we can examine the potential shortcomings of the third criterion taken in isolation. Here the worry is that an overemphasis on stability fails to grant adequate importance to issues of freedom, both autonomy and liberty. It may look as if a seamless totalitarian state would meet the third criterion, as might a society in which some group was thoroughly excluded and oppressed, but in which this was regarded by all as an appropriate response to natural differences. Each of these societies would, by hypothesis, form people who would come to see their ends as best realized within its confines. But neither would it protect individual freedom (at least not everyone's individual freedom), and at least the second could not be seen as the embodiment of a shared will of all its members. It is thus necessary for all three criteria of legitimacy to be met if a society is going to realize its members' freedom. A society that does meet all three criteria, however, is one that is just, legitimate, and stable.

3.3. Ethical Life I: The Family

The three main institutions of modern life as Hegel conceived of it—the family, civil society, and the state—together make up the realm of ethical life (*Sittlichkeit*). These institutions along with the spheres of property ownership (Abstract Right) and moral subjectivity (*Moralität*) together serve to meet Hegel's criteria of legitimacy and thus show that the modern social world is worthy of reconciliation. Since the most robust and therefore interesting forms of shared will are embodied in the institutions of ethical life, in particular the family and the state, I will focus my attention on these two institutions. First, though, some general remarks about the sphere of ethical life.

Ethical life has two sides to it. The objective ethical order is the concept of freedom developed in the existing world; roughly speaking, it consists of the institutions and laws that serve to realize freedom. One important feature of these institutions is that they derive their validity from considerations that do not directly involve the will of individuals independent of their place within these institutions. As Hegel puts it, "they are *laws and institutions which have being in and for themselves*."[13] The institutions that make up the objective ethical order can be thought of as those such that in willing their continued existence by playing the role they establish for me, I am thereby actualizing my self-conception as a free being.

Given that they serve to form our self-conceptions, these institutions cannot be justified on the basis of our prior willing of them, because we only come to be the sort of beings we are by living within these institutions. Thus, to evaluate these institutions, we have to compare how we fare under them with how we would fare under other institutions that could play a similar role in our lives but lack the central features of their ethical counterparts. For instance, the question to ask regarding the state is not whether I am more free in the state than in the state of nature, but whether the particular form of state that Hegel defends serves to realize my freedom in a way that other forms of social organization would not. Institutions of the objective ethical order will be institutions that meet the three criteria of legitimacy: they will embody shared wills, protect individual freedom, and serve to reproduce themselves.[14]

The other side of ethical life involves the awareness on the part of individuals that it is in virtue of their membership in the objective ethical order that they realize their deepest self-conceptions. Although it is not up to individuals to shape the institutions and laws of ethical life as they choose—these institutions are not dependent on individual wills in that way—the very structure of these institutions is such that individuals can come to affirm them. In fact, Hegel claims, the subject comes to see these institutions as something to which he is intrinsically linked: "the subject bears *spiritual witness* to them as to *its own essence*, in which it has its *self-awareness* and lives as in its element which is not distinct from itself—a relationship which is immediate and closer to identity than even *faith* or *trust*."[15] It is as a result

13. PhR, §144.
14. Although each institution meets each criterion to some degree, it is only in combination, and indeed in combination with the realms of Abstract Right and *Moralität*, that they most fully satisfy the three criteria.
15. PhR, §147.

of this side of ethical life that the institutions Hegel defends satisfy aspects of the second and third criteria of legitimacy: they serve to protect individual freedom and self-expression and form us in a manner that allows us to become reconciled to them.[16]

Before turning to the family, I want to highlight three distinctive characteristics of ethical life. First, the institutions of ethical life give us a series of substantial identities rather than merely a series of interests and goals. The connection between shared wills and shared identities is one of the central features of deliberative liberalism as well, and one of the means by which it can address the concerns of a politics of identity. Second, by justifying the institutions of ethical life in virtue of the ways their structural features allow them to satisfy the criteria of legitimacy, Hegel offers a justification for a set of institutions without relying on a theory of fundamental natural interests. Finally, although each institution of ethical life contributes to the satisfaction of each of the three criteria, they do so to different degrees. All three institutions embody shared wills, but the family is primarily a sphere of education and reconciliation, whereas civil society is primarily a sphere of individual expression. The state, insofar as it synthesizes the strengths of both the family and civil society, balances these two characteristics.

The family is the first institution of ethical life. It serves three primary functions within the modern social world: it provides for our needs for sex and intimacy in a manner that is liberating rather than constraining, it provides one significant outlet for individual self-expression through choice of marriage partner, and it provides for the biological and much of the social reproduction of the population through the bearing and education of children. Each of these, of course, corresponds to a different criterion of legitimacy. I focus here on the first and the third.

Families begin in marriage, and it is in marriage that we find the most important form of shared will within the family. We can see how marriage serves to realize a deep form of freedom by comparing it with the shared will embodied in contract. The first important difference between marriage and contract is the self-conception of the relating parties. In contract, the individual parties remain self-subsistent individual persons even in positing their common will in the contract.[17] In the family, in contrast, "one is present in it not as an independent person but as a *member*."[18] That is, insofar as

16. Neuhouser discusses the distinction between the objective and the subjective aspects of what he calls Hegel's conception of "social freedom" in *Foundations of Hegel's Social Theory*, chaps. 2 and 3, where he also argues that Rousseau makes use of a similar distinction.
17. PhR, §74, 75.
18. PhR, §158.

I am a member of a family, I come to see myself not as an independent person with no substantial ties to other members of the family, but as part of a larger whole. I come to see myself as a son or father, husband or brother, and these identities make no sense outside of my relations to my parents or children, spouse or siblings.

As a result of this self-conception, certain sorts of relationships with other people are not restrictions on my self-actualization but necessary aspects of that self-actualization. For instance, if I conceive of myself as an independent person, then finding myself sacrificing my own projects in order to help my spouse realize some of hers will seem like a restriction on my freedom. Part of being a husband, however, involves occasionally sacrificing my personal projects in order to help my spouse. Furthermore, part of being a couple will involve forming ends that are truly shared in the sense that they can only be understood as "our" ends, and not as either yours or mine, or even, in some sense, both yours and mine. If I think of myself as a husband, and not simply an independent person, then these are also my ends, and so I am free insofar as I pursue them. The point here is not that I do not have to sacrifice my personal projects any more, but that doing so realizes my conception of myself as a husband. Thus, insofar as I conceive of myself as a husband, making these sacrifices serves to realize my freedom rather than restrict it. Hegel thus describes the "objective origin" of marriage as lying in the "free consent of the persons concerned, and in particular their consent to *constitute a single person* and to give up their natural and individual personalities within this union. In this respect, their union is a self-limitation, but since they attain their substantial self-consciousness within it, it is in fact their liberation."[19]

It is easy to think that something unsavory is going on here.[20] Hegel is telling us that marriage does represent a form of self-restriction on the individuals who marry, and yet that from another point of view, it represents the realization of their freedom. Why is this other point of view not a form of false consciousness? To see why not, compare two couples, one bound by

19. PhR, §162.
20. In Hegel's case, there is something unsavory going on. As he goes on to explain, although both parties renounce their personality in favor of the personality of the couple, it is only the husband who in a certain sense truly gets his own personality back again, insofar as he also participates in the institutions of civil society and the state. This sort of problem is, of course, not exclusive to Hegel's theory—it appears throughout much of the history of actual marriage. Since my aim in this chapter is not to develop a Hegelian theory of marriage, but to understand Hegel's conception of citizenship and his strategy of political justification, in part by understanding how they are similar to his understanding of marriage, I will for the most part bracket these more unsavory aspects of his theory.

love, and the other by mutual need only. Doing so will allow us to focus on the transformation brought about by a true marriage (one bound by love), and to see whether it serves to realize our freedom. It allows us to ask whether, given similar circumstances, the transformation that love creates is a liberating one or not.

Each member of the couple bound together by mutual need requires things from the other and is willing to provide things in return. Nevertheless, they do not see themselves as a unit. They are two complete individuals with their own projects and plans. In order to count on the other one being there when needed, however, the first member of the couple has to also be available for the second member when needed. Being there for her partner, however, is not one of her essential projects; it is merely a means of guaranteeing the availability of her partner's help and support when she needs it. The demands placed on her insofar as she is part of a couple, then, will be in a position to clash with the demands of her projects. Fulfilling her responsibility to the couple will then come to seem like a sacrifice, a restriction on her own self-actualization and thus on her freedom. Even if she receives the support and comfort she needs from her partner, she will see the relationship as a necessary burden and a compromise.

For the loving couple, things will be different. Hegel describes love as

> the consciousness of my unity with another, so that I am not isolated on my own, but gain my self-consciousness only through the renunciation of my independent existence and through knowing myself as the unity of myself with another and of the other with me. . . . The first moment in love is that I do not wish to be an independent person in my own right and that, if I were, then I would feel deficient and incomplete. The second moment is that I find myself in another person, that I gain recognition in this person, who in turn gains recognition in me.[21]

My love for my wife means that I would feel incomplete without her because an important part of who I am is bound up in being married to her. As a result, her needs shape the couple's needs, which in turn shape my needs, and so when her needs pull me away from pursuing some personal project, I feel this not as an outside force preventing me from doing what I wish to do, but as an internal conflict. It is not like when a stranger at the door pulls me away from my work; it is more like the situation when I want to work in the library and I want to sit outside and enjoy the beautiful day. In fact, insofar as my identity is bound up with my being part of this couple,

21. PhR, §158A.

it would represent a greater restriction on my ability to be who I am if, when my wife needed me for something important, she hid the fact from me in order to let me continue working. What prevents the reciprocal satisfaction of each other's needs from being a restriction on our freedom, this argument concludes, is our love for one another. Thus, it turns out to make sense to say with Hegel that marriage represents a form of liberation.

The transformative effect that marriage has on our identity and self-conception turns out to allow for the formation of shared wills that cover our entire lives without obliterating our differences. There are two basic reasons for this. First, an institution need not be homogenous. People may play different roles within an institution and yet in virtue of these roles all be members of that institution, and thus contribute to the constitution of the shared will it embodies. Second, people have many different identities at any one time. Being a spouse may be a role that infuses my entire life in, say, the way that having contracted to buy a mango for fifty cents at the supermarket yesterday does not. And yet, being a spouse is perfectly consistent with also having a career, belonging to various associations, and being a citizen. As a result, my sharing one identity with my spouse need not prevent me from having all sorts of other identities I do not share with her.

Because marriage allows for both of these kinds of difference, it can serve to govern our lives in a much more pervasive sense than contract. As Hegel puts it, the "*ethical* aspect of marriage consists in the consciousness of this union as a substantial end, and hence in love, trust, and the sharing of the whole of individual existence."[22] Unlike contracts, which can only unify our wills with regard to external things, the institutions of ethical life can govern our entire existence as individuals, as marriage does, and yet in the process realize our freedom. As a result, they need not be optional in the way contracts must be. In fact, they cannot be optional in that way, for being optional in that manner would leave them vulnerable to individual caprice. Thus, while love plays a central role in Hegel's view of marriage, he is adamant that it cannot play the only role.[23] He says that marriage "should . . . be defined more precisely as rightfully ethical [*rechtlich sittliche*] love, so that the transient, capricious, and purely subjective aspects of love are excluded from it."[24]

The idea here is to turn what would otherwise be only an immediate relationship based on feeling alone into one mediated by an institution and thus based on the more solid foundation of reason. Marriage is a contract to

22. PhR, §163 (emphasis in original).
23. See PhR, §161A, 162R.
24. PhR, §161A.

transcend the standpoint of contract because it involves, in addition to the ties of love, a commitment by each spouse to surrender his or her personality to the unity of the couple for their entire lives. Each partner commits to be bound by the ties of love even in the absence of the feeling of love. For such a commitment to be possible, there must exist an institution of marriage that makes it in principle impossible and in actuality difficult to dissolve a marriage once it is formed. The concession to actual circumstances is necessary because even if marriage is not only about love, it has love, and thus feeling, for one of its moments and thus "is not absolute but unstable, and it has within it the possibility of dissolution."[25]

I now turn to the educative function played by the family. First, the family is a stable institution in that it serves to reproduce itself. Hegel claims that one of the effects of growing up in a loving family is that it shapes our natural desires for sex and companionship into a desire to get married and have a family. People who grow up in such families think that love and marriage go together, as in the old Frank Sinatra song, "like a horse and carriage." Thus, even before they find their spouse, they conceive of themselves as people whose substantial ends include marrying and having and raising children. Moreover, the family plays an important role in educating children so that they will come to develop ends that can best be realized in civil society and the state.[26]

Although the family plays important roles in satisfying the three criteria of legitimacy, it cannot do so alone. Members of a family are bound together by the feelings of love and trust. And while these allow the family to realize a form of freedom in the context of mutual interaction and dependence, the family's reliance on such feelings also make it inherently fragile. In addition, the family alone does not provide sufficient space for individual freedom (and this is particularly true for Hegel's traditionally sexist family). By placing the family within the structure of ethical life that includes civil society and the state, we address these shortcomings. The state is held together by more rational, less contingent and fragile ties, and civil society provides a realm where the principles of individual freedom are given their fullest expression.

3.4. Ethical Life II: The State

Hegel takes the separation of civil society from the state to be one of the chief advances of modern society, and his own conceptual separation of them

25. PhR, §163A.
26. PhR §174 &R, 175 & A & R.

is one of his lasting contributions to political thought. For my purposes, however, it is Hegel's discussion of the state that is of most importance.

In discussing Hegel's theory of the state, I focus only on his introductory remarks about the state, and in particular on four essential features of the state that I tie to the three criteria of legitimacy. First, the state is self-reproducing, and thus meets part of the third criterion. Second, it unifies rights and duties, which allows it to preserve individual freedom and thus meet the second criterion. Third, the state is held together by a feeling of trust that Hegel calls patriotism. Patriotism is the glue that binds the citizens into the shared will embodied by the state. In patriotism, then, we see how the state meets the first criterion of legitimacy. In addition, the discussion of patriotism sheds light on how people can form a shared will without the sort of face-to-face interaction that underlies the formation of a shared will in marriage. Finally, the state is transparent to rational insight and thus worthy of reconciliation. These final features allow the state to meet the rest of the third criterion.

For the state to be self-reproducing, citizens must, in freely willing as individuals, not will in a manner that undermines the universal will of the state. That is, their universal will must be their own will and must will the conditions of its possibility. The state must also meet certain requirements, so that in realizing the autonomy that comes from its embodying a shared will it does not trample on the individual wills of its citizens. The institutions of ethical life are self-reproducing because their members develop identities as a result of growing up and living within institutions that lead them to play their roles freely within those institutions. Their playing these roles serves to perpetuate these institutions. This, in turn, enables these institutions to continue to form them as they have come to be.

Hegel claims that the state meets this requirement because "the universal is simultaneously the concern of each [individual] as a particular [entity]": "It is the self-awareness of individuals which constitutes the actuality of the state, and its stability consists in the identity of the two aspects [the universal and the particular] in question."[27] This requirement, when satisfied, provides for the distinctive strength of the modern state, which lies "in the unity of its universal and ultimate end with the particular interest of individuals, in the fact that they have *duties* towards the state to the same extent as they also have rights."[28] That is, what ensures that the state is stable is that citizens are warranted in the attitude they take toward the state, in which the universal affairs of the state are seen as their particular concern. They are warranted in that attitude insofar as their duties and rights are unified.

27. Both quotes are from PhR, §265A. The phrase in brackets in the second is my addition.
28. PhR, §261.

We might describe the duties an individual owes to the state, or to any other institution of which she is a member, as stemming from the interest that the institution itself has, whether merely in its own preservation, or in carrying out its particular task. Duties thus appear to be imposed from above. They are the costs that individuals must pay in order to secure membership in the institution. Rights, on the other hand, open up possibilities for the individual to pursue. Insofar as rights are also guaranteed by institutions, they involve not a commandment but an opportunity. They are part of the benefits we get from belonging to a given institution.

For instance, if I belong to a food cooperative, I have certain duties, which require me to do a certain amount of the work necessary for the cooperative to function. Perhaps I have to inventory groceries once a week. I have these duties insofar as I am a member of the cooperative; they are determined by the needs of the cooperative. But in return for the performance of my duties, I also have certain rights: I can buy my food there at a discount. That these benefits count as rights of mine depends on two things. First, it is something that flows from my membership in the cooperative. Second, it is something I take to be a benefit. Of course, I take it to be a benefit not insofar as I am a member of the cooperative, but rather insofar as I am a person attempting to meet his needs for food as cheaply as possible. Thus, although my performance of my duties entitles me to this right, my duty with regard to the cooperative and my rights with regard to it touch different parts of my identity. In addition, although I gain the right because I perform the duty, these are two separate things: one involves taking inventory, and the other involves buying food.

Hegel claims that in the state the connection between rights and duties will be closer: "in the process of fulfilling his duty, the individual must somehow attain his own interest and satisfaction or settle his own account, and from his situation within the state, a right must accrue to him whereby the universal cause becomes *his own particular* cause."[29] Thus, insofar as we are citizens, our performance of our duties as citizens is supposed to realize our rights as citizens. The point, Hegel emphasizes, is not that the interests of the state outweigh our particular interests, but that our particular interests "should be harmonized with the universal."[30]

This final comment has an ominous ring to it. We need to see it in the right light, however. Insofar as I live in a just state, I come to think of myself as a citizen. One of the things it means to be a citizen is that I take the affairs

29. PhR, §261R.
30. Ibid.

of the state to be my business as well. Thus, in acting in accord with my self-conception as a citizen, I need to direct some of my personal interests toward public issues. Doing so is part of what it means to be a citizen. Acting in this manner, I thereby make it the case that in performing my duty to contribute to the upkeep of the state, taken broadly to include everything from paying taxes to contributing to public discussion of political issues, I also make use of what from my side of the situation looks like a right to do these things.

To a certain degree this is only possible because of the nature of the duties of citizenship in a modern state. Unlike in Plato's *Republic*, the particular role we play in the state is determined by the role we play in civil society, a role we choose.[31] In addition, the state serves not only to realize our freedom as citizens, but to secure once and for all our freedom as persons, moral subjects, family members, and burghers. Consequently, in upholding the state we make possible our free occupation of all these other roles. On the other side, since the state requires that people play all these roles, we do a certain amount of our duty to the state by acting out these roles in the proper manner.

Because it unifies our rights and duties in this fashion, the state serves to protect our individual freedom and thus meets the second criterion of legitimacy. Notice that it does this by meeting both aspects of that criterion. The state allows for difference within its framework: not only do citizens occupy different roles within the state due to their positions in civil society, but they are allowed to express different opinions about matters of state and to have those opinions taken into account in political debate.[32] At the same time, the state opens up room for the flourishing of the other institutions of ethical life in which we can pursue our own projects and plans. As we will see when we turn to deliberative liberalism, what allows for a liberal state to preserve individual freedom while embodying a shared will is precisely that the state is liberal and therefore leaves a great deal of room for diversity both within its institutions and in the rest of society. In addition, it is precisely deliberative liberalism's ability to unite rights and duties in this way that contributes to its stability.

Patriotism can be seen as the result of my becoming aware of my relation to the state as I have outlined it above. A citizen, like a spouse, has a consciousness of himself as a member of a larger whole. Unlike a (Hegelian) spouse, however, he sees that it is up to him to choose just what role to play

31. PhR, §262A.
32. See Neuhouser, *Foundations of Hegel's Social Theory*, chap. 7, for a lengthy and compelling discussion of the degree to which the space made within the state for moral subjectivity makes the Hegelian state more liberal than many commentators have interpreted it as being.

in this greater whole. This gives a citizen a greater distance from the institutions of the state than the spouse has from her partner or from the institution of marriage. Instead of the immediacy of love, citizens are bound together by an attitude Hegel calls patriotism and defines as a sort of trust:

> This disposition is in general one of *trust* (which may pass over into a more or less educated insight), or the consciousness that my substantial and particular interest is preserved and contained in the interest and end of an other (in this case, the state), and in the latter's relation to me as an individual. As a result, this other immediately ceases to be an other for me, and in my consciousness of this, I am free.[33]

Citizens, then, not only have the right sort of particular interests (those that are collectively realizable in the state); they have an awareness that their interests and those of the state are not at odds. In fact, as citizens, we "trust that the state will continue to exist and that particular interests can be fulfilled within it alone."[34] To illustrate his point, Hegel mentions what makes it possible for us to walk the streets in safety at night. We often forget that it might be otherwise; the feeling of safety becomes habit. And yet, were we to reflect on just what makes it possible for us to pursue our particular interest in walking the streets at night, we would realize "that it is solely the effect of particular institutions." Hegel concludes by claiming that states are held together not by force, but by "the basic sense of order which everyone possesses."[35] Because we all possess a basic sense of order, which we acquired through growing up under the institutions of ethical life, we have formed particular interests that do not require us to disturb the peace, to attack people on the street, and so forth, and thus we can live freely together. In large part, what allows the citizens of the modern state to form a shared will about political matters is that they share this background basic sense of order. This sense of order is then reinforced through their everyday activity within the state.

Here we can begin to tease out a model for the formation of a shared will that does not require all the citizens to come together face to face in order to affirm the activities of the state. Rather, through countless everyday interactions with one another and the institutions of the state, citizens form opinions and attitudes (such as the basic sense of order). This process of opinion formation is done together rather than side by side.[36] The

33. PhR, §268.
34. PhR, §268A.
35. Ibid.
36. I will discuss and develop the contrast between reasoning together and reasoning side by side in chapter 4.

result of all of these interactions is that citizens come to share certain opinions and attitudes. They also come to share a view about which political reasons are authoritative, and thus to share a will.[37] Patriotism is thus nothing other than the attitude of citizens who share in the will that animates the state.

In his discussion of patriotism, Hegel is quick to distinguish it from forms of mere opinion. It is "certainty based on *truth*" and a product of the rationality of the state.[38] I take his point here to be that it is necessary not only that citizens come to have this sort of trust in the institutions of the state, but that the state warrants their trust—and here we come to the final feature of the modern state I want to highlight. This final condition requires not only that the institutions of the state serve both to harmonize particular and universal interests and to form people into citizens, but that they do so in a manner that is rationally transparent. That is, it is necessary that an individual citizen be able to understand the reasons behind the organization and functioning of the state. Without the possibility of such insight, we can never be fully reconciled to the workings of the state, and thus can never be fully subjectively free. Imagine a state that is opaque to rational insight. Even if it creates citizens who have individual interests that allow them willingly to act to uphold and recreate the institutions of the state, they will nevertheless fail to be individuals. Hegel in fact argues that the states of ancient Greece where citizens, lacking the notion of individual moral subjectivity, see the laws of the state as otherworldly and thus not open to human scrutiny, are less fully ethical for this very reason.

On the basis of the social freedom argument alone, then, we can draw the following conclusions about what allows the modern state to meet the three criteria of legitimacy. The institutions of the state reproduce themselves because they serve to educate and construct people living under them as citizens. Being a citizen means having particular interests that cohere with the public interest, and taking public affairs as in an important sense one's own. It also involves standing in a relation of trust toward the institutions of the state, and thus requires a recognition of the role of the state in making possible the life you lead as a citizen (as well as the life you lead insofar as you are a person, moral subject, family member, and burgher). Finally, to ensure that this trust is not a form of false consciousness, it is necessary that the institutions of the state be accessible to rational scrutiny and insight and be able to stand up under such scrutiny.

37. Something like this process of opinion and will formation is at the heart of what is generally called, following Habermas, the public sphere. See Jürgen Habermas, *The Structural Transformation of the Public Sphere*, trans. Thomas Burger (Cambridge: MIT Press, 1989).
38. PhR, §268.

3.5. Conclusion: The Lessons of History

I have examined the political thought of Rousseau and Hegel in order to motivate and prepare the ground for the formulation of deliberative liberalism in the rest of the book.[39] We have seen how we can justify a political structure without presuming uniformity among individuals. In concluding this historical detour, I highlight eight aspects of Rousseau's and especially Hegel's views that resonate with what I develop in later chapters.

First, the conception of reason found in Rousseau and Hegel provides the grounds for the theory of reasonable deliberation developed in chapter 4. The further connection Hegel draws between shared wills and shared identities that is distinctive of the institutions of ethical life helps shape the account offered in chapter 4 and its application to the political deliberation of citizens in chapter 5.

Second, it is important for Hegel's defense of these institutions that they are stable. That stability is achieved in large measure because the institutions of ethical life include an educative function and are also transparent to rational inquiry. Deliberative liberalism also regards stability as a necessary criterion of justice. The process of reasonable deliberation that serves to form the shared will of citizens also plays an educative role. Through deliberating reasonably with those of our fellow citizens with whom we differ, we come to be aware of the diversity that characterizes our society. That awareness in turn leads us to become reasonable. I discuss the educative role of deliberation and its contribution to the stability of deliberative liberalism in chapter 8.

Although reasonable deliberation serves to form us into reasonable citizens, it also serves to determine the content of the state. And this leads to a third aspect of deliberative liberalism that is partially occluded in Hegel's theory: we cannot determine ahead of time precisely the nature of the will we can come to share as citizens. Insofar as deliberative liberalism takes a political approach, this result is desirable. This feature is occluded in Hegel's view because of his metaphysical freedom argument. As a result of the metaphysical freedom argument, we can tell ahead of time (i.e., prior to the actual deliberation of citizens) what would constitute the structure of a

---

39. Both Hardimon and Neuhouser point out a number of ways in which Rawls's political liberalism has deep affinities with Hegel's view. I wholeheartedly agree with their claims, and in fact hope to show that these affinities are perhaps even more pervasive than either Hardimon or Neuhouser recognizes. One of my aims for the book as a whole is to bring to the surface some of the Rousseauvian and Hegelian roots of Rawls's project.

just state. The open-ended quality of political deliberation is discussed in chapter 5.

Fourth, the attitude Hegel calls "patriotism" will have an analog in deliberative liberalism: the attitude of "reasonableness." Like patriotism, reasonableness on the part of the citizens will lead them to recognize that a state guided by just political principles is one in which they can preserve their differences from others, and yet at the same time share with them an identity as citizen. Achieving both of these results allows them to have more than merely instrumental relations with one another, and at the same time to realize their freedom, not only as citizens, but also as members of particular cultures, and as individuals. I discuss these issues in chapters 7 and 8.

Fifth, the identification in the Hegelian state between our rights and our duties will find resonance in two aspects of deliberative liberalism. The ideal of public reason demands of us that in arguing for particular policies, we do so on the basis of reasons all citizens can accept as authoritative. In doing so, it creates a duty of civility, of respect for the differences between ourselves and our fellow citizens. At the same time, it provides us an identical right: not to submit to the coercive force of the state, except in accordance with reasons we can accept as authoritative. Public reason is introduced in chapter 5, and discussed at some length in subsequent chapters. Furthermore, a set of arguments that grows out of the ideal of public reason and invokes the need for citizenship to be nonburdensome also sets up this sort of identification. Such arguments are the focus of chapter 7.

Sixth, the importance of stability and rational transparency finds echoes in deliberative liberalism's concern with what Rawls calls "stability for the right reasons." This form of stability is discussed in chapter 8. Deliberative liberalism achieves this sort of stability in the way the Hegelian state does, by setting up institutions that create roles and identities that realize our freedom through our affirmation of them.

Seventh, returning to Rousseau, deliberative liberalism will be concerned that power not be distributed asymmetrically within society. This concern arises, as it does in Rousseau, because of the worry that asymmetrical levels of power will serve to undermine the possibility of freedom, here through their interference with reasonable political deliberation. These matters are discussed in chapters 5 and 6.

Finally, deliberative liberalism holds on to a structure that plays a large role in Rousseau's theory but not in Hegel's: the two-tiered system set up by the social contract and the general will. It is this two-tiered system that allows for a democratic form of government that simultaneously entrenches certain rights and other legitimating principles. Deliberative liberalism will also make use of this structure in order to defend a requirement that levels of power be reciprocal and that citizenship be nonburdensome. Each of these requirements will be defended as being a necessary precondition for the possibility of reasonable political deliberation. They will thus fill the role played by the social contract in Rousseau's theory.

4

Reasonable Deliberation

The deliberative strand of Rousseau's argument, which Hegel develops, relies on an aspect of practical reason other than that relied on by the natural law strand. The natural law strand sits rather comfortably within the confines of rational choice theory. The deliberative strand, however, is likely to be misunderstood if it is placed within the framework of rational choice theory. Its distinctive qualities are best appreciated within the framework of a theory of what I call reasonable deliberation. In this chapter I develop the outlines of a theory of reasonable deliberation and, by way of illustration, contrast it with the better-known theory of rational choice.[1]

4.1: From Rational Choice to Reasonable Deliberation

Theories of rational choice focus on the question of how to choose what to do. That is, they are concerned with the selection of one among a set of possible actions. Furthermore, they tell us how to make such a choice rationally. They accomplish this aspect of their task by telling us how to choose "in order to achieve our aims as well as possible."[2]

---

1. This chapter reproduces much of the material in my "Outline of a Theory of Reasonable Deliberation," *Canadian Journal of Philosophy* 30 (2000): 551–580. Several of the issues treated here are discussed at greater length there.

2. Jon Elster, "Introduction," in *Rational Choice*, ed. Jon Elster (New York: New York University Press, 1986), 1.

Theories of reasonable deliberation, as I describe them here, analyze a different domain of reasoning in the service of action. First, their subject matter is the deliberation that leads to action, rather than the final selection of the action itself. Second, they ask about the intrinsic character of a deliberative path, rather than its likely outcome. That is, they are theories of the reasonableness of deliberation, rather than of its rationality. To see the distinctiveness of this theoretical domain, it helps to back away from the domain of rational choice theories one step at a time.

Beyond the question of which action to select, there is the question of what method to use in determining our selection. The world does not confront agents in the form of neatly packaged decision problems, with clearly identified options each bearing a value tag. Even if our sole criterion in choosing what to do is to choose rationally as this is defined by our favorite theory of rational choice, we will need to adopt a deliberative strategy to determine what to do. A theory of rational deliberation will help us make this choice. Such a theory is likely to call our attention to two related features of a deliberative strategy. First, is this strategy likely to produce the rational choice? Second, is this strategy likely to produce this result in a manner that is efficient and otherwise instrumentally appropriate? Deliberation can be hasty or overly cautious, and when it is, it can be open to rational criticism even if the end result is the otherwise rational choice. Different strategies require different investments of time or effort in gathering and analyzing information. The marginal benefit to be gained by using more thorough strategies might be outweighed by their extra costs. Someone who investigates options and weighs costs and benefits with the same care when buying a house as when buying shampoo is likely to deliberate badly in at least one of these cases. A theory of rational deliberation, then, will guide the choice of a deliberative strategy by identifying which is the most likely and efficient means of pursuing my aims as well as possible. We can, of course, easily expand rational choice theory to cover choice of strategies as well as choice of options.[3]

But there is a further concern we might have with our deliberative path to action. Sometimes we will be concerned with the character of our deliberation itself. Spelling out just what such concern amounts to and why it should fall under the purview of a theory of practical reason will be one of the primary aims of this chapter as a whole. But I can indicate briefly what I have in mind. Deliberation is a process of taking certain matters into consideration before deciding what to do. The result of deliberating is not only that I

---

3. David Schmidtz makes this sort of move in chapter 2 of his *Rational Choice and Moral Agency* (Princeton, N.J.: Princeton University Press, 1995).

make a choice, but that I have attended to a set of considerations. In some instances, it may be as important that I have attended to the right set of considerations as that I have decided upon the right choice. The importance of such attention is most noticeable in cases where we deliberate with others. In such cases, we attend to our deliberative partners in large part by attending to their reasons. The most clear-cut failures of deliberative attention have a moral quality to them: deliberation can be insensitive, ruthless, or unfair, even if it is a reliable generator of rational choices. The question of whether the deliberative path we take to our choice of action is sufficiently sensitive to the appropriate reasons is the question of whether the deliberation is reasonable. A theory of reasonable deliberation thus analyzes the intrinsic character of deliberation rather than its reliability or the choices it yields.[4]

Theories of reasonable deliberation share at least three features, all of which distinguish them from most rational choice theories. This section sets out these features and contrasts them, by way of illustration, with the corresponding aspects of rational choice theories. It is worth emphasizing, however, that these contrasts are meant solely to clarify the features of theories of reasonable deliberation, and not to set the stage for a criticism of rational choice theories or any particular rational choice theory.

Theories of rational choice and theories of rational deliberation regard deliberation on the model of calculation. For instance, Jon Elster describes rational choice theories as composed of a three-part characterization of a choice situation, and a simple function that selects the highest ranked action as rational.[5] Within such a theory, deliberation is captured by the application of the function to the choice set. Even when rational choice theories are broadened to include choice of strategies, the deliberative strategies are characterized as different choice functions. In contrast, theories of reasonable deliberation do not reduce deliberation to calculation. For these theories, the archetypal example of deliberation is not a single agent applying a function to a choice set, but rather a group of agents exchanging reasons.

The import of this difference becomes clear when we contrast it with the standard means by which rational choice theories treat of choice situations involving multiple agents. In such cases, rational choice theories treat the

---

4. Of course, a theory of reasonable deliberation will not be wholly insensitive to the choice a deliberation yields. The end result of deliberation will serve, however, not as a direct criterion for the deliberation being reasonable, but as a kind of evidence of the reasonableness or unreasonableness of the deliberation.

5. Elster, "Introduction," 4. The three components are a feasible set of possible actions, a set of beliefs about the likely outcomes of taking these actions, and a subjective ranking of these actions, often in terms of the ranking of their likely outcomes.

agents as reasoning side by side. Elster, for instance, describes the difference between one- and many-person decision situations as involving the difference between parametric and strategic decisions. When making a parametric decision, the agent can treat the choice environment as fixed. The relevant aspects of that environment are given ahead of time and are unaffected by the agent's choice. In strategic decisions, however, the environment is not fixed. Rather, the environment is subject to change as a result of the agent's actions because the environment includes other agents who will react to the agent's choice, or even to what they anticipate his choice will be. Nevertheless, even with strategic decisions, each agent reasons alone. The other agents still enter the picture merely as part of what is admittedly a more complicated choice environment.

In contrast, the theory of reasonable deliberation takes cases where a number of people reason together as paradigmatic.[6] When we reason together, we exchange reasons. That is, we offer up to one another considerations we take to be relevant to the choices at hand. The reasonableness of such deliberation will depend, then, on the way that exchange proceeds. For now, I merely note that focusing on the exchange of reasons among agents rather than on their individual calculations about what to do means that the decisions we each take are not merely strategic. Rather, to deliberate reasonably together, each agent must regard his fellow deliberators as more than particularly complicated pieces of the furniture of the universe.

This first contrast leads to the second, which can be thought of as spelling out the difference between the reasonable and the rational. As a result of being rational, according to rational choice theory, I can choose my ends wisely and pursue them more efficiently, more effectively.[7] A well-wrought theory of rational choice will help me to choose my actions in the light of my goals, as well as in light of my other concerns, commitments, and values. Nevertheless, on this picture, rationality is basically a tool I use to find my way in the world.

The theory of reasonable deliberation, by contrast, focuses on the role reasoning together plays in structuring our relationships, and on the contexts in which we form, alter, and maintain those relationships. Being reasonable, on this picture, makes it possible for people with divergent ends

---

6. It need not thereby conclude that we never deliberate alone. For a rich account of individual practical reasoning that includes not only rational choice but also reasonable deliberation, see Barbara Herman, *The Practice of Moral Judgment* (Cambridge: Harvard University Press, 1993), esp. chaps. 7 and 9.

7. I am assuming here a rational choice theory that is not purely instrumental. Instrumental rational choice theories will of course limit the role of rationality to the efficient and effective pursuit of given ends.

and interests to live together in ways that preserve their autonomy. It makes such relationships possible by giving us the capacity to form shared wills.[8] When our relationships are open to revision via reasonable deliberation, then we can share a space of reasons. When these reasons guide our action, we are guided by reasons we recognize as our own, and thus are autonomous. Asking whether a deliberation is reasonable, then, is not a way of asking whether it reliably produces a collectively desired outcome, nor is it a way of assessing the rationality of the ends pursued. Rather, it is a way of asking about the inner constitution of the relationship among the deliberators and the way that relationship is altered or maintained as a result of the process of deliberation itself.

What determines whether we are investigating the rationality of a deliberative process or its reasonableness are the questions we ask and not the phenomena we examine. A group of people might deliberate together in order to reach a collective decision about what to do. If we are interested in the rationality of their deliberation, we will look at their exchange and ask if it served the cause of their coming to select the best available alternative. If we are interested in the reasonableness of their deliberation, we will look at the same exchange and ask whether it properly respected the relationships that obtained among them.

Finally, each theory focuses on a different role reasons play in our deliberations, and thus each takes up a different aspect of the nature and authority of reasons. Rational choice theory regards reasons on the model of points in a game. The game, we might say, is to realize as many of your ends (perhaps weighted for importance) as possible given your environment. As a result, something counts as a reason for you to act one way rather than another if it indicates that something about either the configuration of your ends or the choice environment will affect the point total associated with a given action. Depending on what content is added to a given version of rational choice theory, very different sorts of considerations will count as reasons. Nothing, for instance, rules out the possibility that rational choice theory will regard the desires and ends of others as giving rise to reasons for me to act. It is important to note, however, that they will only give rise to reasons to act if they fit into my chosen set of ends or serve to reshape my environment. In this sense, even those rational choice theories that allow my ends to include the well-being of others regard rational choice as a solipsistic exercise.

Theories of reasonable deliberation, however, focus on reasons that act as

8. Note the parallels between the role of reasonable deliberation here and in Rousseau's theory.

claims and considerations we urge on one another in the course of forming, altering, and maintaining our relationships.[9] According to the theory of reasonable deliberation I sketch below, claims take on the normative authority of reasons when they find support in those relationships, and in consequence, in our "practical identities."[10]

Whether or not one person has a claim on another may depend on the nature of their relationship. Thus, in many cases, whether something counts as a reason for the purposes of assessing the reasonableness of deliberation will depend on who is offering the reason to whom. As a result, theories of reasonable deliberation will be likely to pay heed to the sorts of details that are routinely ignored by rational choice theories.

In addition, seeing reasons as claims requires that we adopt a slightly more detailed psychological picture than that relied upon by rational choice theories. Claims are by their nature not always something we desire to fulfill, and so in order to imagine people capable of acknowledging and acting on claims, we have to imagine people capable of acting in ways not determined by their desires or preexisting ends.[11] Recall that Rousseau emphasizes precisely this point about our psychic structure as one of the central transformations that result from the development of human reason.

Finally, it is important to note here that a claims-based theory of reasons changes the relation between reasons and ends. If we conceive of reasons as claims, then it turns out that we need not think of our ends and environment

9. What I call a claims-based theory of practical reason can be found in the work of a variety of philosophers. See, for instance, Charles Taylor, "Explanation and Practical Reason," in *The Quality of Life*, eds. Martha Nussbaum and Amartya Sen (Oxford: Oxford University Press, 1993); T. M. Scanlon, "Contractualism and Utilitarianism," in *Utilitarianism and beyond*, eds. Bernard Williams and Amartya Sen (Cambridge: Cambridge University Press, 1982); Christine Korsgaard, "The Reasons We Can Share," in *Creating the Kingdom of Ends* (Cambridge: Cambridge University Press, 1996), and *The Sources of Normativity*; and various writings of Jürgen Habermas. In addition, I would argue that Rawls has a claims-based theory of reasons, and that certain of Kant's remarks can be read as endorsing this view of reasons. For an elaboration of this view of Kant, see Andrews Reath, "The Categorical Imperative and Kant's Conception of Practical Rationality," *Monist* 72 (1989): 384–410. Of course, as is suggested by the preceding chapters, both Rousseau and Hegel invoked this conception of reasons as well.

10. Although my account of the relationship between identities and the normative authority of reasons is in many ways similar to Christine Korsgaard's, whose term this is, we arrive at our concerns via somewhat different paths and use them toward different ends. One important difference to flag is the degree to which I regard all important aspects of our practical identities as relational.

11. They may nevertheless sometimes act reasonably in ways that satisfy their desires. Sometimes, our desires give us reasons to satisfy them. In addition, there are many things we want to do that we have, all things considered, good reasons for doing, quite apart from the fact that we want to. The presence of such reasons, however, means that even if we didn't want to act in this way, we would still have good reasons for doing so, and it is in that sense that the action has a claim on us.

as more or less fixed elements that give rise to reasons. The question of whether or not a claim has authority for me (or perhaps should have authority for me) cannot be reduced to the question of whether it relates to an end I have or to the environment I face. For instance, on the theory I develop below, the claims of others have authority for us because of the relationships we form with them. When these relationships give rise to further ends (including the preservation and maintenance of the relationship), these ends are best seen as products of the reasons, and not their source.

4.2. A Theory of Reasonable Deliberation: The Bare Bones

This section offers the barest outline of a particular theory of reasonable deliberation. I defend and further develop this outline in later sections. As I said above, the particular theory developed here locates the normative authority of those claims that count as reasons in the relationships that obtain between those making the claims and those on whom they are made. In particular, it regards the shared warranted understanding of relationships as the source of the normativity of reasons. Thus, for example, when someone makes a claim on me, that claim has the authority of a reason if it finds support in an aspect of our relationship that we are both warranted in acknowledging. While this approach has the advantage of directly tying the normative status of the reasons analyzed by the theory to the functional role of reasonableness in forming and maintaining relationships, it has two potential problems. Both point to the apparent flimsiness of shared understandings of relationships as the source of normativity. The first points to the practical flimsiness of relationships. Relationships are not fixed once and for all. They are subject to sudden change, and change that is not itself the result of reasonable deliberation among all parties to the relationship. Relationships thus seem like poor candidate grounds for the normativity of reasons. The theory developed below addresses this concern by connecting the relationships in which we are members with our practical identities. This connection highlights the stability of relationships while acknowledging their flexibility. The flexibility that remains, however, is an advantage in a source of normativity.

The more serious concern points to what might be called the normative flimsiness of relationships. Many relationships are one-sided and oppressive. Such relationships seem not only bad but downright dangerous candidates for housing a source of normativity. Many people accept their lot in abusive relationships, and it would be wrong to say that their acceptance thus legitimates the abuse because it is supported by the nature of their relationship. Nor, the worry continues, is this problem helped by the connection between relationships and identity that served to forestall the first worry. Many people's identities are wrapped up in socially constructed roles that are demeaning or oppressive. Clearly someone's identity as a woman in a sexist society that defines a woman as a kind of subperson cannot ground the normative authority of claims that invoke her identity to exploit her status.[12]

In response to this worry, the theory developed below attempts a robust but nonfoundationalist answer that will no doubt be controversial. Rather than providing an external set of criteria by which we can distinguish good relationships from bad, it claims that these criteria are to be found in the criteria for reasonable deliberation itself. I argue below that only certain kinds of relationships admit even the possibility of truly reasonable deliberation. In particular, reasonable deliberation requires that all participants be allowed to reject claims made upon them, and that such rejection have an effect on the future course of the deliberation. In the case of oppressive relationships, then, we can say that even though the parties make claims on one another that rest entirely on their shared understanding of their relationship, their deliberation is nevertheless not reasonable. This approach has two advantages over a more foundationalist external approach. First, it is theoretically parsimonious: we need not develop a theory of relationships in addition to a theory of reasonable deliberation. Second, it makes possible a non-normative use of the term "reason" that parallels the normative one. In the case of oppressive relationships that are accepted by all parties, we will be able to explain the interactions that take place in the absence of brute force in terms of the reasons exchanged by showing how the claims being made rest on the parties' understanding of their relationship.

4.3. Reasons as Claims

Pat is trying to get some work done. Sandy, noticing what a beautiful day it is outside, suggests that they go for a walk together. Pat responds that the work is going well and it needs to get done, and that taking a walk now would interrupt things at a crucial point. Sandy asks how much longer Pat has to work, and Pat responds, "Only an hour." Since it is only one in the

---

12. The term "subperson" comes from Charles Mills, who uses it to analyze the nature and harm of racism and white supremacy. See, for instance, his "Non-Cartesian *Sums*," in his *Blackness Visible* (Ithaca, N.Y.: Cornell University Press, 1997).

afternoon, they agree to go for a walk in an hour, and Sandy leaves Pat at the computer and goes out on the porch to read a book.

Pat and Sandy have deliberated together about how to spend the afternoon. They have, of course, also each come to a decision about how to spend the afternoon, and so we can ask whether their decisions were rational, and even whether the deliberative process they engaged in on their way to making their decisions was rational. The theory of reasonable deliberation, as I stressed above, asks a different question: was their deliberation reasonable? Did they each properly attend to the reasons they had for deciding what to do? In particular, did each of them properly attend to the reasons for acting that stemmed from their relationship to the other and the claims each made that rested on that relationship?

To answer these questions, we need to start by determining what reasons each has for acting one way rather than another. Answering this question requires working out what counts as a reason for each of them, and in particular, whether the claims made in the course of their discussion have the normative authority of reasons. What, then, are those claims?

Sandy expresses a desire to go for a walk with Pat. Pat takes up Sandy's utterance as a reason by regarding it not as a mere piece of information about the world, but as the urging of a claim that Sandy, at least, takes to have authority. Pat can regard Sandy's claim in this way without necessarily accepting it, however. Pat sees Sandy's claim as defeasible and mentions the work that needs to get done. Sandy takes this up as a reason by understanding it as urging a counterclaim. Sandy's wish to go for a walk together carries some weight, but in the presence of Pat's desire to work, it may not carry enough. When Sandy now asks how much longer Pat must work, it is not merely an attempt to find out new facts, but also, and more centrally, an attempt to understand the precise nature of Pat's claim. The question, then, stands as an implicit recognition that Sandy has at least a *prima facie* reason to let Pat work. Finally, Pat can take up Sandy's question as a move in their activity of reasoning together by understanding it as a qualified reiteration of the original claim. They have both then acknowledged that Sandy's desire to go for a walk and Pat's desire to work place both of them under conflicting claims. Thus, the rest of their exchange can be understood as working out together how to reconcile those claims, how to acknowledge and adequately respond to their normative authority, rather than deciding on the appropriate allocation of costs.

In order to know what reasons they have for acting we need to determine (as do they) which of the claims urged have normative authority, which rise to the status of reasons. Claims, I argue, derive their normative authority from warranted shared understandings of relationships. You and I stand in a certain relationship. If I offer you a reason for acting in a certain way, then I am urging a claim on you to act that way based on what I take to be our shared understanding of our relationship. In particular, I am relying on our shared understanding of our relationship as being able to support the claim in question. Perhaps we are only related insofar as we are both human beings, and then our relationship might only sustain basic moral claims.[13] Perhaps we are professional colleagues but not especially close, and then I can claim certain kinds of conduct from you, such as a willingness to evaluate my work, but perhaps not tenderness. The important point is that claims become reasons because they derive authority from our relationships and the authority we give them, rather than directly from their ability to contribute to the realization of our already given ends.

We can see the difference it makes to think of reasons as claims by thinking about the response that is appropriate to someone making a claim on us, and how it differs from the response appropriate to the presence of a reason on the model of rational choice theory, where reasons are regarded as a subclass of facts about the world (including the people reasoning). On the claim-based view, Sandy offers a *reason* to go for a walk by asserting a claim on Pat, a claim based on their relationship to one another being the sort of relationship it is. For this reason to be effective, Pat must take Sandy's utterance up as a reason. Such uptake involves acknowledging something about their relationship: that it supports the claim that Sandy is making. Such acknowledgment need not involve taking the claim to be decisive, but merely as warranted, as reasonable.

This sort of response stands in contrast to Pat taking up Sandy's expression of desire as merely a fact. Uptake of facts need not require any acknowledgment about their relationship, but merely the recognition of the fact that Sandy wants to go for a walk and how it changes the nature of the choice situation Pat faces. Reacting to Sandy's expressed desire as a new fact about the choice situation is thus not essentially different from reacting to any other new piece of information. On this interpretation, Sandy's desire changes Pat's choice situation in precisely the same way that a notice that the server will go down in an hour or a suddenly recalled plan to watch the Bulls game does.

13. It might sound strange to say of our relation to our fellow humans and the reasons this supports that it depends on any sort of shared understanding. As I see it, in making basic moral claims on fellow members of the species I am relying on a particular (though perhaps unarticulated) understanding of the meaning of our common membership, whether it is as fellow inhabitants of a planet with limited resources, as fellow rational creatures, as fellow creatures made in the image of God, or whatever. Making such a claim in good faith thus involves the thought that this understanding is one we either share already or could come to share.

In what could be termed a successful exchange of reasons, Sandy urges a claim that finds support in their shared understanding of their relationship, and then Pat takes up this claim as a reason. It is important to note, however, that these two steps are not entirely independent. That Pat takes up Sandy's claim as a reason will in some cases be sufficient to reaffirm that claim's already constituted normative authority. In other cases, however, Pat's uptake will play a role in constituting the normative authority of the claim. Relationships do not have lives over and above the attitudes, commitments, behaviors, and understandings of those who form the relationship. What makes it the case that a relationship supports a certain claim is to a large degree the fact that the parties to the relationship understand it that way. That understanding, however, may be nothing more than the disposition to take up claims of this sort as reasons in deliberation. Deliberation is thus a somewhat self-reflexive process.

One important consequence of this self-reflexivity is that the sort of reasons to which theories of reasonable deliberation draw our attention can be constructed as well as discovered. Moreover, they can be constructed through the process of reasonable deliberation itself. Pat and Sandy construct the space of reasons they share in virtue of their relationship by making claims on each other in the process of building, developing, and maintaining that relationship, a process that includes but is not limited to episodes of reasonable deliberation.[14] That relationship, in turn, is partially constituted by their shared recognition of what sorts of claims it can support. Thus, when Pat takes up Sandy's claim as a reason, this very action can make it a reason, by (re)establishing the ground of its normative force.

Imagine, for instance, that Pat and Sandy have just moved in together, and that they have therefore not come to a shared understanding of what sorts of claims override the need to work. If Sandy suggests going for a walk even though it is clear that Pat is working, this suggestion can be taken to offer up for consideration a kind of claim that could override work. Whether this consideration has the force of a reason will depend on whether or not Pat shares the understanding of the relationship on which it is based. If Pat does not share this understanding of the relationship and thus fails to take up Sandy's utterance as a reason, then this renders it not a

14. I hasten to add here that in most cases when we construct relationships through reasonable deliberation, it is not via reasonable deliberation about the relationship, but about all sorts of other matters: what to have for dinner, what causes to support, where to live, how to divide joint responsibilities, whether a joke was funny or insensitive, whether forgiveness forced or sincere.

reason, since it turns out not to have been a claim based on their shared understanding of their relationship.[15]

Because reasons can be constructed in this way, we need not think of the space of reasons in which deliberation takes place as already determined by the content of our ends, even where these ends include being in certain relationships or certain kinds of relationships. In forming relationships we undertake normative commitments: commitments to regard certain claims of others as having the force of reasons for us. One consequence of undertaking such normative commitments is that we come to form new ends. These ends, however, are best seen as the byproducts of our commitments rather than as the source of those commitments or their authority. A claims-based account of reasons need not, then, start with a given set of ends. It can explain the generation of ends as the byproduct of our coming to be in certain relationships. That is, we have reasons to adopt certain ends, to see certain interests as properly our own, because we stand in relationships that authorize certain reasons. An important consequence of this feature of reasonable deliberation is that it makes it possible for people whose ends conflict to nevertheless come to an agreement that is more than a mere compromise.

A focus on reasonable deliberation reveals not only a rich taxonomy of possible agreements, but also a rich array of possible failures to reach agreement that do not signal the hopelessness of further deliberation. There are several ways in which Pat can fail to accept Sandy's reason. Perhaps the relationship supports Sandy's claim *prima facie*, but in the face of Pat's conflicting claim it does not. In such a case, Pat will be able to acknowledge the relationship but contest the authority of the reason: "I'd love to go for a walk, but I just have too much work to do." And then Pat and Sandy will be reasoning together. Even if Pat fails entirely to take up Sandy's utterance as a reason ("Can't you see I'm working?"), we are not stuck imagining a complete breakdown of deliberation. Rather, we can conclude that they have more serious problems to work out than how to spend the afternoon. Instead of imagining that their conversation breaks down, we can see how they might be led to a more extensive conversation about the nature of their relationship and the sorts of claims it supports.

---

15. At least, the above paragraph represents one way of interpreting what has happened. As I clarify below, there may be times when the appropriate interpretation of a failure to take up a reason as a reason is not that there was no reason, but that the deliberation or one of its participants was not reasonable.

4.4. The Practical and Normative Flimsiness of Relationships

If the normative status of the claims we make on one another rests on nothing more solid than our shared understandings of our relationships, it may seem as though this theoretical castle of reasonable deliberation has been built on a heap of sand. There are, at first glance, a number of potential problems with this account of reasons. It turns out to be unclear how, on this account, uptake can be either sufficient or necessary to render a claim a reason.

Actual uptake looks like it cannot alone be sufficient, since if it were, all deliberation that resulted in agreement would have to be correct. A claim might contain propositions represented as factual, and these could be false. In such cases, if my deliberative partner takes up my claim as a reason, we want to say that she has made a mistake, rather than that her uptake somehow renders the error correct. In dealing with this problem, it helps to distinguish two sorts of errors. My claim might involve errors about the world or it might involve errors about the nature of our relationship. For now I will bracket the question of what to do about false claims about the world. It is a serious issue, but it is one all theories of practical reason have to address, and how we address it will not fundamentally change the structure of the view I am defending. At the very least, it seems as if reasonable deliberation will require that the deliberators be open to revision in light of new information about the truth or falsity of the factual content of their claims.

Errors about the nature of our relationship require us to have some way of establishing the facts of the matter about our relationship, which can at times be independent of what each of us says here and now about the relationship. Some of these problems can be handled in a relatively straightforward manner for relationships that involve social roles. There are, for instance, social rules and even laws that define the employer/employee relationship. Insofar as a boss is urging a claim on her employee within the confines of this relationship, there is an independent fact of the matter as to what this relationship authorizes even if that fact is currently vague or hard to see without third-party investigation.[16] In the case of personal

---

16. Note that the presence of social roles is meant to address the practical flimsiness of relationships and not their potential normative flimsiness. That is, we do not have any guarantee at this point that the socially or legally defined roles will be just or reciprocal in any way. They may turn out to be ones the full theory will say do not allow for reasonable deliberation. Even such cases, however, will solve the problem of practical flimsiness, since they will provide determinate and stable answers to the questions of what claims a particular relationship supports.

relationships and relationships less well governed by social norms or laws, the solution I offer to the second problem will help.

The second problem is that uptake as such cannot be necessary. There will be cases where we will want to say that someone's rejection of a claim is unreasonable, rather than that it undermines the reason-status of the claim. Imagine that Pat is less accommodating than I have been suggesting. Sandy expresses a desire to go for a walk with Pat and takes this utterance to offer a legitimate claim. Now if the normativity of this claim rests on nothing firmer than Pat recognizing that their relationship supports Sandy's claim in this instance, it is hard to see that it has any normative force at all. What is to stop Pat from insisting that their relationship supports no such claim and thus sloughing it off?

This case actually raises two problems. The first has to do with the practical flimsiness of relationships. That is, the possibility that Pat rejects Sandy's claim on a whim and thus undermines the normative force of Sandy's claim would appear to be a further indication that relationships are not sufficiently stable to provide the grounding for normativity. The second has to do with the purported normative flimsiness of actual relationships. Grant that Pat cannot undermine the normative status of Sandy's claim on a whim. Nevertheless, Pat's rejection of Sandy's claim might be grounded in Pat's unilateral conclusion that their relationship needs to change in fundamental ways. Furthermore, Sandy might accept Pat's rejection as decisive because part of the structure of their relationship is that Pat has the authority to shape its contours unilaterally. The problem here would not be that Pat has reacted in an ill-considered manner, but that the normative bite of Pat's rejection flows from the dominant role Pat plays in their relationship. If we are wary of relations of domination grounding normative authority, then we will want to say that the actual character of Pat and Sandy's relationship turns out not to serve as a source of normativity. I take each of these worries in turn.

4.5. Shoring Up Our Claims: Reasons, Identities, and Relationships

Although I have been investigating the authority of reasons by considering the role they play in deliberation, it is possible to approach the issue of their authority via a different route. Start from the fact that characterizes reasonable people: we have wills separable from our desires. In other words, our wills are not completely determined by our desires. Faced with desires, we can choose to endorse them and thus to will the actions necessary to their satisfaction; or we can fail to endorse them, though in a way that need not make them disappear. But if our wills are not completely determined by our desires, then something else must determine our wills because we do, in fact, will and we do, in fact, act. If our wills remained undetermined, then we would not be able to will anything or to act at all. Thus, even if it turns out that I always will to endorse the strongest of my desires at any given moment, this still requires that my will be determined by some principle: the principle of always acting on the strongest desire of the moment.

What, then, determines our wills? In order to will in line with a particular principle, I have to endorse it, regard it as somehow an appropriate guide to my will. In order to conceive ourselves as acting at all, then, we have to think that we are determining our wills ourselves. To conceive our wills as being determined outside ourselves would be to conceive ourselves as being acted upon, and it is simply impossible to actually act under such a conception. If we sit around presuming that something external to us determines our wills and causes us to act, then we sit around waiting for something to happen. We do not act. The consequence of this fact about the nature of human action is that I must regard that which determines my will as in some deep sense me. We can then think of the principles that determine my will as constituting a sort of practical identity—my identity insofar as it determines my actions.[17] My practical identity is my conception of myself, my view of what about me makes my life valuable: it captures those aspects of my self that have the authority to determine my actions.

We might say, then, that in forming a stable identity over time, I come to give authority to certain facts about myself (or at least to recognize this authority when it arises prior to my willed endorsement of it). In doing so, I determine my will in particular ways. Claims have authority over me insofar as they appeal to facts about myself that have authority over me, so they will rise to the status of reasons if they appeal to some or other aspect of my practical identity.

The connection between the authority of reasons and practical identity helps provide a response to the worry about the practical flimsiness of claims-based reasons. Grounding the normative authority of claims on relationships seemed to leave normativity up to the whims of individual deliberators. We are less likely to have that impression when thinking about the relationship between reasons and practical identity. Identities are stable, if

17. For a detailed discussion of the connection between practical identities and the authority of reasons, where it is tied to more explicitly Kantian roots, see Korsgaard, *The Sources of Normativity*, esp. lecture 3. The argument above generally follows hers. It is, of course, also one way of filling in Kant's claim in the *Groundwork* that rational beings must act under the idea of freedom.

not static. I cannot merely change what I value about my life by deciding to do so or declaring that I have. As a result of that stability, however, we can be sufficiently sure, at any given moment, that when we offer a claim based on a certain well-founded understanding of some aspect of another's practical identity, we will be in a position to assess its fate properly. That is, we can determine whether the rejection of our claim is warranted, thus rendering the claim not a reason, or unwarranted, thus rendering our deliberation partner unreasonable. If we attend to our situation, then, we will generally be in a position to know if we should regard our claim as a proposed reason or an already well-grounded one, and that will help us to determine the appropriate response to its rejection.

The connection between practical identities and the authority of reasons serves two purposes: it shores up the potential practical flimsiness of the claims-based account of reasons, and it provides the foundation for a connection between identity and normative authority that is central to understanding the importance of the claims of the politics of identity from within a reason-based political theory such as liberalism. In the rest of this section, I further develop both of these lines of thought, by connecting my account of identity with my account of relationships. Doing so will show that relationships are no more practically flimsy than identities. It will also set out rather explicitly the nature of the claims made by the politics of identity in a language with which liberals are more likely to be familiar and thus comfortable.

I start by distinguishing two sorts of practical identity and two senses of relationship.[18] I then set out the connections among these four notions and the authority of reasons. Distinguish, first, between personal and social aspects of a practical identity. Personal aspects of a practical identity are particular aspects, things that serve to differentiate and thus individualize us. So, for example, personal aspects of a person's practical identity include that they are this person's spouse or that person's parent or these people's friends or colleagues. Social aspects of an identity are better thought of as arising from membership in various and sundry socially salient groups: being of a particular gender or race or ethnicity or religious group or profession. As this list is meant to suggest, social aspects of our identity come in both chosen and unchosen forms. What is distinctive about them is that they locate a person socially, as an intersection of types, we might say. Personal aspects, on the other hand, locate her as a particular individual. Clearly, this distinction is not hard and fast, neither in its application to real life nor in its purely

18. These two distinctions are further refined in chapter 5, section 2.

abstract usage. Nevertheless, it serves a useful heuristic purpose in setting out the connections between identities, reasons, and relationships.

Turn now to relationships. I distinguish between relationships we form and relationships in which we stand. We form relationships with others through interacting with them, building up piece by piece a set of expectations and understandings. In short, in the course of forming relationships with others, we come to share a set of reasons with them, to all give together a certain normative authority to particular claims. The sense, then, in which the authority of reasons rests on our relationships is the sense of relationships we form.

In contrast, we can stand in relationship to another in virtue of the social positions we occupy, regardless of whether we have ever interacted with that other. Such relationships exist only via the mediation of a social structure that sets out the social positions we occupy, their relationship and the criteria that determine who occupies which position. As I said in chapter 1, I agree with Iris Young's basic account of social groups as determined not by the essential characteristics their members have in common, but rather by their members' shared place within such a social system. One consequence of this is that membership in such groups leads us to stand in relationships both with other members of that group and with members of complementary groups. Thus, for instance, we can say that women stand in a relationship to one another on the basis of their joint occupation of the social position marked by their gender, and that they stand in a different relationship to men in virtue of the relative social positions set out for each gender in our social system.

In much of my discussion so far I have focused on the relationships we form and the personal aspects of our identity. The connection between them is rather straightforward. To get from identities to relationships, we need only note the ways in which even personal aspects of our practical identities are often public, and this in two senses. First, they are epistemologically public: we can know facts about other people's identities.[19] We rely on such knowledge in making judgments about the grounds of people's actions and about whether those actions are hypocritical or lacking in

---

19. Of course, this knowledge can never be perfect: it can all too easily be wrong or incomplete. This is also true of our knowledge of our own identities. We may not, for instance, think that we value something about ourselves until threatened with its loss, and even then our unease may not strike us as the result of our having had a certain identity all along. I don't think these ever-present possibilities need cause embarrassment for a theory of reasonable deliberation. They have parallels in the theory of rational choice: we can never have perfect knowledge of other people's ends, or of our own, and yet this is not taken to suggest that rational choice is an incoherent notion.

integrity. Second, our identities are ontologically public: they are publicly formed and they are constituted in large part by our relationships to others, both to other individuals and to organizations and institutions. This feature holds even of the personal aspects of our identities. In characterizing these aspects of our identities, I suggested that they involved relationships to particular people. Such relationships are generally mediated by some or other social institution. I cannot be your colleague if we are not both members of a well-defined profession or project. I cannot be your friend unless we live in a society in which this is an accepted relationship.[20] When asked to describe ourselves, we often cite our relationships, our associations and memberships, our allegiances to causes or countries or institutions. Even the personal aspects of our identities take this public form. They are public facts about us, even if they are secret ones. They are not irretrievably stuck inside us, they are communicable and graspable by others.

It is in virtue of the ontological publicity of our practical identities that we can move back to a theory that grounds the authority of reasons in the nature of relationships. That is, reasons derive their authority from both the relationship the reasoners form and the personal aspects of their identities because these are not two separate sorts of things. The personal aspects of our identities are wrapped up in our forming certain relationships. In order to deliberate with others, I must regard them as (potentially) forming some or other relationship with me that can serve to support the claims we make on one another. Doing so, however, is tantamount to taking one personal aspect of my practical identity to include my membership in this relationship. In reasoning together, we establish certain commitments that have normative consequences. We can say, then, that in forming and maintaining relationships, we shape the personal aspects of our identities insofar as our practical identities are constituted by constellations of normative commitments.[21]

Sandy asks Pat to go for a walk, and regards the question as implicitly offering Pat a reason to stop working and come for a walk. We can then say that this reason has authority because their relationship is such that each is obligated, under conditions like these, to regard the other's desires as

20. My point here is not that we cannot have all the attitudes, expectations, interests, and so forth that characterize a friend relation in a society bereft of the concept, but the more mundane point that in such a society our relationship would not be characterized as friendship.

21. The tone of rampant freedom in this passage is bound to be misleading. To say that we can construct relationships and identities is not to deny that we do this, when we do, in the context of a whole lot of background baggage. Some parts of our identity are imposed on us through various and sundry social processes, and these clearly affect the sorts of relationships and identities we can and do construct. See below for an elaboration of this point.

authorizing reasons (though not necessarily decisive ones) to act. This is just part of what it means to be a couple. But we can also say that it is in virtue of having as one aspect of a practical identity being in a couple with Sandy that Pat really does have a reason to stop working. In failing to acknowledge Sandy's claim, Pat would be denying part of who she is.[22]

Turning now to the pair of social identity aspects and the relationships in which we stand, things are a bit more complicated. Since these relationships need not involve interaction with others, they cannot generate normative commitments in the way that the relationships we form do, if they can generate normative commitments at all. A great deal of the resistance and hostility to the politics of identity on the part of liberals stems, I think, from the assumption that the only way in which the social aspects of our identity could have normative significance is on the model above that links relationships we form to personal aspects of our identity. I want, however, to suggest another route by which social aspects of our identity come to take on normative significance, one that I think can be recognized as fitting into the general framework of a claims-based account of reasons. In doing so, I hope both to elaborate further my understanding of the structure of the claims made by advocates of a politics of identity and to set up the possibility that such claims can be made within the confines of a theory built on reasonable deliberation.

The basic point is that the relationships in which we stand play a role in determining what relationships we can form and with whom because both sorts of relationships are mediated by the social system in which we find ourselves. For my purposes, the most important interactions of these kinds involve the ways some of the relationships in which we stand, because they are hierarchical, undermine the possibility of our coming to form reciprocal relationships. We can think here of feminist analyses of heterosexual relationships in a patriarchal society.[23] According to such analyses, gender is a hierarchical relation in which men are dominant and women subordinate. The result is that it is impossible for any particular man, no matter how well-meaning, and any particular woman, no matter how enlightened and willing to speak up, to form a truly reciprocal relationship. The man cannot,

---

22. Given the presumed importance of her work, she also has reasons to keep working. We might say that were she always to drop her work at Sandy's slightest whim, she would also be denying part of who she is. In particular cases, determining which acts are reasonable will often require knowing not only about the aspect of someone's practical identity that authorizes the claim under investigation, but how it fits together with the other aspects of their identity.

23. Although I think such analyses are more or less on target, nothing in my argument here depends on their being right. I aim here to make a merely structural point about how two sorts of identities relate to one another.

no matter how he tries, completely shed his gendered identity and the power it gives him over the woman. It is always there, so to speak, hiding in the shadows, waiting to be called on when things get rough, and as a result, he always has that threat advantage over her. And even were he to be so psychologically constituted as to be clearly incapable of resorting to the force and violence that society would allow him to use, he can pretty much rely on her disempowered position as a woman to have the same effect. In such a case, the implied threat is not that he will use his social power to harm her, but rather that if she does not submit, he will abandon her to other men who will.[24]

It is because some of the relationships in which we stand to one another in virtue of some of our social identities make it impossible for us to form certain sorts of relationships with others that those social identities have normative significance. Deliberation occurs among people who have formed or are in the process of forming a relationship. That deliberation can only be reasonable if that relationship is marked by a certain degree of reciprocity. Thus, to the extent that they prevent our forming such relationships, the social aspects of our identities make some forms of reasonable deliberation impossible. And it is on those grounds that we can raise a complaint about them from the perspective of a theory of reasonable deliberation.

The most important case of this sort for my purposes involves our political relationships to one another. As Rousseau and Hegel both saw, we have no choice but to form political relationships with others. Our social identities will then have political relevance if they constrain our ability to form certain kinds of political relationships with others. As I argue in the next three chapters, many of the social identities that are of concern to the politics of identity do, in fact, prevent us from forming a reciprocal relationship with one another as liberal democratic citizens. It is for this reason that our social identities have political significance, and it is for this reason, ultimately, that liberals can and should take the politics of identity seriously.

4.6. Addressing Normative Flimsiness: Reasonable Relationships

The worry about normative flimsiness demands that a theory of reasonable deliberation include grounds on which to distinguish those relationships

---

24. See, for instance, Robin West, "Legitimating the Illegitimate," *Columbia Law Review* 93 (1993): 1442–1459; Catharine MacKinnon, *Towards a Feminist Theory of the State* (Cambridge: Harvard University Press, 1989); Adrienne Rich, "Compulsory Heterosexuality and Lesbian Existence," *Signs* 5 (1980): 631–660.

that have normative authority from those that do not. The problem is that actual uptake alone cannot be considered the sole determinant of the legitimacy of a claim. Sometimes we accept claims made upon us because we have accepted demeaning or oppressive identities or roles in relationships. Rather than search for an external theory of relationships by which we could give substance to a notion of hypothetical uptake of claims, I will offer a condition under which actual uptake will be sufficient to secure the normative status of a claim.

The condition, simply put, is that the deliberation in which the claim is made must be structured such that the rejection or acceptance of the claim makes a difference. Thus, if I accept a claim made on me in the context of a deliberation where I was not only free to reject that claim, but where my rejection would alter the further course of the deliberation, then that claim has the status of a reason. Deliberations will need to satisfy this condition if they are to be reasonable. We will then be able to say that relationships within which reasonable deliberation is possible are reasonable, and that only reasonable relationships can ground the normativity of claims.

At first glance, this condition may appear far too weak to overcome the normative flimsiness of actual relationships. It turns out, however, to pack quite a normative punch. Relationships, for instance, marked by severe asymmetries of power turn out to undermine the conditions under which rejection can matter, and thus undermine the possibility that they can be sites of reasonable deliberation.[25] The problem in such cases is that one of the parties lacks the option to challenge the shape of the relationship and thus the identities it constitutes. Even if the subordinate party can issue such a challenge, the deliberation will be reasonable only if it treats such a challenge as worthy of consideration. If you make a claim on me based on your view of our relationship, and we are deliberating on that claim, there must be room for me to reply that while that reason is indeed authorized by that identity, it is not an identity I can or wish to adopt, at least not in that form. I can do so by making clear why, for instance, other aspects of my identity that you ought to respect prevent me from inhabiting the identity as you have constructed it, or by showing why the choice of whether to make this aspect of my identity relevant in this context ought to be mine and that you have failed to respect that. Thus, for instance, it should be open to a woman to reject claims made on her on the grounds of some aspect of the identity "woman" as it is defined within a sexist culture. She might reject them by calling attention to the incompatibility of this oppressive identity with some other identity she claims, such as that of human or citizen. She might also

25. I address this issue at greater length in chapter 6.

reject the claim as incompatible with her own understanding of her gendered identity: perhaps being a woman does not, in her eyes, require her to be the primary caretaker of her young children. What is crucial to determining the possibility of reasonable deliberation between men and women, however, is whether, were she to make any of these deliberative moves, they would be accepted as themselves legitimate. Contexts that make it impossible for women to offer such reasons, or to have them seen as reasonable moves within the deliberation, are contexts in which reasonable deliberation is impossible. Thus, for instance, reasonable deliberation between men and women will not be possible so long as men are allowed to ignore women's rejection of their claims on the grounds that such rejection is just further evidence of women's unreasonableness. Whether men have this deliberative power may depend on factors beyond their own willingness to listen and take seriously what individual women say. It may lie in the general social climate that brands women who reject such claims as unreasonable—as uptight or overly ambitious or too radical, as unable to take a joke or to regard even unwanted sexual attention as flattering.

In offering a response to the concern that relationships are normatively flimsy, I have suggested that we can find criteria for distinguishing those relationships that can ground normativity and those that cannot within the structure of reasonable deliberation itself. One upshot of this approach, however, is that the factors that determine whether or not deliberation is reasonable may extend beyond the exchange of claims and reasons that makes up any given act of deliberation. They may, for instance, depend not only on whatever relationships the deliberators (attempt to) form, but on the various and sundry other relationships in which they stand.

4.7. A Model of Reasonable Deliberation

I conclude this chapter with a basic model of reasonable deliberation that is informed by the discussion to this point. My aim is not to provide the kind of precise formal characterization of the theory that is the norm among rational choice theories, though it is my hope that this model will move us in the general direction of being able to provide such a precise formulation. It is rather to bring together the points made over the previous several sections in order to flesh out the bare-bones picture I sketched in section 4.2.

Part of the difficulty in sketching a model of reasonable deliberation arises from the fact that there is no clear order of priority between our relationships and our deliberations. We form and shape and maintain our relationships in part through reasonable deliberation, and yet we undertake reasonable deliberation in the context of those very relationships. Even in the context of a given piece of deliberation, we may undertake the deliberation from within a particular understanding of a relationship, and then over the course of and as a result of the deliberation we may come to find ourselves with a very different understanding of our relationship.

In fact, we sometimes engage in deliberation with someone in the hopes of forming a relationship that does not yet exist.[26] Offering claims in reasonable deliberation ought not to be seen on the model of premises in a practical deduction. Rather, we should see it as inviting (with a greater or lesser degree of insistence) one's deliberative partner to share a kind of world-view—a space of reasons. Such an invitation can be extended both to someone with whom I already share a well-defined and mutually understood relationship and to one with whom I do not yet share anything but the possibility of forming such a relationship.[27]

Both ends of a deliberation are thus in flux. The course of a deliberation can alter the relationship that supports the deliberation, and it can alter the agreement, the shared will, that the deliberators eventually form. To circumvent this problem, I introduce a kind of presumed fixed point that sits between the relationship of the deliberating parties and the shared will they may come to form. I describe this fixed point as a "plural subject."[28]

The term plural subject is meant to capture something special about the first-person plural pronoun; it is a way of analyzing what is involved in our speaking or acting as a "we."[29] People form a plural subject when they not only form some recognizable relationship with one another, but also share

26. Peace negotiations are the most prominent example of such cases. In light of the discussion so far, it should not be surprising that many successful peace negotiations begin by getting the parties to the same place for long enough that they have to talk to one another, about anything. Such dialogue helps create a relationship on which later deliberation can rest and build.

27. My thoughts on this point have benefited from several discussions with Avner Baz.

28. I borrow the term "plural subject" from Margaret Gilbert, who places it at the center of her analysis of social groups. See Margaret Gilbert, *On Social Facts* (Princeton, N.J.: Princeton University Press, 1989), esp. chap. 4. Gilbert's analysis is aimed at determining the relationship between the intentional states of a group and those of its members, and so her account of when a group of people form a plural subject involves claims about members' intentional states. Since I am primarily concerned with questions of reasons and identity, I will define plural subjects differently than Gilbert, though I think in roughly the same spirit.

29. There is a vast literature in the philosophy of action about the possibility and character of what are often called joint or shared or "we"-intentions. See, for instance, Michael Bratman, "Shared Intention," *Ethics* 104 (1993): 97–113, and "Shared Cooperative Activity," *The Philosophical Review* 101 (1992): 327–341; J. David Velleman, "How to Share an Intention," *Philosophy and Phenomenological Research* 57 (1997): 29–50; and Gilbert, *On Social Facts*. Oddly enough, nowhere in that literature is there much discussion of the relationship of forming a joint intention and coming to share a set of reasons. It seems to me likely that a theory of reasonable deliberation would be able to shed light on the phenomena of joint action and intention formation, though no such direct illumination will be provided here.

an understanding of their relationship and the claims it authorizes. In many cases, it will not be necessary that they agree on the full extent of the claims it authorizes, so long as there is significant overlap in their understanding and that overlap covers the reasons being urged in the deliberation.

Deliberation is reasonable when two conditions are met. First, each of the deliberators must offer reasons to the others on the presumption that they together form a plural subject, and that their deliberations are the deliberations of the plural subject they form together. This presumption leads them to offer what I call "we"-reasons. "We"-reasons are reasons deliberators presume to be authoritative for those with whom they comprise the plural subject engaged in deliberation (the "we").[30] Second, there must be appropriate space for the reasonable rejection of proffered "we"-reasons to affect the further course of the deliberation. Rejection of a given "we"-reason is reasonable if it rests on a warranted criticism of the presumption that sustains the original claim. As I suggested in the last section, such criticism might rest on a rejection of the identity in virtue of which one is being presumed to be a member of the plural subject, or its particular contours, or its presumed relationship to other aspects of one's practical identity that themselves have a claim on others' recognition and respect. Thus, a wife might reject a claim made by her husband that is supported by her identity as a wife on any of these three grounds. First, she might object to their marital relationship being understood as a relationship between two unequal partners (a husband and wife rather than two coequal human life partners). Second, she might accept this general interpretation of their relationship but contest the particular obligation he claims comes with being a wife (she might accept that it includes giving emotional support but not providing complete and constant sexual access). Finally, she might even accept the traditional subjugated sexual role of a traditional wife and yet reject this particular entreaty on the grounds that it would conflict here and now with some other aspect of her identity that he does or is bound to respect ("Not now, honey, the children need me.").[31] In all of these cases, we can understand her

---

30. This description requires a slight modification to deal with cases where the identity of the plural subject is heterogeneous, so that the identities that are relevant to the deliberations are not all the same, such as deliberation between parents and children within a family, or between management and workers within a company. Nevertheless, the points that follow will not substantially change when the plural subject in question is heterogeneous.

31. Note that in the latter two cases the relationship between husband and wife, if it is in fact reasonable, is not so traditional after all, as it gives the wife the authority to effectively reject proposals in ways that traditional marital roles do not.

rejection of the reasons her husband offers as involving a challenge to his presumption about the nature of the plural subject they form. Unless these challenges affect the further course of the deliberation, that deliberation is not reasonable.

Deliberation that is reasonable in this sense thus sustains while potentially reshaping our relationships and allows us to form shared wills together. When I offer others a "we"-reason, I in part suggest that such a reason is supportable by the identity I take us to share (or to be capable of coming to share) insofar as we form a particular plural subject. That others accept such a reason serves both to confirm that we do in fact share the identity in question and that the identity we share does in fact support such a reason.[32] Depending on whether or not we understood already that our shared identity had that feature (of supporting that reason), we will be able to say that this process of deliberation served either to establish or to reaffirm some aspect of our shared identity.

At the same time, the process of reasonable deliberation involves, in the ideal case at least, coming to a shared understanding as to which reasons are relevant to the question at hand. Thus, as a result of deliberating reasonably, we can come to form a shared will if the balance of these reasons yields a determinate answer.[33] In addition, a joint commitment to reasonable deliberation means that our deliberation itself embodies a shared will, a will to privilege the reasonableness of our deliberation over the need to reach a (possibly imposed) consensus.

In outlining this theory of reasonable deliberation I have tried to map the space in which deliberation takes place, and to thus point toward a set of questions we will need to ask when assessing the reasonableness as opposed to the rationality of deliberation. We can, for instance, assess whether a given deliberation is reasonable by making explicit the presumptions involved in any offering of a "we"-reason. In doing so, we need to focus on the shape of the identity being invoked, the context in which that identity is said to be relevant, and thus the conditions under which rejection of offered reasons might both be warranted and make a difference. Doing so might involve asking some of the following questions: What is the content of the plural subject we are presumed to share? What are the grounds of that pre-

32. I assume here that the deliberation is reasonable, and so the acceptance is, as it were, genuine. It is acceptance in a situation where rejection would have mattered.

33. And even when it fails to yield a determinate answer, the fact that we generally agree on which reasons are relevant will mean that even decisions we reach through deliberatively approved but nondeliberative procedures such as voting that are not directly supported by our shared will can be considered legitimately the will of the plural subject we form.

sumption? How dependent is that presumption on the actual responses of the people to whom the reason is offered? Is there sufficient space for the rebuttal of a deliberative presumption to make a difference? It is in large part by looking at these and related questions about political deliberation that I motivate the discussion of the rest of the book.

5

Reasonable Political Deliberation

This chapter sets out the main elements of reasonable political deliberation and the conception of citizenship on which it relies. In so doing, it provides the main element of the defense of the possibility of a legitimate liberal democratic regime by showing how such deliberation, when reasonable, can serve as the basis of legitimate consent, in large part by embodying a shared will among citizens without relying on either exclusion or assimilation.

5.1. Political Deliberation

Political deliberation, as I shall use the phrase, is the deliberation of citizens about how to use the coercive power of the state with respect to what Rawls calls matters of basic justice and constitutional essentials.[1] It consists of an exchange of public reasons, those reasons that are authoritative for citizens in virtue of their identity as citizens. In this section I fill out this characterization, and distinguish it from other sorts of political activity that might also be thought to fit under such a heading. Doing so is important, because deliberative liberalism, like Rawls's political liberalism, revolves around the claim that only public reasons are properly

---

1. See John Rawls, *Political Liberalism* (New York: Columbia University Press, 1996), 227–230.

invoked in political deliberation, and the strength of this claim depends to a great extent on the limitation of the realm of political deliberation proper.[2]

I discuss four general features of political deliberation. The first three cover ways in which political deliberation is political: it takes place in political fora, it concerns political topics, and it takes place among people insofar as they are political agents. These serve mainly to distinguish political deliberation from other political activity. The final feature of political deliberation is a direct consequence of deep diversity: political deliberation is plural, in the sense that people engaged in political deliberation need not all have the same conception of citizenship, and thus may not share in any complete sense a set of public reasons they regard as authoritative for them as citizens. This final feature of political deliberation shapes to a large extent what will count as reasonable political deliberation and what we can expect of such deliberation.[3]

Political deliberation takes place in properly political fora: in legislative debates, electoral campaigns, political demonstrations, and the decisions of appeals courts, to name the most prominent examples. Political deliberation is thus to be distinguished from public or private deliberation about political questions. The point of this distinction is not to deny that these latter forms of deliberation are of political importance, or even that they influence political deliberation proper. Rather, it is to highlight a realm in which we act most clearly as citizens, a realm that plays a central legitimating role. Although some government institutions will necessarily be part of the political realm in this sense, I do not mean to suggest that these institutions exhaust that realm. Ordinary citizens also take part in political deliberation. We do so first in our role as the audience to whom political deliberation is ultimately addressed. It is in large part up to ordinary citizens to accept as authoritative only public reasons offered by candidates and government officials and to reject those candidates and officials who do not respect the bounds of public reason.[4] In addition, ordinary citizens can act and deliberate politically in a variety of ways, from speaking out at public hearings and debates to participating in political demonstrations. When the institutions that serve to legitimate law are not open to such

2. Rawls makes this point in his "Idea of Public Reason Revisited," reprinted in his *Collected Papers*, ed. Samuel Freeman (Cambridge: Harvard University Press, 1999), 574–576.

3. This fourth feature of political deliberation leads to a fourth sense in which such deliberation is political: as I argue in sections 5.2 and 5.3, what I call deliberative liberalism's "political conception of citizenship" is in part a response to the plurality of political deliberation.

4. Rawls makes this point in "Idea of Public Reason Revisited," 577.

participation by ordinary citizens, then political deliberation cannot be reasonable.[5]

For citizens who do not occupy positions of authority within the government, whether a form of political action counts as participation in political deliberation may depend on what they reasonably take themselves to be doing and how they expect to be understood by others. Are they acting as concerned citizens or as partisans or members of a particular group or association? Is this gathering a rally, meant to enthuse a base, or a demonstration, meant to raise an issue in the political forum? The point of distinguishing such cases is to be able to say that in those that take part in political deliberation, the appropriate reasons to invoke are public ones.[6]

The wider realm of public deliberation about political matters includes not only discussion in the media, but the countless interactions between citizens in our daily routines: the full panoply of what Habermas calls the "bourgeois public sphere."[7] Within this wider sphere of debate, people deliberate sometimes as citizens, and sometimes from more partisan perspectives. Such shifting and mixing of roles and perspectives is important for a healthy democratic society. But it is precisely because of the importance to a democratic society of a fully open public sphere that this wider public sphere be distinguished from the loci of political deliberation. For within the public sphere, not only do we offer reasons to one another as citizens, but we work out other aspects of our identities as members of all sorts of associations and institutions. Furthermore, and most importantly for deliberative liberalism, we work out the way in which all these identities relate to our political identity. It is thus both impossible and undesirable to separate out those aspects of public deliberation in which we act merely as citizens from those in which we act in other capacities. It is impossible because these roles often merge in public debate, and it is undesirable because it is in large part as a result of this merging that we come to see how the various aspects of our identities and the identities of others fit together. As a result, limiting deliberation within the public sphere as a whole to public reasons would

5. William Greider's *Who Will Tell the People* (New York: Simon and Schuster, 1992) offers an eye-opening and depressing catalogue of the myriad ways in which the input of ordinary citizens is choked off or ignored by federal officials in the United States.

6. It is not to make the criteria of political participation intentional. Rather, it is to note that many almost identical actions can fall on either side of the line I am drawing between participation in political deliberation and other forms of political action without undermining the conceptual distinction I am drawing between these sorts of activities and the roles they play in legitimation.

7. Jürgen Habermas, *The Structural Transformation of the Public Sphere*, trans. Thomas Burger (Cambridge: MIT Press, 1989).

undermine the role of deliberation as the forge of public opinion and reasonable citizens. While public deliberation will be enhanced by the values of mutual respect that support a restriction to public reason in political deliberation, it will not be furthered by the narrower requirements of the principle of public reason and the rest of the requirements that make reasonable political deliberation possible.

Finally, political deliberation plays a fundamental role in legitimation. If political ideas generated within the public sphere are to determine in any way the nature of political institutions they will have to be taken up and endorsed by precisely the fora in which political deliberation proper takes place. Thus, if we are interested in what can legitimate political principles and the regimes based on them, we will need to focus our attention on properly political fora.[8]

The second sense in which political deliberation is political is that it is the deliberation of citizens (and of their representatives), and thus of people in their political identities. Thus, not even all debates in political fora will count as political deliberation. In many cases, such discussions are not best thought of as taking place between people in their capacities as citizens (or their representatives). Certain strategic deliberations with an eye toward the next election will be best seen as involving people in their identities as partisans or backers of this or that party or candidate and thus will not count as political deliberation in my sense of the term. Similarly, if we enter public debate on political matters with the aim of defending some narrow interest, say of a particular religious group or of a certain profession or class, we are deliberating not as citizens, but as members or advocates for the narrower group in question. The point of this distinction is not to suggest that such interventions ought to be banned from politics, whatever that might mean. Rather, it is to suggest that such forms of political action and speech do not form part of what I am calling political deliberation. An important consequence of this point is that such political actions need not be limited to public reasons, as I characterize them below. At the same time, such interventions cannot serve the legitimating role played by political deliberation.

To see how these roles fit together, consider cases where members of a religion seek exemptions from certain state requirements on the grounds that they interfere with their ability to practice their faith. Sikh barristers in Britain, for example, have been excused from the requirement that they wear wigs in court, as these cannot be worn on top of turbans. More contro-

8. I do not mean to deny here that illegitimacy can also arise from a sort of disjunction between political and public fora and their deliberation.

versially, some Muslim girls in French schools have demanded (and have been alternately granted and denied) the right to wear headscarves in class in contravention to French regulations that prohibit the ostentatious display of religion in the public schools. In these cases, we can distinguish two roles that religious authorities might play in public deliberation about the matter. In the first, the religious authorities act as citizens, and restrict themselves to public reason arguments in favor of a change in the rules that would accommodate their members. They might, for instance, claim that such rules unfairly burden their members in ways that they do not burden the members of other religions, rather than citing religious doctrine to support the practice.[9] If political deliberation is reasonable, then such public reason arguments will have to be taken up by other citizens, and if they are to be ultimately rejected, it will have to be because of other public reasons that either outweigh or undermine the concern with unfair and undue burden.

But there is also a second way in which the religious authorities might enter public (but not political) deliberation that would nevertheless have an effect on political deliberation. Religious authorities could act as expert witnesses, as it were. They might merely explain publicly the religious significance of the practice in question. Doing so would involve citing the reasons for the practice that were internal to the religion itself, and thus were clearly not public reasons. By making clear to citizens who are not members of the religion just what significance a particular practice or symbol has within the religion, they might then provide support for members of the religion, acting as citizens, to make a public reason argument from undue burden themselves. Imagine that the Muslim girls object to the regulations regarding dress in school on the grounds that it unfairly burdens Muslim students by preventing them from acting appropriately in the eyes of their religion in a way that it does not prevent non-Muslim students from doing. The force of such an argument will in part depend on just what kind of burden these regulations turn out to be in their religious life. Thus, their public reason argument might be strengthened by the nonpublic reasons made clear by the religious authorities, which set out why, on religious grounds, this practice is of great importance. The point of drawing this distinction between two ways of entering public, but not necessarily political, deliberation is to make clear what other citizens are obliged to do in response. When a fellow citizen enters political deliberation and urges public reasons on us, we are obliged to take these up as reasons, and thus to offer counter-reasons if we do not wish to accept their reasons. When a fellow citizen merely explains

9. I discuss public reason arguments from "burdensomeness" in chapter 7.

the relation of her practices to her religious belief in nonpublic terms, we are not obliged to regard those reasons as having even a *prima facie* claim on us.

The third sense in which political deliberation is political concerns its subject matter: political deliberation concerns political questions in two rather narrow senses. First of all, political deliberation is directed toward questions of the common good, the good of the public. Rawls, for instance, claims that the subject of the reason of citizens is "the good of the public."[10] In this he follows Rousseau, who claimed that the general will was always directed at the common good.[11] So, we can say that we take part in political deliberation when we deliberate as citizens in political fora about the common good of the plural subject we form with our fellow citizens.

The second sense in which the topic of political deliberation is political is that it concerns exercising the role of the state in securing that good. That is, when we deliberate with one another about the good of the entire population but do so as a question of philosophy, or as a way of ascertaining the best way for us to make individual contributions to the common good, we are not, properly speaking, engaging in political deliberation as citizens. What makes our deliberation the political deliberation of citizens is that we are discussing, *inter alia*, how best to use the power of the state, which in a democracy is our collective power. Since the power of the state is always coercive, the political deliberation of citizens turns out to be about how to direct a form of coercive power that is ours collectively toward particular ends designed to protect and promote the common good.

It is this fact about the political deliberation of citizens that requires that they honor the principle of public reason in such deliberations. To see why this is so, we need only imagine what a failure to do so would look like. Return to the case of the Muslim girls. Imagine that they demand an exemption from the dress code in part on the grounds that conforming to the dress code (i.e., not wearing a headscarf in class) will offend Allah. Imagine that they make this argument as a move within political deliberation. They do not, however, try to determine whether their reasons are public or not. From their point of view as both citizens and Muslims, their reasons seem to provide overwhelming grounds for granting them this exemption. But now we can ask what sort of presumptions they are thus making about the plural subject they form with their fellow citizens. To what extent are the reasons they offer truly "we"-reasons? They are either entering this debate not as

10. Rawls, *Political Liberalism*, 213.
11. See, for example, Rousseau, *Of the Social Contract*, in *The Social Contract and Other Later Political Writings*, trans. and ed. Victor Gourevitch (Cambridge: Cambridge University Press, 1997), Book 2, chap. 4, ¶1; and Book 4, chap. 1, ¶1.

citizens but only as religious believers, or making the assumption that all their fellow citizens would find their religious reasons authoritative for them in virtue of their citizenship.[12] But, given the fact of deep diversity, such an assumption is definitive of unreasonableness.[13] In making it, they are either disregarding the fact of reasonable pluralism or assuming that the coercive power of the state, which is the coercive power of its citizens, can be invoked for reasons not all of their fellow citizens could see as sufficient. In either case, they are being unreasonable. As we have seen, political legitimacy requires that the state act only on the basis of reasons all citizens can reasonably accept. A government that acts on nonpublic reasons as if they were public reasons requires that some citizens submit to its authority without consenting to it. It is thus not acting legitimately.

The final feature of political deliberation is a result of the fact of deep diversity. One of the consequences of such diversity is that people will not only have widely different sets of nonpolitical identities, but will also disagree about what reasons are properly authoritative for them insofar as they are citizens. I will describe this feature by saying that political deliberation is plural. At first glance, it may seem as if acknowledging the plurality of political deliberation would undermine any attempt to use the theory of reasonable deliberation to work out a theory of political deliberation, insofar as the theory developed in the last chapter requires that people share an identity in order to deliberate. It might look, then, as if the plurality of political deliberation will render any purported political deliberation somewhat of a sham. Imagine, for instance, that we identify a set of public reasons based on one group's conception of citizenship and what it authorizes and then assess the reasonableness of political deliberation by asking whether it takes place in terms of these reasons. Any consensus reached on the basis of such a deliberation will necessarily be partial, since it grows out of a particular description of the set of public reasons that is not shared by all. To claim that such a consensus could secure political legitimacy would then be tantamount to excluding those who do not share the conception of citizenship from having a say in their society on their own terms.

One way of interpreting the actual deliberations that took place in France over *l'affaire du foulard* (the affair of the headscarves) was that it involved the

12. The second half of this claim depends to some degree on their attitude in making these claims. It is conceivable that they make these arguments in good faith as public reason arguments. In such a case, the reply of their fellow citizens that these arguments rest on premises they do not accept will be sufficient for them to drop their argument. The case I am imagining here is one where they do not make this argument tentatively, and assume that their fellow citizens will accept it.

13. For a fuller discussion of "reasonable pluralism" and its connection to "unreasonableness," see Rawls, *Political Liberalism*, 48–54, 61, 138.

failure of the French government and the French public generally to recognize the plurality of public reason. Through the mid-1980s, the French confronted a range of problems surrounding the increasing multiethnic and multicultural makeup of the French population. The result was the adoption of what is generally referred to as a republican conception of citizenship, which was both comprehensive and voluntarist.[14] That is, being a French citizen was understood as completely separate from one's ethnic background or religious affiliation, but at the same time was rather fully theoretically defined to specify most if not all of the values it was thought to include. Having developed this comprehensive ideal of citizenship, the government then gave the French school system a central role as an institution within which future French citizens would be molded to identify with this conception of citizenship, regardless of their other nonpolitical affiliations. This was to be done in part by making schools entirely secular.

It was in this context that the expulsion of three Muslim schoolgirls for refusing to remove their headscarves in a small suburban town outside of Paris blew up into a national incident that occupied the French public on and off for several years. From the French perspective, which did not fully recognize the plurality of political deliberation, there was a clear conflict between a religious requirement and a requirement of citizenship, and any attempt to accommodate the religious requirement would serve to undermine the universality of citizenship. From the perspective of the Muslim girls and their supporters, however, and from any perspective that recognizes the plurality of political deliberation, the French consensus that wound up insisting on enforcing the dress code in schools that forbids the wearing of headscarves in class was a consensus that relied on either the exclusion or the assimilation of the Muslim students.

The consequence of political deliberation being plural, however, is that any attempt to take the French route will meet with similar consequences. That is, it will always be the case that given a particular comprehensive conception of citizenship and an accompanying set of public reasons, the best one can hope for is a partial consensus masquerading as a universal one. Rather than concluding that the plurality of political deliberation undermines the project of basing legitimacy on deliberation, or that we must set-

14. Both *l'affaire du foulard* and the more general background of French discussions of citizenship that preceded it are addressed in Adrian Favell, *Philosophies of Integration* (New York: St. Martin's Press, 1998). Further details of the case, and reflections on its implications about issues of toleration, can be found in the debate between Anna Elisabetta Galleotti and Norma Claire Moruzzi in *Political Theory*: Galleotti, "Citizenship and Equality"; Moruzzi, "A Problem with Headscarves."

tle for a partial consensus, I argue in the rest of this chapter that the fact of plurality merely changes the way we should understand how political deliberation proceeds, what constitutes its being reasonable, the nature of the shared will it can produce, and how we understand our identity as citizens.[15] In particular, the plurality of public reason means that the difficult part of ensuring that political deliberation is reasonable stems not from ascertaining in advance the content of our identity as citizens and thus the space of reasons we share, but rather from ascertaining whether or not our political relationships to one another are structured so as to allow our uptake and rejection of proffered reasons to matter in the right way. In the terms I laid out at the end of chapter 1, it means that deliberative liberalism must take a political approach to its conception of political deliberation.

In the French case this would involve understanding the claims made by the Muslim girls as more complicated, as possibly reflecting a different understanding of the balance of public reasons, one to some degree shaped by their position as members of a religious minority in a country where the drive to secularize citizenship was accompanied by a long-standing tendency to see religious practice only when it wasn't that of the Catholic majority. Coming to such an understanding requires adopting a political conception of citizenship—one that both grounds public reasons and allows for their plurality.

5.2. A Political Conception of Citizenship: The Structure

Our identities are multiple at two levels. Our practical identities have many aspects. I am a parent, a spouse, a philosopher, a Jew, a vegetarian, a member of various associations and groups, a resident of Chicago, and a citizen of the United States, among many other things. Each of these is an aspect of

15. This concern about the problem posed by the plurality of political deliberation as well as the hope that there are liberal democratic solutions to it is an ongoing feature of the work of James Tully, and I have benefited greatly from discussing these matters with him. See, for instance, Tully, *Strange Multiplicity: Constitutionalism in an Age of Diversity* (Cambridge: Cambridge University Press, 1995), "Democratic Constitutionalism in a Diverse Federation," in *Ideas in Action: Essays in Politics and Law in Honor of Peter Russell,* eds. Joseph Fletcher and Jennifer Nedelsky (Toronto: University of Toronto Press, 1999), "Multicultural and Multinational Citizenship," in *The Demands of Citizenship,* eds. Iain Hampsher-Monk and Catriona McKinnon (London: Continuum International, 2000), and "The Unattained Yet Attainable Democracy," © Programme d'études sur le Québec de l'Université McGill, 2000. Accommodating such plurality is also one of the main aims of James Bohman's *Public Deliberation* (Cambridge: MIT Press, 1997). Deliberative liberalism overlaps in many ways with the view developed there, although he starts from a more Habermasian perspective than I do.

my practical identity. In addition, each aspect of my practical identity can be multifaceted insofar as it serves to authorize a whole variety of different reasons. Among the features of such identity aspects I distinguish between form and content features. Furthermore, given any feature of an identity aspect, we can ask about the source of that feature. That is, we can ask on what basis that feature is properly understood as a part of that aspect of someone's identity. I distinguish two answers to that question: features of an aspect of practical identity can be externally dictated or deliberatively constructed. Before examining deliberative liberalism's conception of citizenship, it will help to explore these two distinctions in some detail. As I make clear below, they serve to refine the distinctions introduced in chapter 4 between personal and social identity aspects, and between relationships we form and those in which we stand.

The content of an identity is the set of reasons it authorizes.[16] A content feature grounds at least some of the reasons authorized by the identity aspect in question in a direct fashion. Content features are intrinsic to the identity in question in the sense that they may be completely independent of the relation the identity aspect they characterize bears to other identity aspects, whether those within a person or those of others. Nevertheless, the content features of an identity might vary widely without the identity itself having changed. They can, in this sense, be contingent features of the identity they characterize.

Form features, however, derive from the place a given identity occupies in a more complicated social system. The form characteristics of an identity are determined by the part it plays, and by what is required of someone playing that part, within a larger social context. Although form characteristics shape the set of reasons a given identity authorizes, they do so less directly, generally by constraining the processes that serve to generate the content characteristics of a given identity.

Consider the identity of "father" as it has been traditionally understood in our society (i.e., as exemplified in the ideals of fatherhood within white, middle-class nuclear families portrayed in the mainstream media of the 1950s). Among the content features of this particular conception of fatherhood are such things as financial provider; household authority; role model; emotionally distant, yet wise; firm, yet reasonable and understanding; and so forth. This list includes a combination of ideals to be striven for, markers of

16. While it is in general helpful to distinguish between a complete identity and its various aspects, I will sometimes use "identity" where I mean only a particular aspect to avoid unnecessarily lengthy phrases. When it is not clear from the context whether I mean to be talking about a complete identity or a mere aspect, I will use more precise language.

being a good father, and certain privileges and opportunities that automatically come with the identity. Nevertheless, all of them can be thought of as helping to ground directly the reasons that are authoritative for fathers (at least on this conception) insofar as they are fathers. In contrast, the form features of fatherhood on this conception derive from the place fathers occupy in a larger social system and the way this shapes what fathers must be like. Thus, to the extent that fathers on this model are different from and complementary with mothers, fatherhood will have to have a shape that fits together well with that of motherhood. Thus, if there are attributes necessary for child-rearing that mothers do not have, fathers will have them. Similarly, fathers, on this conception, must be men, and being a man carries with it certain identity requirements in this social world. From these two considerations, we can conclude, for instance, that one set of form-features of fatherhood will involve the fact that fathers are male child-rearers.

Of course, form and content features are related. In this case, much of the content of fatherhood is determined by its form features. One might argue, for instance, that fathers have to be financial providers because children have material needs, and given a certain sexist economic structure, it is only men who can earn enough money to meet these needs adequately. Thus, the content feature of financial provider arises out of the form feature of male child-rearer.

Several things should be noticed about this example. First of all, while a given set of form features can serve to ground certain content features, they may not uniquely determine them. Further determination may involve other form features, or it might be a matter of contingent aspects of social development. If, for instance, taking out the garbage, but not dusting, is taken to be a content feature of fatherhood, it is hard to see how this is necessarily tied to maleness, although once it becomes so associated, the form feature of maleness might serve to explain this content feature. The point is that form features might constrain the content features, while leaving their final form open to determination by other means, including (as I will discuss below) deliberative construction. It is in this regard that the distinction between form and content features of an identity diverges from the distinction Rawls draws between concepts and conceptions, to which it bears certain important similarities.[17] The concept/conception distinction, as it is generally understood, links its two components via some particular theory. That is, in virtue of some theory, we move from a particular concept to a

17. See John Rawls, *A Theory of Justice* (Cambridge: Harvard University Press, 1971), 5. I am grateful to Tamar Schapiro for pushing me to think about the relationship of my form/content distinction to Rawls's concept/conception distinction.

particular conception of that concept. The theory is taken to determine the conception uniquely. In contrast, it is not always the case that given a particular theory of a given identity, we can move from a set of form features to a unique set of content features, although this will sometimes be possible. The possibility of such theoretical indeterminacy lies at the heart of the second distinction, which I discuss below.

Second, since content features can rest on a whole constellation of form features, which themselves are the result of a wide set of social relationships in which a particular identity places one, it may be that changes in one of those relationships have a significant effect on the content features of the identity. Thus, for instance, changing the nature of the economic system to make it less sexist might change radically what features are associated with fatherhood in particular rather than with parenthood in general.[18]

Third, although I have been presenting the order of explanation as going from form features to content features, I think the ultimate order of influence is less one-sided. That is, the incompatibility or unattractiveness of a certain set of content features might put pressure on a society to reorganize, and thus to shift the form features of the unattractive role. One might suggest, for example, that one of the pressures that has shifted the form features of fatherhood over the last several decades is the distastefulness and difficulty of occupying the role as it was previously defined, and perhaps more relevantly, women's parallel reaction against traditional content features associated with motherhood and femininity. Since the unattractive collection of content features was supported by the form features, which in turn were supported by the relationships in which mothers and fathers stood, rejection of the content features has led to a reconceptualization of the form features, and this in turn has applied pressure to shift the structure of family and gender and workplace relations.

Note that this distinction refines the distinction between personal and social identities I made in chapter 4. Personal identities are identities with minimal form features. Social identities are identities all of whose content features are determined by their form features. As I argue below, citizenship is best thought of as an aspect of our identity that has some determinate form features that do not, on their own, fully determine its content features.

I turn now to the second distinction. Just as the form/content distinction refines the personal/social identity distinction, the externally-dictated/delib-

---

18. Although distinguishing cause and effect here is notoriously difficult, it seems obvious that there is a relationship, however complicated, between greater sex equality in the workplace and greater sex equality in the domestic sphere, and that relationship is tied to the relationship between form and content characteristics of both motherhood and fatherhood.

eratively-constructed distinction serves to refine the relationships-we-form/relationships-in-which-we-stand distinction. About any given feature of an aspect of an identity, we can ask on what basis it is included among the features of that aspect. Some features will be externally dictated. Such dictation can take place through any number of different processes. I mention two. It might be that certain social structures in place in a society determine the nature of a given aspect of an identity. For instance, in the example I gave above, certain features of the identity of father were dictated by the fact that fathers (on the conception in question) are male, and by the way in which the social structure determines the social position, powers, and responsibilities of men. When social structures serve to dictate features of an identity aspect, they do so by determining its form features. Nevertheless, it is also possible for content features of an identity to be dictated in this manner, insofar as external factors uniquely determine the move from form features to content features.

A second form of dictation is through what might be called theoretical derivation. Here features of an identity aspect are worked out theoretically by considering the nature of the aspect, its general social function, or its relation to other identities. Such a form of identity determination plays a larger role in the development of normative theories and so is of particular importance in working out a political theory. Thus, for instance, the conception of fatherhood I have been discussing might be justified in part by working out a theory of sexual difference that claimed that men naturally possessed certain characteristics that justified a society in giving certain roles and responsibilities to men and others to women. We might argue, for instance, that the emotional distance I suggested as characteristic of fathers on the conception in question is the result of the natural emotional distance of men. Similarly, many accounts of citizenship, such as those implicit in the natural law strand of the social contract tradition or in much of contemporary comprehensive liberalism, are theoretically derived, relying as they do on some or other theory of human nature.

In contrast to the ways features of an identity can be externally dictated, they might be deliberatively constructed. Think, for instance, of the specific contours of the relationship that Pat and Sandy develop in the course of their interaction and deliberation. Many of the particular features of their relationship are not determined prior to their own construction and development of that relationship, and it is only through the deliberation that develops their relationship that they acquire certain features as members of that couple. These features are deliberatively constructed; their authority stems from their being given authority by the deliberating parties in the course of deliberation. It does not rest on anything beyond those deliberations past and present, and within certain limits, it is always open for someone in the deliberation to contest the authority of such a feature.

This distinction refines the distinction laid out in chapter 4 between types of relationships. We can thus say that all of the features of the relationships in which we stand are externally dictated, while in the relationships we form many, if not all, of the significant features are deliberatively constructed. In line with my claim that deliberative liberalism takes a political approach, and with the meaning I assigned to this term, I will say that a conception of a particular identity aspect is political if at least some of its features are deliberatively constructed.[19]

5.3. A Political Conception of Citizenship: The Details

Deliberative liberalism conceives of citizenship as an identity aspect with theoretically derived form features and deliberatively constructed content features, where the construction of the content features is constrained by the form features. In this way, deliberative liberalism addresses two dilemmas that any account of citizenship must face. Before discussing the derivation of the central form features of citizenship, it will help to explain how this general approach solves these dilemmas.

The first dilemma involves the competing demands of democracy and liberalism. To be democratic, a conception of citizenship must regard citizens as the ultimate source of political legitimacy, and thus give them the final say in the determination of the political system. According to democratic conceptions of citizenship, whatever citizens decide about the nature of the political system goes. For a conception of citizenship to be liberal, however, citizens must be bearers of certain inalienable rights and liberties. These rights and liberties are not up for debate in the political process. They thus appear to be beyond the reach of the collective power of citizens to change. In this way, liberalism can appear to contain an antidemocratic element at its core, while unbridled democracy can serve to undermine liberal values and protections. Deliberative liberalism resolves this dilemma by conceiving of citizenship as having a dual nature. Insofar as they are theoretically derived, the form features of citizenship are in an important sense beyond the reach of politics. Since (as I argue in later chapters) the standard set of liberal protections can be understood as arising from the form features of citizenship

19. As I said in chapter 1, this usage is in general agreement with Fred D'Agostino's use of the term "political conception." See his *Free Public Reason: Making It Up as We Go* (New York: Oxford University Press, 1996).

as conceived by deliberative liberalism, this conception of citizenship will be liberal. At the same time, however, deliberative liberalism relies on a political conception of citizenship, in which the content features of citizenship are deliberatively constructed. In this way, it meets democratic demands. The nature of citizenship is nothing that is fully determined prior to the collective political activity of citizens.

The second tension involves the status of a conception of citizenship. On the one hand, my aim in setting out a conception of citizenship is to give shape to a principle of public reason. It is in this sense a sort of personal identity that is meant to set out what reasons someone acting as a citizen should take as authoritative. It is thus a description of a self-conception I am claiming members of a properly functioning liberal democratic state will and should have. At the same time, citizenship is a legal category, and one's being a citizen is, in this sense, quite independent of whether or not one values certain features of oneself or regards certain reasons as authoritative. In this sense, it is more like a social identity, defining a relationship in which I stand to others, not a relationship I form with them. One of the main aims of chapters 7 and 8 is to show the importance of linking these two conceptions of citizenship and to argue that they are so linked in deliberative liberalism. Here I am primarily concerned with the first sense of citizenship, as I work out an account of political deliberation that can ground the legitimacy of political principles. Nevertheless, the structure I am outlining here already gives us some reason to think that an account of citizenship developed with an eye to the sense in which it serves as a self-conception will also provide an adequate account of citizenship qua legal category. Since the content of citizenship is deliberatively constructed, any content feature that places us under some legal obligation or other will have to gain the ongoing endorsement of citizens and to find a way into their self-conceptions. To the extent that the legal obligations constrain that process of endorsement, it will be through the determination of form features. Nevertheless, this is a complicated problem whose solution does not lie in the drawing of philosophical boundaries. My point here is rather that this approach has the resources to reduce the chance of a split occurring between any citizen's self-conception of their political identity and the state's determination of their political identity.

I now turn to four central form features of citizenship as it is conceived within deliberative liberalism and give brief accounts of their nature and derivation. I do not claim this list to be exhaustive. I discuss these features because they play a large role in the argument of subsequent chapters and because they illustrate what is involved in providing a theoretical derivation for form features that nevertheless leave room for the deliberative construction of content features. The four features come in two groups. Freedom and equality play a central role in my discussion of exclusion in chapter 6. Overridingness and obligatoriness play a central role in my discussion of assimilation in chapter 7.

The derivation of all four features of citizenship follows a similar route. Each begins from the role citizens play in a liberal democracy as it is conceived by deliberative liberalism: legitimating political principles through their ongoing participation in reasonable political deliberation. Each form feature is thus justified by showing how it enables citizens to perform this role.

The presence of both freedom and equality among the form features of citizenship arises from the role of uptake in securing the reasonableness of political deliberation. In offering public reasons to our fellow citizens in the course of political deliberation, we are to regard their uptake of those reasons as relevant. Political deliberation is reasonable only when we both offer public reasons and are prepared to enact only those principles and policies that are supported by reasons taken up and endorsed by our fellow citizens. Treating the uptake of our fellow citizens in this way is what is involved in treating them as free and equal. It is to treat them as free because it involves recognizing that it is up to them to endorse or reject the reasons we have offered and that their doing so is reflective of their capacity for self-determination more generally. Since one of the ways we may come to have a different conception of citizenship and its potential obligations than our fellow citizens have is as a result of our occupying different nonpolitical identities, our willingness to accept their rejection of our public reasons because they do not in fact find support in their conception of citizenship is to regard their conception of citizenship, and the nonpolitical identities that shape it, as worthy of respect.[20]

Taking uptake seriously treats our fellow citizens as equals because it assumes that we are working together as coauthors of our political system, each with an equal say and equal rights to reject a system she sees as oppressive. As I argue in chapter 6, the failure to take seriously or to let matter others' rejection of our proffered reasons is one important way we treat people as inferior. To regard someone as inferior is in part to think that their reasons matter less (or not at all), and is thus to be willing to ignore the reasons they actually give or their rejection of our reasons. Thus, if we are to deliberate reasonably with our fellow citizens, we must regard them as equal.

Counting obligatoriness among the form features of citizenship captures the fact that citizenship is not only a way of conceiving of oneself, but also a

---

20. The conditions under which we can treat our fellow citizens as free in this sense, and the consequences of the requirement that we do so, are explored in greater depth in chapter 7.

legal category. But we can also see it as arising from the role citizens play in legitimating a single political structure.[21] Understood as a form feature, obligatoriness serves to constrain the scope of political deliberation by grounding its limitation to public reason. Thus, while it does not exactly flow from the requirements that ensure that political deliberation is reasonable, it serves to shape the special qualities political deliberation, as opposed to other forms of deliberation among non-obligatory identities, must have in order to be reasonable. The very need to restrict political deliberation to public reason stems from the fact that citizenship is obligatory: it can be neither freely adopted nor easily abandoned—it is an identity the state takes you to have whether or not you come to affirm its reasons for action.

I turn now to overridingness. Part of what makes political deliberation reasonable is that participants offer one another reasons they regard in good faith as authoritative for others insofar as they are citizens (i.e., public reasons). Thus, one essential aspect of citizenship is that citizens, when engaged in political deliberation, restrict their arguments to what they take to be public reason arguments. Restricting the kind of arguments I make in this manner implies that I do not always make political arguments on the basis of the whole truth as I see it, especially if that basis is not supported by the balance of public reasons as I see it. Notice, however, that this requirement is tantamount to the requirement that in political deliberation I allow my identity as a citizen to override my nonpolitical identities. Considered as a form characteristic, overridingness holds that citizens argue only on the basis of public reasons when engaged in political deliberation. Such a requirement does not lead to a denial of the plurality of public reason. I am not in violation of this requirement if what I take in good faith to be public reasons turn out to be reasons you as a citizen cannot accept. All the requirement of overridingness demands is that I first make political arguments in terms of what I regard as public reasons, and then take seriously your rejection of my reasons if they turn out to be reasons you cannot affirm. We can thus see the fact that citizenship is overriding within the political domain as nothing more than the requirement that citizens uphold the ideal of public reason, where this ideal is understood to include not only an ideal of how to make claims within political deliberation, but also an

---

21. I do not mean with this remark to take a stand on the legitimacy of secession. It seems clear that one move within political deliberation should be a suggestion that a single political unit devolve into multiple units. If that suggestion is endorsed by all citizens, then secession seems completely unproblematic from the point of view of democratic legitimacy. The difficulties arise, of course, when those to whom the suggestion is made reject it. At that point, what needs to be worked out is whether that rejection is reasonable or not, and if it is not, whether the rejection itself constitutes a kind of secession.

understanding of how to respond to the claims of others and to their responses to our claims.

5.4. The Principle of Public Reason

Public reasons are the reasons appropriate to offer in political deliberation—the "we"-reasons that are authoritative for citizens. Rawls describes the content of public reasons in two ways. He says at times that public reasons are those reasons we can "reasonably expect that others might endorse as consistent with their freedom and equality."[22] That is, they are the reasons that can be made good, in the sense of clearly authoritative, to citizens generally.[23] According to this general description, a reason will count as a public reason if fellow citizens can be made to see that it is supported by the political identity they can and do share. I will call this his general definition.

Rawls's "official" definition of the content of public reason is slightly different. He defines, within political liberalism, public reasons as those reasons that only invoke a reasonable political conception of justice supported by an overlapping consensus of reasonable comprehensive views.[24] Since I have not made anything of the distinction Rawls draws between comprehensive and political conceptions, and the way it is possible to work up a free-standing political conception, I will not make use of his official definition. In addition, there is a danger in using a conception of public reason modeled on Rawls's official definition that I want to avoid.

I take it that using the contents of a political conception of justice is one way of working out the determinate content of public reason from the general ideal of political deliberation as involving the exchange of public reasons among citizens. Rawls has been criticized for this method on the grounds that such a method fails to appreciate adequately the plurality of

22. Rawls, *Political Liberalism*, 218.
23. Rawls talks of claims being "made good" to citizens generally (Ibid., 61).
24. Ibid., 223. This definition relies on various quasi-technical terms of Rawls's. Since I will be using his general definition of a public reason rather than his official definition, nothing in what I say will ride on the precise definition of these terms. Nevertheless, a rough translation might help. A political conception of justice is one that can be developed without reliance for its justification on aspects of comprehensive world views not shared by all citizens. The overlapping consensus is an area of common ground among the different comprehensive conceptions in a society; its content comprises those ideas of political justice shared by practically all members of a society. Insofar, then, as reasons derive their authority only from a political conception of justice, which in turn relies for its justification only on ideas found within the overlapping consensus, these reasons will be public because we can reasonably expect our fellow citizens to endorse them.

political deliberation.[25] Such criticism fails to notice Rawls's claim that even within this method citizens are bound to disagree about the precise content of what they take to be the best political conception of justice and that this is "inevitable and often desirable."[26] What is required, he says, is that each of us "must have, and be ready to explain, a criterion of what principles and guidelines we think other citizens (who are also free and equal) may reasonably be expected to endorse along with us."[27] In "The Idea of Public Reason Revisited," Rawls stresses that in any well-ordered democratic society, there will not be a single political conception, but rather a family of reasonable political conceptions. As a result, different people might draw the set of public reasons differently. What is important, however, is that in offering public reasons, everyone recognizes a criterion of reciprocity, which "requires that when those terms are proposed as the most reasonable terms of fair cooperation, those proposing them must also think it at least reasonable for others to accept them, as free and equal citizens, and not as dominated or manipulated, or under the pressure of an inferior political or social position."[28]

Acknowledging that there will always be a family of political conceptions on which citizens draw in formulating arguments in terms of public reasons is Rawls's way of recognizing what I have called the plurality of political deliberation. Nevertheless, in order to avoid being misread in the way that Rawls has been misread, I will stick with an account of public reason based on something more like Rawls's general definition of public reason. Rather than generating a substantive account of public reasons via a particular political conception of justice, as Rawls does, I will derive some substantive constraints on what could count as a public reason by attending to the form features of citizenship laid out in the previous section. (Note that Rawls actually employs a similar method in the passages quoted above, insofar as he claims that public reasons are those that could be made good to citizens "consistent with their freedom and equality.")

This method of derivation respects the plurality of political deliberation in two ways. First, as I stressed above, the form features of citizenship leave a great deal of the content of citizenship open to deliberative construction. Since that content ultimately serves to ground public reasons, there is much room for plurality within this conception of public reason. Second, even the constraints that derive from the form features are not entirely out of the

25. D'Agostino makes this sort of charge in *Free Public Reason*.
26. Rawls, *Political Liberalism*, 227.
27. Ibid., 226.
28. Rawls, "Idea of Public Reason Revisited," 578.

reach of deliberative consideration. As I argue in chapter 8, for a society to be stable, the constraints that flow from the form features of citizenship need to meet with the deliberative endorsement of actual citizens in actual political deliberation.

With these initial remarks in place, we can set out the principle of public reason. I state the principle in two steps. First I provide an official definition of public reason. Then I state the principle of public reason, which relies on that definition. Define public reasons as the reasons that are authoritative for us insofar as we are citizens. In practice, this definition requires that a claim meet one of two conditions in order to be public. Either it must meet with actual deliberative uptake by citizens in reasonable political deliberation, or it must rest on the form features of citizenship. For the most part, this second possibility serves to authorize the rejection of claims made by others that rely on an understanding of our political relationship that violates one of the form features of citizenship. Such arguments will occupy most of my attention in chapters 6 and 7.

The principle of public reason then reads as follows: political deliberation is reasonable only if it involves the exchange of public reasons. In other words, it must involve the good faith effort on the part of citizens to offer only reasons they take to be genuinely public and to reject those claims they regard in good faith as nonpublic in some fashion or other. This principle sets out a necessary condition for the reasonableness of political deliberation. It is not, on its own, sufficient to guarantee that political deliberation is reasonable. In chapters 6 and 7, I look at cases where the principle of public reason is met and yet political deliberation is not reasonable. Such cases point to the need to adopt certain structural constraints on aspects of the wider society to prevent conditions from arising under which reasonable political deliberation is impossible even in the face of good faith efforts by all citizens.

Most readers will have noted that this principle is rather abstract, and may seem of little direct help in providing here and now a test for the publicness of particular reasons and arguments. Such open-endedness is not, however, a shortcoming of this principle. The plurality of political deliberation means that we cannot generally know in advance what fate our proffered public reasons will or should meet in actual deliberation. All we can do, and all that deliberative liberalism asks us to do when we take part in political deliberation, is offer in good faith reasons we reasonably expect others to regard as authoritative insofar as they are citizens. As we will see below, part of that good faith, and thus part of what makes political deliberation reasonable, is a willingness to take as relevant to the publicness of our proffered reason whether it is taken up or rejected by our fellow citizens.

Our obligation cannot be entirely discharged by filtering our reasons through a theoretically derived sieve, so any principle of public reason that purported to offer us such a sieve would be misconceiving what reasonable political deliberation requires of us.

5.5. Three Misunderstandings

Though the abstractness of my formulation of public reason is principled, it can nevertheless lead to misunderstandings. In this section, I want to head off three common misapprehensions. Doing so will also allow me to further characterize political deliberation. The first misunderstanding is based on a mistake about the role that can be played by particular nonpolitical identities in public reason arguments. The second involves cases where public reason is indeterminate. The third involves the way the principle of public reason is supposed to function in a well-ordered society.

It is often thought that the restriction to public reason serves to sterilize public political deliberation in an unfortunate way. On this view, the ideal of public reason leaves people's deepest convictions and their most firmly occupied identities outside the realm of political deliberation. This line of criticism is common among people who come to these issues from the perspective of Jürgen Habermas's discourse ethics. For instance, Thomas McCarthy asks: "Can individuals reasonably be expected to divorce their private and public beliefs and values to the extent required by an ideal of citizenship which, according to Rawls, demands that we not even vote our consciences on fundamental political issues?"[29] In the same vein, Seyla Benhabib complains that "all contestatory, rhetorical, affective, impassioned elements of public discourse, with all their excesses and virtues, are absent from [Rawls's] view."[30]

These criticisms raise several related problems. First, the principle of public reason seems to exclude people who are motivated by nonpolitical aspects of their identity from participating in political deliberation. Benhabib's worries that an ideal of public reason would serve to cut off all the messy passionate cries for justice that flow from our nonpolitical identities figure in here. Second, it seems to prevent people's political deliberation

29. Thomas McCarthy, "Kantian Constructivism and Reconstructivism: Rawls and Habermas in Dialogue," *Ethics* 105 (1994): 44–63, 52. Although Rawls says something to this effect, I think it ought to be read not as McCarthy reads it, as forbidding votes of conscience, but rather as demanding of us that when our conscience as citizen conflicts with our conscience as some other aspect of our identity, we follow our conscience as citizen in political matters.

30. Seyla Benhabib, *Situating the Self* (New York: Routledge, 1992), 102.

from being shaped by their nonpolitical identities. McCarthy's disbelief that we could ever reasonably expect people not to vote their conscience on matters of fundamental justice expresses this concern. Third, it imagines that the principle of public reason treats political deliberation as ideally dispassionate.

The principle of public reason I set out in the previous section does not require that we eschew motivation from other parts of our identities in order to enter political deliberation as citizens. Nor does it preclude a crusade for social justice that has its roots in a deep religious commitment and belief. First of all, the claim that to be reasonable political deliberation must be carried out in terms of public reasons is a claim about the way political deliberation proceeds, and not about the motivations of various political actors who participate in that deliberation. Nothing in this account of political deliberation prevents people from being moved to support a given position as a result of their deep religious faith or their lived experience as a member of this or that minority or excluded group. It merely says that in offering reasons to other citizens in support of such a position, we must attempt to offer reasons we think they would also find authoritative as citizens. Since we are understood to be reasoning together as citizens, public reasons are the appropriate sorts of reasons to offer.

Perhaps, however, as McCarthy suggests, even if this ideal permits me to enter the political debate as the result of some aspect of my nonpolitical identity, upholding the ideal of public reason will still prevent that aspect of my identity from shaping my contribution to that debate. On such a view, the civil rights activist who is led to join the cause as a result of his religious beliefs must, having joined up, bracket those beliefs, and argue only in ways sanctioned by his political identity as a citizen. This view is neither Rawls's nor mine, however.

Imagine that as a result of his comprehensive religious view the activist sees the importance of civil rights legislation as securing the dignity of members of an oppressed minority rather than, say, increasing their economic opportunities. Nothing in the ideal of public reason as I understand it prevents his arguing in terms of dignity rather than economic opportunity as the source of this understanding of the importance of civil rights. For political deliberation to be reasonable, he must not rely in arguing for the importance of human dignity on premises that derive from his comprehensive doctrine alone, premises he could not reasonably expect his fellow citizens to endorse as well. Thus, it is perfectly consistent with the ideal of public reason that our nonpolitical identities shape our political participation. Reasonable political deliberation requires rather that our political identities do so as well, and in a particular way. Upholding the principle of public reason requires the recognition that what we consider to be the whole truth in matters of political import may not be what others consider to be the whole truth, and so deliberating with them in good faith requires discovering and sometimes constructing a shared basis of support that often will not include what we take to be the whole truth.[31]

Finally, we may worry that the principle of public reason requires that our political deliberation be calm, cool, and dispassionate. When defenders of the status quo fend off radical challenges in the name of reasonableness, they rely on such a picture. Deliberative liberalism does not, however, draw a distinction between the passionate and the reasonable. What the principle of public reason asks is that we not let our passionate commitment to a given position deafen us to the claims our fellow citizens make on us. It is, however, only human to become impassioned when discussing issues of fundamental importance, and for our passion occasionally to interfere with our ability to attend properly to the claims of others. Such moments of passion cannot, then, be grounds for excluding someone from deliberation or ignoring their claims. They do, however, require that we remain collectively aware of such possibilities so that when they arise we can all step back for a moment until our ears clear. In doing so, we respect each other's passions without letting those passions interfere with our respect for each other.

I turn then to the second worry. On many properly political matters, what we regard as purely public reasons may not be sufficient to determine a unique outcome. It might be thought that upholding the principle of public reason on these occasions would require citizens to make important decisions arbitrarily, in the face of further nonpublic reasons they regard as decisive.[32] In order to address this concern, we must first distinguish two forms in which the problem of indeterminacy might arise. In the first, although each citizen is able to reach a definite conclusion on the basis of what she reasonably takes to be public reasons, citizens do not agree in their conclusions. In such a case, the indeterminacy of public reason is due to its plurality, not its paucity, and the solution is not to supplement public reasons with nonpublic ones, but to find an agreed upon procedure such as voting for reaching decisions under conditions of disagreement.

31. Note that this requirement stems from the form feature of overridingness. I think one source of McCarthy and others' reading of Rawls on this point might be a failure to distinguish overridingness as a form feature from overridingness as a content feature of citizenship. (I discuss the importance of keeping these two attributes separate more fully in chapter 7).

32. This sort of worry seems to be one of the prime motivations for Kent Greenawalt's claim that citizens and legislators ought to be allowed to let their religious convictions affect their political choices. See his *Religious Conviction and Political Choice* (Oxford: Oxford University Press, 1988). As will become clear, I am in general agreement with his position, especially given the restrictions he places on the sphere of activity I have called political deliberation.

Such a procedure will satisfy the principle of public reason and thus give rise to legitimate law if it meets three conditions. First, the procedure, its manner of invocation, and its domain must themselves be supported by an agreement that rests on public reasons. If citizens consent to the rules that govern such procedures, then they can be said in an important sense to endorse the reasons for the policies the procedure generates, since the reasons for supporting such policies include the fact that the policy resulted from a legitimate procedure legitimately applied.[33] Second, if the participants in the procedure can in fact determine their conclusion on the basis of public reasons alone, then they must do so. Thus, for instance, each citizen must vote on the basis of what she regards, at the end of deliberation, as the most reasonable balance of public reasons, even if this yields a different result than that arrived at by considering all the reasons she regards as authoritative.[34] Third, the procedure and its results must remain open to deliberative challenge. One of the ways in which what Rawls calls matters of basic justice and constitutional essentials can be distinguished from the stuff of ordinary politics is that when they fail to meet high standards of legitimacy, some people's ability to make effective deliberative challenges is undermined. When a decision is not of this august sort, it will not prevent people who disagree with it from offering deliberative challenges to it. Of course, mere defeat of your position is not sufficient reason to offer a challenge to laws enacted as a result of democratic processes. One of the signs of a properly functioning democratic society is that people are only moved to make deliberative challenges to actions by the majority when they have grounds for thinking the majority has overlooked a reason it ought to have considered. Thus, for instance, one might challenge a majority decision if the voices of those who opposed it could not be heard adequately or were not taken seriously, or if there is reason to think that the majority's judgment was clouded by factors that ought to have been irrelevant to their decision. It seems to me that in most, if not all, cases where public reasons are claimed to be indeterminate, they are so for this first reason. For a theory like deliberative liberalism that explicitly accepts the plurality of public reason, such cases pose no embarrassment.

The second sort of case arises when public reasons are insufficient for at least some citizens to reach definite conclusions. In these cases, such citizens may feel pressure to rely on nonpublic reasons to reach a decision on how to

33. Henry Richardson makes a similar point about the reasons why nondeliberative decision procedures might nevertheless carry deliberative legitimacy in "Democratic Intentions," in *Deliberative Democracy*, eds. James Bohman and William Rehg (Cambridge: MIT Press, 1997).

34. Rawls stresses this point in " Idea of Public Reason Revisited," 605–606.

vote or what policies to support. Such citizens will claim that a failure to invoke nonpublic reasons will require them to act hypocritically before their fellow citizens, and thus to undermine precisely the mutual respect that the principle of public reason is meant to realize. In order to ascertain what the principle of public reason demands in such a case, we need to be precise about just where the pressure is felt. By hypothesis, the issue in question will not admit of a purely deliberative resolution; some nondeliberative but deliberatively endorsed decision procedure will need to be employed. So, the question becomes whether citizens can rely on nonpublic reasons when deciding how they will vote in such situations. Note, furthermore, that there exist no decisive public reason arguments against any of the proposals the citizen is considering voting for. If there were, public reasons would not be indeterminate. In such cases, where public reason supports equally a number of different options and the only way of deciding among them is to rely on nonpublic reasons, the principle of public reason will permit citizens to decide how to vote among those options on the basis of nonpublic reasons as well.

To see why the outcome of such a vote would still be legitimate, note that from the point of view of the citizen in the eventual minority, this vote looks no different from the kind of vote I claimed was legitimate in the first case. If the majority is swayed by reasons I do not regard as authoritative, my endorsement of the result of a vote relies entirely on my endorsement of the procedure and my willingness to forgo deliberative challenges to it. It is not based on my positive endorsement of the reasons that sway the majority. Thus, if the majority's reliance on nonpublic reasons is going to undermine the legitimacy of the outcome, it must do so by giving me grounds to object to the procedure or to raise a deliberative challenge to its outcome. By hypothesis, there are no decisive public reasons that reject the outcome, and so I do not have substantive grounds for raising a deliberative challenge. This leaves the possibility that I might object to a decision procedure that allowed people to rely on nonpublic reasons as tie-breakers. Since the alternative in this narrow range of cases is that people vote hypocritically or arbitrarily, it seems as if I have good public reasons to allow some nonpublic reasons to play this kind of limited role. At the same time, I have reason to reject allowing just any nonpublic reasons to play this role. Reasons of narrow self-interest, for instance, might still be unacceptable.

Finally, I think these remarks help illuminate Rawls's own reasons for restricting the principle of public reason to constitutional essentials and matters of basic justice. These are matters in which the presence of nonpublic reasons at any level of justification provides grounds for dissenting citizens to raise legitimate deliberative challenges. In doing so, they assert that in matters of such fundamental importance, we as a society are better off making no decision than one that rests, even indirectly, on reasons we cannot share as citizens.

The third misunderstanding holds that an ideal of public reason, implemented in the legal structure of a society, would serve unwittingly to exclude certain voices or means of advocacy. James Tully makes a compelling case that what he calls the "language of modern constitutionalism" excludes aboriginal voices from political deliberation in accordance with their own customs and ways, and in their own languages and frameworks.[35] In its most plausible form, this criticism worries that there is no way for us, as we set out an ideal of public reason, to know in advance what reasons can be made good to citizens generally, or in what terms and languages such reasons can be urged. A strong form of this concern suggests that there is a worrisome similarity between the arguments here urged by liberal theory and those used to justify certain forms of imperialism. In both cases, a set of allowable means of entering public debate are worked out by some small segment of a population: colonial administrators or political philosophers, as the case may be. These restrictions have the effect, intended or not, of preventing some people from adequately making claims of justice. Perhaps tribal land claims based on the importance of a particular piece of land to the religious and cultural life of the tribe cannot be articulated in the language of public reason, which has been set up with a different conception of the relation of individuals to the land. We can summarize such concerns as follows: making the use of public reason necessary for political deliberation to be reasonable, deliberative liberalism fails to take seriously the plurality of political deliberation.

I think this worry gets its plausibility from a failure to see that the concept of citizenship that grounds the principle of public reason is in large part deliberatively constructed. This failure leads to a mistaken view of how reasonable political deliberation would work in real life. This view imagines that the principle of public reason is to be enshrined in some sort of prior restraint law that checks every intervention into a debate that is supposed to be guided by the ideal of public reason. But it ought to be clear that even if we could make sense of this idea (who would pronounce on such matters? where would their authority come from? how would it actually prevent people from intervening illicitly in such debates?), it does not capture the point of the principle of public reason.

35. See Tully, *Strange Multiplicity*, 71–78, for example, where he discusses how Lockean conceptions of property served the interests of European conquest and disenfranchisement of the aboriginal peoples of North America.

The point of making the use of public reason a necessary condition for reasonable political deliberation is to authorize a sort of argument that can be made in political deliberation as a way of blunting the force of certain other arguments. That is, once we have brought to bear the considerations raised here in favor of honoring such an ideal, then we have at our disposal a presumably powerful argument to make at certain times. If, in political deliberation, other citizens urge an argument for a particular view that does not satisfy the principle of public reason, we can now, as a legitimate move within the debate, point out to them why their argument fails to meet this criterion of reasonableness and why as a result it does not carry the weight they thought it did. In a society where the principle of public reason is generally honored, such a counterargument will be decisive. Seeing that the ideal can function in this manner makes clear why it need not be enshrined in the form of a prior restraint law to be effective in shaping public debate.

Furthermore, the principle of public reason plays a positive role in our participation in political deliberation. Striving to limit ourselves to public reasons in political deliberation helps us to overcome what Tully calls "diversity blindness": the failure to see that our point of view is just one among many possible reasonable points of view.[36] Insofar as political deliberation will involve people invoking the fact of their various nonpolitical identities and the roles these play in their lives, our collectively upholding the principle of public reason will help us to see the reasonableness of other points of view.[37] Thus, in contrast to the worry of exclusion voiced above, it turns out that we will be led to see others' political demands as worthy of consideration and respect precisely through attempts to deliberate in terms of public reasons. Return to the aboriginal land claim. The tribe explains the nature of their tribal identity and its ties to a particular piece of land. Rather than leading us to dismiss the demands that flow from this connection as the result of "primitive" or "superstitious" beliefs, the ideal of reasonable political deliberation conducted in public reasons asks us to work to understand the importance these connections have for them and the reasonableness of demands that might flow from them.[38]

36. Tully discusses "diversity blindness" in his "Diversity's Gambit Declined," in *Canada's Constitutional Predicament after 1992*, ed. Curtis Cook (Montréal: McGill-Queens University Press, 1994). I discuss in chapter 8 how reasonable political deliberation fosters diversity awareness.
37. As mentioned before, I take up in chapter 7 the question of just how nonpolitical identities can figure in public reason arguments.
38. Tully discusses a number of such cases where judges have managed to accommodate the claims of both sides (*Strange Multiplicity*, 167–176). I discuss some of these and others in chapter 7.

5.6. Political Uptake and the Deliberative Shared Will

In this section, I focus on the sense in which reasonable political deliberation helps to meet Hegel's first criterion of legitimacy: that legitimate institutions embody a shared will. I argue that rather than seeing the shared will
of citizens as something deliberation produces over and above itself, we
should see the shared will of citizens as something the very practice of deliberation constitutes. The will citizens share is not a will to enact the agreements that result from political deliberation, but the will to resolve all
political conflicts by reasonable political deliberation.

When citizens disagree about which political principles to endorse and
enact, they deliberate. When that deliberation is reasonable, any agreements it produces will be backed by reasons all of them regard as authoritative insofar as they are citizens. If the positions the society takes on
matters of basic justice and constitutional essentials are the result of and
are continually reaffirmed by reasonable political deliberation, then the
state will have reasons for its action (at least in these fundamental cases)
that all citizens can regard as authoritative. The state will satisfy a reason-
based criterion of consent, and thus, if consent is central to legitimacy, it
will be legitimate. What differentiates such a theory from the kind of view
I criticized in chapter 1 for failing to accommodate diversity properly is
that it rests the claim of legitimacy not on the nature of the agreement
reached, but rather in the fact of its continued reaffirmation through
ongoing reasonable political deliberation. That is, what confers legitimacy
on any given result of deliberation is the reasonableness of the deliberation and the ongoing openness to challenge via such deliberation. Thus,
we do not have to distinguish between two sorts of result: unanimous
results, which are unproblematically legitimate; and other results, which
arise from deliberatively approved nondeliberative procedures such as
majority voting, where the legitimacy of the result rests solely on the legitimacy of the procedure. Rather, in all cases, legitimacy rests on the reasonableness of deliberation. Nondeliberatively attained results, such as
from majority votes, trace their legitimacy not only to the original deliberative approval of the procedure as a means for reaching decision, but to
the ongoing deliberative environment in which the result could be challenged at any time.[39] In this way, the results of voting are no different from

39. These two grounds of legitimacy will be related in a properly functioning democracy,
since a vote gives citizens a further reason in support of the winning policy: that it was supported by an appropriate majority. In many cases, reasonable citizens will take this reason to
outweigh other reasons they have for opposing the policy and will thus forgo deliberative challenges they might otherwise make. See Richardson, "Democratic Intentions."

the results of more widespread consensus; they trace their legitimacy to their ongoing survival of the deliberative process rather than to their original pedigree.

What this means, however, is that if we want to find a shared will that serves as part of the source of legitimacy, we will find it not in particular results, not in the products of deliberative agreement, but in the commitment to the ongoing process of deliberation itself. The will citizens share, then, the will that serves to satisfy the first criterion of legitimacy, is the will to continue deliberating reasonably about political questions. Institutions will be legitimate when they embody this shared will, which means that the institutions of a legitimate liberal democratic state will have to provide for reasonable political deliberation as the means by which political conflicts are resolved. In addition, their legitimacy will stem from this provision, and thus from whether they enable truly reasonable political deliberation in society.

Resting legitimacy on openness to deliberative challenge does not mean that a legitimate society can never make political progress, that all issues will always remain matters of live political debate. What contributes to such progress, however, is not merely the quality of the reasons on either side of the debate, but a whole host of complex sociological factors. Keeping the contingency of those factors in mind is important. First, as John Stuart Mill argued, one of the things that keeps the reasons that support settled policies alive is the need to rehearse them from time to time in order to argue against opposing positions.[40] Second, keeping in mind the contingency of the factors that lead to what looks to us like progress can keep us from falling into a kind of moral triumphalism that excludes others who disagree with us in the name of a supposedly reasonable consensus.[41]

Reasonable political deliberation can be undermined both directly and indirectly. Political institutions and the behavior of politicians can directly hamper political deliberation by leaving ordinary citizens out of political deliberation altogether—either by failing to inform them of matters of great importance or by failing to heed their demands on such matters. An example of this sort of derailing of political deliberation was the U.S. government's failure to make public the growing crisis in the savings and loan industry in the run-up to the 1988 elections. Here, a

40. Mill, *On Liberty*, ed. Currin V. Shields (New York: Liberal Arts Press, 1956).
41. I take it that Stanley Fish charges Amy Guttman and Dennis Thompson with something like this mistake in his "Mutual Respect as a Device of Exclusion," in ed. Stephen Macedo, *Deliberative Politics: Essays on Democracy and Disagreement* (Oxford: Oxford University Press, 1999).

matter of clear significance, which ultimately cost taxpayers several hundred billion dollars, was kept from public notice because it was in the interest of those who knew about it, bankers and politicians alike, not to let the electorate find out and possibly express their views about the matter. Notice that the problem here is not that politicians violated the principle of public reason by defending their actions with nonpublic reasons. Rather, they circumvented the whole process of political deliberation by not even raising the subject in a public forum, and by doing what they could to prevent other, more civic-minded colleagues from doing so. In such a case, reasonable deliberation and citizen consent is impossible, because the people in a position to initiate such deliberation refuse to do so.

Political deliberation is often further undermined when problems are initially presented to the public alongside a set of predetermined possible solutions, all of which are the result of meetings between powerful lobbyists, interest groups, and government officials. Once again, the savings and loan crisis provides a stunning example. Once George Bush had won the 1988 election, his transition team began to consult with bankers and other powerful forces in the financial industry about how best to solve the problem. They did not consult with ordinary citizens or citizen groups, and such groups did not take their own views on the matter public because they had not yet been informed that there was a problem to begin with. When the Bush administration finally announced that there was a problem, they also set out the parameters in which debate then proceeded about a solution. Such ability to set the terms of subsequent debate provides a further way of undermining the reasonableness of political deliberation by making the actual deliberation of citizens somewhat of a foregone conclusion. As William Greider writes:

> This transaction represents another critical juncture in the governing process where democracy breaks down—the moment when the dimensions of the public problem are first defined and before any visible action has begun. . . . In some ways, this moment is when the public at large has the most to contribute—when the discussion is still generalized instead of technical, when the arguments are about broad political choices and public aspirations. In the routines of modern Washington, this is the point where the public is nearly always excluded.[42]

42. William Greider, *Who Will Tell the People*, 76. My discussion of the savings and loan issue is based on Greider's. See esp. 60–78.

Although the various and sundry ways in which a government can directly undermine the reasonable political deliberation of its citizens need investigation and elucidation, such work is not primarily philosophical. I take it that the framework provided here can guide such investigation: it helps us to see where the problems lie and why they undermine legitimacy. But the possibility that governments act to secure their power by compromising their legitimacy does not undermine the possibility of legitimate democratic government. A more serious threat to the very possibility of such government comes from the ways in which reasonable political deliberation can be indirectly undermined.

Indirect hampering takes place when certain social conditions exist that render it impossible for citizens to engage with one another in reasonable political deliberation. The details of those conditions will be the focus of chapters 6 and 7, but it will help to wind up the discussion in this chapter with an overview of the sorts of problems such conditions present.

Under what conditions is reasonable political deliberation rendered impossible, and how can these be avoided? As we saw in chapter 4, the reasonableness of deliberation depends on the relevance of uptake of proffered reasons. Two of the central ways in which uptake can be rendered irrelevant are by ignoring it and by assuming it. Ignoring uptake requires having the power to render rejection of a reason irrelevant. In such cases, we exclude others from our deliberations. Their uptake of our reasons has no effect because their rejection could have no effect. Assuming uptake requires being blind to the fact of deep diversity and how it shapes the plurality of political deliberation. In such cases, we assimilate others to our own perspective. We take for granted that because we find a reason authoritative, they will too. In my outline of the defense of the possibility of legitimate liberal democracy in chapter 1, I suggested that according to deliberative liberalism, exclusion and assimilation would be fundamental forms of injustice, rather than necessary evils required in order to secure unanimous consent. We can now see what this claim comes to. Taking seriously the role of fully reasonable political deliberation as the means of forming and maintaining a shared will among citizens, and thus of securing their consent to political principles, means that practices, policies, and institutions that threaten the reasonableness of political deliberation count as grave injustices, even if they do help us to reach agreement. Because it rests legitimacy on the reasonableness of deliberation and not on its results, deliberative liberalism must regard exclusion and assimilation as injustices to be avoided rather than necessary evils to be tolerated or justified. In chapters 6 and 7, I look more closely at exclusion and assimilation and how they threaten the possibility of reasonable political deliberation. The principles I develop there that help to avoid exclusion and assimilation thus play a central role in the proper functioning of deliberative liberalism and help to strengthen the case that liberal democratic legitimacy is possible in the face of deep diversity.

6

Exclusion

This chapter and the next have a variety of interrelated aims. Foremost among them is to work out some of the more radical implications of the picture of reasonable political deliberation as the source of democratic legitimacy defended in chapter 5. In particular, I argue that a commitment to securing legitimacy through reasonable political deliberation requires a commitment to a variety of measures generally associated with the politics of identity and thought to be incompatible with liberalism. This chapter argues that robust norms of equality are necessary if political deliberation among all citizens is to be possible. Chapter 7 argues that deliberative liberalism must endorse a rather broad range of cultural autonomy in order to enable all members of society to identify ourselves as citizens.

These chapters complete the defense of the possibility of democratic legitimacy in the context of deep diversity, by showing how deliberative liberalism can and must avoid exclusion and assimilation. This chapter investigates the forms of exclusion that might seep into reasonable political deliberation and discusses how these undermine the reasonableness of such deliberation. It concludes with the claim that a liberal state can address these forms of exclusion without betraying its liberalism by attending to asymmetrical distributions of constructive social power. The next chapter takes up the issue of assimilation in a similar fashion.

Exclusion and assimilation often appear to be two sides of the same process: the two options offered, for instance, in the sentiment "America—love it or leave it." In order to motivate my taking them up as separate issues with rather different implications (implications that may even appear to be in tension with one another), I distinguish them briefly here. The problem of exclusion is the result of social conditions undermining political activity. When social practices, attitudes, or institutional structures prevent some group of people from participating as free and equal citizens in reasonable political deliberation, those people are excluded. The prime examples of this phenomenon are the ways in which women and people of color are unable to speak politically in a way that is properly heard as a result of pervasive forms of sexism and racism in the wider society.

Assimilation, in contrast, concerns a set of phenomena that work in the opposite direction: people are assimilated when being a citizen constrains unfairly the breadth of possible ways of occupying the broader social culture. When being a citizen requires endorsing a set of comprehensive philosophical beliefs or taking part in a set of nonpolitical cultural practices, then people who do not endorse those beliefs or who do not follow those practices face a choice their fellow citizens do not. For them, citizenship requires assimilation. I argue in chapter 7 that political deliberation can only be reasonable when the state refrains from exerting, and citizens can effectively resist, assimilationist pressures.

Finally, these two chapters continue the project of showing that deliberative liberalism meets Hegel's three criteria of legitimacy. Chapter 5 showed how a state animated by reasonable political deliberation embodies the shared will of its citizens. Here I argue that the institutions supported by deliberative liberalism embody the shared will of all members of society and not just a select and privileged few. Chapter 7 argues that deliberative liberalism meets the second criterion, which requires that a legitimate state provide for a robust form of individual self-determination.

Before turning to substantive matters, a final general comment about the status of my arguments in these two chapters is in order. As I have suggested in earlier chapters, I am not, in articulating and defending the principles of deliberative liberalism, offering particular policy prescriptions. Rather, when I do make remarks about the potential practical implications of deliberative liberalism, I aim to show how arguments for particular policies might be formulated within the framework of deliberative liberalism. Doing so is meant to further my claim that deliberative liberalism provides a framework in which the concerns of both liberals and advocates of a politics of identity can be articulated in a manner that can be understood as reasonable by those of a different political mindset. Whether or not the illustrative arguments I mention in passing would receive proper endorsement in actual reasonable political deliberation is a question that goes beyond the scope of my discussion here. Such issues turn on too many empirical considerations to be obvious on the basis of philosophical principles alone.

6.1. Exclusion and the Impossibility of Reasonable Political Deliberation

We have seen that the reasonableness of any deliberation rests in part on factors beyond the comportment and interaction of those deliberating. If we are to ensure that the political deliberation of citizens is reasonable, then, we will need to attend to matters beyond their exchange of public reasons in political deliberation. Recall that reasonable deliberation requires a context in which no one who deliberates is denied a say in determining the relationship formed by those deliberating. In the case of political deliberation, this requires that the wider social structure not include social identities that place people in nonreciprocal relationships of the sort that undermine the possibility of forming the political relation of citizenship—a relation marked by, among other things, the form features of freedom and equality. When these conditions fail, some citizens are excluded from reasonable political deliberation, because they cannot be treated as citizens, as free and equal, within that deliberation, even if it appears that they are accorded full status in political deliberation.

I distinguish four levels of exclusion that undermine the possibility of reasonable political deliberation. First, deliberation must be universal. Deliberation fails to be reasonable (in fact, it fails even to be deliberation) if reasons and decisions are unilaterally announced rather than offered. In such cases, the party to whom they are announced is not regarded as having any standing to take up the claim as a reason; it is given as a command. Political deliberation fails to be universal when citizenship is not universal. In this case, noncitizens are not even formally given standing to participate in political deliberation. I call this "legal exclusion" and discuss it in section 6.2.

The second case involves claims that are offered but cannot be meaningfully refused. There are a number of ways in which the possibility of rejection can be foreclosed. The party offering the reason might be able to structure the situation so that the consequences of rejection are unbearably high. When the robber says, "Your money or your life," he is not making a reasonable offer to unburden you of some extra cash, because he has set the costs of rejection unbearably high. Somewhat differently, it might be the case that the party to whom the reason is offered is unable to make her rejection heard, either because she is unable to speak (or speak loudly enough) or because the one offering the reason does not listen to her or take her words seriously. In either case, even when claims offered are genuine reasons in the sense that they are adequately supported by the nature of the relationship between the parties, the exchange does not amount to reasonable deliberation. Notice that this level of exclusion involves structural features of the relationship and is thus independent of whether the excluded party would accept the reason offered. The question asked here is "could she refuse?" It is possible that she both would accept and could not have refused. In such circumstances, deliberation is still not reasonable. Political deliberation excludes some people in this sense when some citizens are socially placed in such a way that their voices are not heard or not heeded. In such cases, a combination of social and political factors will serve to prevent people from effectively participating in political deliberation at all, even if they are granted the legal status of citizen. When this happens, the political relationship they form with others who are not so excluded is not one characterized by freedom or equality. Exclusion of this kind is often the result of economic poverty or dependence. Even when it is not it leaves those excluded in what might be called deliberative poverty.[1] I thus call this type "economic exclusion" and discuss it in section 6.3.

In the final two cases, one party determines the nature of a relevant nonpolitical identity of the other party unilaterally. I will describe these as cases where one party imposes an identity on the other. When an aspect of someone's identity is imposed, the source of the authority of the reason is not her own identification but the determination of her deliberative partner. When we stand in such a relationship with others, we are prevented from forming a political relationship with them that is characterized by freedom and equality. Whereas with cases of economic exclusion no rejections matter, in these cases of social exclusion, it is only a particular type of rejection that will be ineffective. When an aspect of my identity is imposed, there is a set of claims I am assumed to have accepted. My actual rejection of these claims will be ignored or taken as evidence of my unreasonableness. Since I have no say over the authority of these claims, no relationship I form in which these claims are made can be considered free.

In such cases, an examination of political deliberation alone may turn up no evidence of exclusion. Everyone can participate and, in many cases, their participation will be effective. Furthermore, in those cases where my participation is not effective, the reason for its lack of effectiveness will appear to

1. This term is suggested by the analysis of the role inequality can play in undermining the reasonableness of public deliberation found in James Bohman, *Public Deliberation* (Cambridge: MIT Press, 1997), esp. chap. 3.

be my unreasonableness, and not the unreasonableness of the context of deliberation. In rejecting a claim made upon me, I will appear to be attempting to reject an obligation that follows from an identity that is in fact mine. The constraint on my freedom in such a case comes at the level of an effective prohibition on my ability to challenge the relevance of the identity itself, or to challenge the particular shape it has been given. In looking only at the particular deliberation in question, however, we may easily miss this limitation, either because those deliberating have internalized the identity and the claims about its relevance, or because others have been trained to see that identity as obviously relevant and to look upon anyone who would question that fact as themselves unreasonable.

An example will help to clarify this point. Many feminists argue that much of the sexism in current society rests in the fact that it is by and large up to men whether or not to treat a woman's gendered identity as relevant in a given situation.[2] Men, according to such claims, impose an identity on women. As a result, men and women stand in a relationship characterized by, among other things, a lack of reciprocity. This characteristic, however, can hamper their ability to form equal relationships. Imagine, for instance, a man and a woman who are professional colleagues, but nothing more. One of the consequences of the structure of gendered identity and the attitudes it produces is that we are likely to think that it is always open for the man to invoke his colleague's gender, to treat her as a woman, and not just as a colleague. Such behavior need not be degrading or hostile; it need not even constitute harassment. He might merely rely on the fact of her gender in making a professional judgment about her by, for example, assuming that she will be primarily responsible for childcare if and when she has children or that she has certain capacities and skills associated with femininity. If we regard our gendered identities as mere facts about us, such behavior will seem perfectly reasonable, and rejection of it will appear unreasonable— overly sensitive, perhaps, or oddly militant. It is only by looking beyond the confines of this particular professional relationship that we can see how it is being constrained by the social structure set up by gender. If the woman's gender forms an aspect of her practical identity even if only in the eyes of others, then it is something over which she ought to have a say, something about which her rejection should matter. When her male colleagues fail to heed that rejection, perhaps by ignoring it or treating it as unreasonable,

---

2. See Marilyn Frye, "Sexism," in *The Politics of Reality* (Trumansburg, N.Y.: The Crossing Press, 1983), and Catharine MacKinnon, "On Difference and Dominance," in *Feminism Unmodified* (Cambridge: Harvard University Press, 1987). I discuss and defend this view in more detail below.

they make it impossible to form a reciprocal relationship with her as professional colleagues because they deny her a voice in determining together with them which claims have the status of reasons within that relationship. If identity imposition renders impossible the formation of reciprocal relationships, then it renders impossible the formation of the political relation of citizenship. It is thus a form of exclusion.

I will distinguish two levels of identity imposition in what follows. The first involves the imposition of a demeaning or degraded identity—one whose content marks it out as inferior and thus unequal. In such a case, both the fact of its being imposed and the content of the identity serve to interfere with reasonable political deliberation by preventing people from relating to each other as citizens. Nevertheless, since the mere imposition of an identity has similar consequences, even the second, milder level of imposition will be a form of exclusion. At this level, there is nothing problematic per se with the content of the imposed identity. To see the failure of reasonableness, we have to see that the identity is imposed.

Since the imposition of an identity takes place in the broader social world, and since it can often take place in the absence of legal support and even in the face of legal doctrines of equality and inclusion, I will refer to these final two types of exclusion as social exclusion. Because these obstacles exist outside political deliberation itself, removing them will require the adoption of principles that regulate nonpolitical realms. It will thus be here that deliberative liberalism will embrace a position often described as radical democracy.[3] I discuss the first type of social exclusion in section 6.4 and the second in section 6.5.

By seeing these distinctive means of exclusion as working at different levels, we can understand why some remedies to the upper-level problem may not ultimately solve the deeper problems. Thus, for instance, the granting of formal legal equality to women and nonwhites has more or less had the effect of eliminating their legal exclusion, but it has not eliminated social or economic exclusion. Societies with greater levels of equality and access to the avenues of political deliberation than the United States have in many cases lower levels of economic exclusion, but may not have lower levels of social exclusion. Similarly, the replacement of demeaning stereotypes of women or minorities with uplifting or empowering stereotypes may prevent the first form of social exclusion, but it will not necessarily address the sec-

3. See, for instance, Chantal Mouffe, "Democratic Citizenship and the Political Community," in *Community at Loose Ends*, ed. Miami Theory Collective (Minneapolis: University of Minnesota Press, 1991); and "Feminism, Citizenship, and Radical Democratic Politics," in *Feminist Social Thought*, ed. Diana Tietjens Meyers (New York: Routledge, 1997).

ond. We can thus understand how even in the absence of barriers to legal exclusion, a democratic state could nevertheless fail to be legitimate.

6.2. Legal Exclusion

Although rather late in being either theorized or realized, universal suffrage is now a rather uncontroversial requirement for democratic legitimacy. There are, nevertheless, forms of legal exclusion that persist in the face of the universal acceptance of universal suffrage. We can divide these into two categories. First, universal suffrage does not mean that every living human being within the geographical boundaries of a given state is given the legal status of citizenship in that state. In different ways and for different reasons, tourists and children are excluded. Second, citizenship is still legally differentiated in various ways that some argue deprive some citizens of the full weight of that status.

What criteria should be used to distinguish citizens from resident aliens? The arguments against assimilation discussed in chapter 7 rule out any criteria for naturalization other than interest, length of residence, and perhaps ongoing commitments to other countries. The question still remains: what is a reasonable length of residence to demonstrate substantial commitment to a society?[4] What is important to guarantee legitimacy is not so much that one line rather than another be drawn, but that it be open to deliberative questioning and change. Such openness, however, may not be easy to achieve, as the deliberative pressure to change the criteria for citizenship is most likely to come from those who feel that they have made a substantial commitment to membership in this society but are nevertheless excluded under current law. These, however, are precisely the people who lack the deliberative standing to make this appeal, because they are not currently citizens. This problem is in part addressed by addressing the other three forms of exclusion, because one principle way in which the deliberative pressure of resident aliens to become citizens can be felt is through nonpolitical public deliberation, in which they *can* have a voice.

If the restriction on adult suffrage is thus limited to excluding recently arrived immigrants, it brings the question of the status of resident aliens

4. Western democratic societies currently differ widely on this question. In addition, they differ on the cumbersomeness of the process of naturalization, the rights of citizenship beyond voting that are extended to resident aliens, what further criteria children born in the country must meet to be citizens in virtue of their place of birth, and whether or not they recognize dual citizenship.

more in line with the question of the status of children. Both groups count as future citizens, and to some degree their interests will be addressed under these terms. In addition, there is not a stable group of people who is disenfranchised over a long period of time. Nevertheless, it seems plausible to think that the ideal of reasonable political deliberation would place certain constraints on what legal standing and obligations could or ought to be granted to these groups by those who are full citizens. Efforts ought, for instance, to be made to make children and recently arrived aliens deliberative participants whenever this is possible, and restrictions on their deliberative or political or legal standing would perhaps have to be subject to particularly high degrees of scrutiny in view of the fact that they do not have standing to effectively reject reasons offered in political deliberations. As we will see in chapter 8, one of the roles reasonable political deliberation plays in securing the legitimacy of a regime is its educative effect on citizens. The third criterion of legitimacy, that a society be self-reproducing, includes the requirement that the institutions of the state lead people living under them to affirm their identity as citizens. If reasonable political deliberation is to play this role for children and immigrants, it cannot wholly exclude them, even if it does not formally include them as citizens. In general, the institutions of the state need to be designed so as to foster rather than hamper the processes by which children and recent immigrants come to identify themselves as citizens.[5]

The second form of legal exclusion involves legal differentiation among citizens. The clearest case of this involves the differential treatment of men and women under certain aspects of the law, most particularly with regard to military conscription. Part of the content of the identity of citizen, as it has generally been understood, includes the obligation to fight and die for one's country if necessary in time of war. That obligation, however, has never been applied to women even when and where they are otherwise full citizens. In the United States, women are not required to register for the possibility of the draft, even though women have begun to fight in combat roles and many noncombat roles would presumably be filled by means of a draft.

---

5. Assuming, especially in the case of immigrants, that this is something they want to do. Many immigrants come to a country for nonpolitical reasons, and may have no interest in becoming citizens. To be consistent with the nonassimilationist policies discussed in chapter 7, it is necessary that this possibility remain a live option for them. Similarly, parents of some children may see their education for citizenship as a threat to their ability to embrace wholeheartedly their parents' religious or cultural community. Worries about education in particular are some of the hardest questions for deliberative liberalism to answer, because they involve a clash between the nonexclusive and the nonassimilationist aspects of the theory. I discuss such cases in chapter 8.

Does such differentiation undermine the possibility of reasonable political deliberation? I think it does. As many feminists have noted, excluding women from military conscription has two troubling effects. The first is to downgrade the importance of women's political resistance to war and thus to downgrade their status as citizens.[6] The United States could not currently fight a war if no male citizen agreed to fight. In fact, were even a sizable minority to insist on being locked up rather than aiding the war effort, it would be practically impossible to fight. A man's resistance to fighting in a war thus has some tangible effect, however small. The United States could, however, fight a war if no women citizens were to report for combat duty; thus the resistance of women citizens to the war necessarily has a different impact.[7]

As a result, in at least some areas, reasonable political deliberation will be impossible. The problem is that the reasons authorized by a man's citizenship will be different from those authorized by a woman's citizenship. Thus, appealing to reasons that are authoritative for men as citizens, but not for women as citizens, will exclude women from deliberation. Alternatively, failure to urge these reasons when they are in fact relevant to the considerations at hand will be to exclude men from the deliberation, given the current content of the identity of citizen for men. Reasonable political deliberation proceeds in terms of public reasons, reasons that can be made good to all citizens generally. Creating differential political obligations for men and women, then, results in the exclusion of a class of reasons whose authority rests on citizenship from the class of reasons that can be made good to citizens generally. Thus, differential qualities of citizenship turn out to be a form of exclusion. Notice, however, that this argument turns on the fact that it is the state and not men and women in their gendered identities who are imposing this differentiation. State-imposed differentiation is thus not analogous to the demands for differentiated citizenship on grounds of cultural autonomy.

6.3. Economic Exclusion

Although economic inequality is the paradigmatic source of what I am calling "economic exclusion" and it is at this level of exclusion more than any other that worries about economic inequality find a home within delibera-

6. See, for instance, MacKinnon, *Feminism Unmodified*, 35; Wendy Williams, "The Equality Crisis: Some Reflections on Culture, Courts, and Feminism," in *Feminist Social Thought*, 699–701.

7. Of course, fighting a war requires more than combat troops, and it is hardly conceivable that a country could fight any protracted conflict faced with the solid noncooperation in any war-related activity of half of its population. Nevertheless, the point made above still stands.

tive liberalism, economic exclusion does not only result from purely economic deprivation. The essential feature of economic exclusion is that it cuts off deliberative options for the excluded group. We can distinguish three forms of economic exclusion, depending on the manner and degree to which deliberative options are denied the excluded group.

My deliberative options may be cut off if my real-life options are severely restricted, either by social practices and expectations or by economic realities.[8] As a result of such limited options, I may be pressured not to voice certain positions or to reject certain reasons within deliberation. This form of economic exclusion worried Rousseau, who argued that economic dependence of some citizens on others was incompatible with legitimate government. In such situations my voice is neither silenced nor misheard, but what I am led to say with it is highly circumscribed by the realities of my situation. Economic deprivation can certainly have this effect. If my livelihood is dependent on my ability to sell my labor power, it might, in the absence of regulations protecting worker political activity, hamper my ability to participate in political deliberation or to represent my own views honestly. The same will be true of the economic dependence of women on men within traditional heterosexual marriage.

But exclusion of this first sort need not be purely economic. Thus, for instance, groups with a precarious social standing within a society might accept restrictions on their rights because making political demands for inclusion would subject them to greater immediate danger than they suffer because of their current exclusion. Violence and the threat of violence against such groups can thus be seen as participating in creating the environment in which these groups are excluded from political deliberation. Violence against recent immigrants, African Americans, and homosexuals, especially those members of these groups who refuse to accept their exclusion quietly, can all be seen in this light.

Arguments in favor of hate crimes legislation can point to the role of such crimes in this form of exclusion. Such arguments need not claim that attaching increased penalties to crimes that fill this role is justified as a deterrent to such crimes. Rather, such penalties serve two functions brought out by the considerations above. First, they are an expression of the society's rejection of the exclusion such crimes serve to enforce. Second, they can provide a way of targeting prosecution by distinguishing between minor criminal acts that do not play this enforcement role and "hate crimes" that, while they involve the same action, do play this role. The foregoing is, of course, not a

8. Such restrictions are central to Marilyn Frye's definition of oppression. See her "Oppression," in *The Politics of Reality*.

complete defense of such legislation, but only an indication of how a policy supported by the politics of identity can be supported by arguments that fit within the framework of deliberative liberalism.

In the second kind of economic exclusion, while my life choices are not so clearly restricted, I am nevertheless unable to participate effectively in political deliberation. Here the problem is more directly with the ways political deliberation takes place in my society. James Bohman suggests that we can think of the threshold of effective participation in deliberation as the ability to have one's concerns taken up within a deliberative framework.[9] There may be several reasons for failing to reach this threshold. Perhaps effective participation requires resources or capacities I do not have or was denied. Getting an agenda item on the political landscape in the United States at the moment requires attracting the attention of powerful legislators or media outlets. In general, gaining such attention requires considerable resources, whether in the form of campaign contributions, issues advertising, lobbying, or organized campaigns of press releases and publications. To the extent that all such avenues to participation in political deliberation have significant costs attached, those unable to bear those costs are effectively excluded from political deliberation. Similarly, if the positions in the society from which one can effectively enter political deliberation require a level of education only available to the very few, or a quality of education not available to all, then political deliberation fails to be universal, and those without the necessary deliberative capacities are excluded. Remedies for this form of exclusion can either aim to lower the threshold for effective participation, or seek to raise people's capacities to pass these thresholds through subsidies or the promotion of social organizing to pool resources. William Greider proposes, among other reforms, that citizens be given a $100 tax credit for donations to political candidates and organizations involved in political activities, donations that are not even tax-deductible under current tax law.[10]

The final level of economic exclusion involves a failure to be heard. In this case, although I am able, on the face of it, to participate in political deliberation, I am prevented from effectively participating, because other people fail to hear me or to take my participation seriously. Even when resources are not required to speak in the public forum, or I have significant resources to speak, my voice may still be drowned out by competing, better

---

9. Bohman, *Public Deliberation*, 125.

10. Greider, *Who Will Tell the People* (New York: Simon and Schuster, 1992), 52–53. For further discussion of these sorts of remedies, see Bohman, *Public Deliberation*, chap. 3; and Joshua Cohen, "Freedom of Expression," *Philosophy and Public Affairs* 22 (1993): 207–263.

funded voices. There is, practically speaking, limited dialogical space, so the more one viewpoint is spoken, the less room there is for others to counter it effectively. In these and the cases listed above, failure on the part of the state to regulate public discourse, whether through public funding of campaigns or through democratically controlled access to certain public media outlets, leads to the exclusion of some from effective participation in political deliberation, and thus rules out the possibility of that deliberation being reasonable.

Even in the face of an economically level playing field for political participation, there may be social forces that serve to silence particular groups. Perhaps there are social barriers to anyone with a given identity invoking that identity in political deliberation. Bohman gives the example of untouchables in India, whose public support for a policy can often lead to its defeat.[11] Gay activists in the United States have had a similar problem, and in many places both within and outside the United States, still do. Members of other groups may not be taken seriously if they choose to speak in their own voice.[12] It has been held until recently in the United States and elsewhere that while various underprivileged or underrepresented groups might have something to say on "their" issues, it is illegitimate for them to weigh in on other questions. Thus, even when women entering into political deliberation were listened to on "women's issues" such as abortion, education, and childcare, they were not taken seriously on broader issues of economic or foreign policy, unless these domains could be spun as women's issues as well. Furthermore, such intervention is often regarded not as the reasonable participation of citizens, but as the special pleading of a particular group.[13] In such cases, members of the group are effectively excluded from full participation in political deliberation: they cannot deliberate as citizens without giving up their particular nonpolitical identities. Notice that the claim is not that citizenship is a nongendered or raceless identity, since similar claims are not being made about the limitation of men's or white people's abilities to make relevant contributions to political deliberation. Such barriers are reflective of a view of citizenship that excludes people who take up certain nonpolitical identities.

Related to this is the phenomenon some feminists call "silencing."[14] As a

11. Bohman, *Public Deliberation*, 111.
12. Susan Bickford discusses a number of such examples in her *Dissonance of Democracy* (Ithaca: Cornell University Press, 1996), 96–101.
13. For a discussion of this attitude and various examples of how it alters deliberation on racial matters, see Derrick Bell, "The Rules of Racial Standing," in his *Faces at the Bottom of the Well* (New York: Basic Books, 1992).
14. See, for instance, Catharine MacKinnon, *Feminism Unmodified*, and MacKinnon, *Only Words* (Cambridge: Harvard University Press, 1992).

result of certain social conditions, some things women say are not heard, not taken up as having the meaning such words would normally have. One of the central feminist arguments for the regulation of pornography, for instance, is that it contributes to social conditions in which women's voices are silenced. In particular, it is claimed, they are not heard when they say no to sex, and so coerced sex ends up not looking like, or being treated legally as, rape.[15]

A commitment to eradicating economic exclusion thus commits deliberative liberalism to three categories of remedy. First are general policies aimed at limiting economic inequality as a way of limiting the exclusive effects of what I described in my discussion of Rousseau as one-way physical dependence and, where this is not feasible, of limiting the effect of economic dependence on political participation.

Second, policies are needed that will secure minimum deliberative capacities. These include not only purely economic programs to ensure that all have adequate material resources to participate, and structural regulation of the avenues through which people can participate effectively, but also programs to provide all citizens with the nonmaterial resources, such as education and time, necessary to participate effectively in political deliberation.[16] As hinted at above, the state may also have to regulate the major outlets of public deliberation to prevent a few voices from drowning out other points of view.

Finally, work needs to be done to remove the social barriers to people being effectively heard. Affirmative action programs, for instance, might be defended on the grounds that they help to break down people's conceptions of citizenship as somehow incompatible with various particular identities and thus help to break down such barriers. Politicians and other government officials also have a responsibility to use their offices in ways that contribute to social attitudes and practices that do not silence some people. I will have more to say about breaking down social barriers in later discussions about social exclusion.

Before turning to social exclusion, I want to make a brief comment about the nature of the workplace, and what, if any, requirements should be placed on it in order to avoid economic exclusion. Looking at the workplace from

15. For the details of such an argument, see Rae Langton, "Speech Acts and Unspeakable Acts," *Philosophy and Public Affairs* 22 (1993): 292–330, reprinted in *The Problem of Pornography*, ed. Susan Dwyer (Belmont, Calif.: Wadsworth, 1995); and Jennifer Hornsby, "Speech Acts and Pornography," also in *The Problem of Pornography*.

16. Samuel Fleischacker offers a rich and nuanced account of these capacities and the policies that might be required to bring them about in *A Third Concept of Liberty* (Princeton, N.J.: Princeton University Press, 1999).

the perspective of its potential role in creating, maintaining, or reinforcing economic exclusion requires a shift from more common ways of thinking about corporations as profit-driven providers of goods and services. Clearly, rules protecting worker organizing and political activity play a role in preventing corporations from exercising their power to keep their workers from participating freely and effectively in political deliberation. Nevertheless, these may not be sufficient.

Given the role that many large corporations play in the economic life of particular communities, they possess enormous threat advantage over the citizens in that community, especially since the executives and shareholders who ultimately make decisions about relocation are also unlikely to live in that community. Such threat advantage tends to distort the nature of political deliberation, and so a deliberatively liberal state has an interest in reducing it. This might be done by giving a veto power to members of the community about relocation of factories, giving a voice on the board of the corporation to worker or community interests, or instituting financial disincentives to corporations who desert communities to which they are vital.[17] Arguments for fuller forms of workplace democracy will also find a foothold in such concerns.

6.4. Social Exclusion I: Demeaning Identities

If a group has imposed on it an explicitly demeaning or degraded identity, then the very content of the identity may interfere with the possibility of forming an equal political relationship. Perhaps the clearest example in the United States of a group of people who have had a demeaning or degrading identity imposed on them are African Americans.[18] Cornel West, for example, claims that the "modern black diasporan problematic" is characterized by "invisibility and namelessness," a condition that "can be understood as the condition of relative lack of black power to represent themselves to themselves and others as complex human beings, and thereby to contest the

17. I am grateful to Isaac Balbus for pushing me to think about some of these issues and the place they might have in my argument.

18. Depending on circumstances, I will sometime refer to this group as "African Americans" and sometimes as "blacks." I move back and forth between these terms because neither of them seems to be perfectly suited to all situations. In favor of "African American" is that it is the way members of the group currently identify themselves, and thus using it respects their self-determination. Nevertheless, it obscures the fact that blacks have been seen as members of a distinct (and subordinate) race. When I am primarily referring to this group in the context of racist and racialist social hierarchies, I use black, whereas in other contexts, I use African American.

bombardment of negative, degrading stereotypes put forward by white-supremacist ideologies."[19] Charles Mills describes blacks as occupying a position of "sub-persons" in mainstream white thought.[20] In this, they follow Ralph Ellison's classic image of blacks as "invisible" because of the inability of whites to see them, specifically to see them as persons.[21] To the extent that blacks internalize such stereotypes, they will come to take up racial identities based on such stereotypes. Such identities, however, are not compatible with also fully occupying an identity as an equal citizen. Such internalization results in what W.E.B. Du Bois called "double consciousness, this sense of always looking at one's self through the eyes of others, of measuring one's soul by the tape of a world that looks on in amused contempt and pity."[22] We cannot measure our souls by the tape of a world that looks on with contempt and still see ourselves as fully equal members of political society. A world in which some people come to see themselves as less worthy of respect than others is a world in which the preconditions for the possibility of also seeing themselves as political equals are lacking.

But it is not even necessary that blacks internalize the "bombardment of negative stereotypes." Reasonable political deliberation requires more than that each citizen regard herself with sufficient self-respect to be able to first-personally identify as an equal citizen. We must also be able to see our fellow citizens in this way. Reasonable deliberation requires not only the uptake of good faith reasons, but that such reasons even be offered. Even if blacks were able to resist the bombardment of racist imagery thrown their way, and thus to avoid internalizing the demeaning regard of white racists, that alone would not ensure that they would be treated as citizens by their fellow citizens.

If those in the dominant group come to accept that people in the subordinate group are as the stereotypes portray them, then they will have no reason to offer them reasons consistent with everyone sharing an identity as citizens. If whites in the United States regard blacks in the United States as conforming to racist stereotypes, then these attitudes will be sufficient to undermine the preconditions for reasonable political deliberation. Here the problem will be not lack of black self-respect, but white disrespect for blacks.

Think here, for instance, of current conservative rhetoric on race matters.

19. Cornel West, *Keeping Faith* (New York: Routledge, 1993), 16.

20. See, for instance, Charles Mills, "Non-Cartesian *Sums*," in *Blackness Visible* (Ithaca, N.Y.: Cornell University Press, 1997), and *The Racial Contract* (Ithaca, N.Y.: Cornell University Press, 1997).

21. Ralph Ellison, *Invisible Man* (New York: Vintage, 1995).

22. W.E.B. Du Bois, *The Souls of Black Folk* (London: Penguin Classics, 1903), 5.

According to thinkers on the Right in the United States, there is no problem with racism in society. Blacks continue to be disadvantaged to the extent that they are not because of embedded racism and oppression, but because of their own cultural shortcomings—or even because of "liberal" remedies such as affirmative action that are claimed to ghettoize blacks and encourage them to think of themselves as victims. Talk of the "pathology" of the black family, addiction to welfare, and other ways in which the wider society blames the victims of racism for their disadvantage obscures the source of black suffering and disadvantage, locating it within the disadvantaged individuals rather than in the structure of the society and its attitudes toward blacks.

Insofar as this image takes hold in the white mainstream imagination, real awareness of the depth of racism in our society and its oppressive effects on persons of color is made virtually impossible. The result is that the more such oppression serves to leave blacks disadvantaged, the less likely they are to receive the equal respect from whites that is necessary for the formation of a truly shared identity as equal citizens. Rather, as blacks become increasingly disadvantaged, they will be seen as that much more unworthy of equal respect, and that much more incapable of making it in a society whites view as sufficiently fair.

At first it might seem as if no self-described liberal theory could provide sufficient remedies for such exclusion. After all, social exclusion takes place outside the political realm and involves the ways people relate to each other in their nonpolitical identities. Deliberative liberalism as a form of political liberalism might be thought poorly placed to interfere in these matters without implicitly relying on a comprehensive conception of the person or the self from which to criticize these social practices. To avoid imposing a comprehensive conception of the person on citizens who might not share it, deliberative liberalism remedies social exclusion by interfering with the imposition of any identity, rather than by regulating the content of particular identities. Furthermore, it derives the justification for such interference not from any comprehensive conception of the person, but from the necessary form features of citizenship—in particular, freedom and equality. Of course, this interference requires regulating the wider social realm such that people cannot impose nonpolitical identities on others, but the grounds for such regulation lie in the commitment to democratic legitimation through reasonable political deliberation, which by hypothesis we take all members of society to share (or to be able to come to share upon reflection). Furthermore, such regulation proceeds not by regulating or prohibiting such forms of speech, but by addressing asymmetrical distributions of constructive social power. Where power is reciprocally distributed, it will be impossible to impose an identity not because certain forms of speech or attitudes are prohibited, but because they can be effectively countered.

Protecting the conditions under which reasonable political deliberation is possible and universal, however, turns out to require that the state play a more proactive role in coming to the aid of some groups rather than others. Nevertheless, since the aim is to bring everyone up to the minimum level necessary to be full citizens, it can rest firmly on public reasons, universal in scope.[23] In general, then, deliberative liberalism will be committed to various forms of affirmative action and special protection (i.e., legislation that makes something a crime only if it is done by or against a particular group). These remedies will be adopted by deliberative liberalism when an argument can be made that in the absence of such legislation the social conditions under which citizens can view themselves and their fellow citizens as equals are lacking.

Such remedies will aim to change the very structure of social relations. They may thus appear to be overly strong. But it is important to see that the problems they address are embedded in the social structure, and do not exist merely at the level of the attitudes of the dominant group. As many writers have pointed out, racism is not a matter of a collection of racist attitudes on the part of individual whites. It is, rather, a result of structural features of the society that serve to maintain and reinforce those attitudes, to make them seem "natural" or warranted by the facts. Thus responding to them will involve more than exhortations to "love everyone" or to drop overtly racist or sexist attitudes. It will require making visible an "alternative" set of facts, or at least an alternative interpretation of the facts that everyone admits.[24]

It is instructive here to consider the work done by feminists over the past three decades to make visible such social phenomena as rape, sexual harassment, and spousal abuse, to make them visible as social phenomena rather than as isolated incidents explainable by individual pathology or as an unobjectionable part of life or work. Making such material visible, far from cementing the excluded group into the role of "victim," as some worry, can play an emancipatory role. When we see the world of gender relations as

23. Drucilla Cornell makes a similar point with regard to legal remedies to sexism. See Cornell, *The Imaginary Domain* (New York: Routledge, 1995), esp. chaps. 1 and 4, and *At the Heart of Freedom* (Princeton, N.J.: Princeton University Press, 1998).

24. For the importance of this point with regard to race, see Charles Mills, *Blackness Visible*, especially "Alternative Epistemologies." Mills's book not only alerts us to the importance of doing this work, but does a great deal of it as well, uncovering the "whiteness" of academic philosophy, and in particular the ways in which standard approaches to ethics and political philosophy betray a willful ignorance that they are often discussing and defending a "*Herrenvolk*" ethics, an ethics of whiteness that implicitly regards nonwhites as "sub-persons." It is my intention and my hope that deliberative liberalism does not fall into this category.

feminists have taught us to see it, we are more, not less, likely to see women as equal citizens, forcibly excluded from that role by an interlocking network of socially sanctioned violence and limitation; more, not less, likely to take seriously their grounds for rejecting certain public reason arguments as not really public, but based on exclusion and nonreciprocal power relations.[25] In practical terms, these considerations commit a deliberatively liberal state to the protection of those spaces in which this alternative epistemological work can develop, and its citizens to the concerted effort to take seriously arguments that begin from such alternative premises as fully reasonable and worthy of serious attempts to grasp them.[26] One of my aims in this book is to help liberals and others who have been generally skeptical of such arguments in such an effort.

To be effective, such epistemological openness requires further structural change. It also requires undermining the inequalities of power that give people in both groups an incentive not to see forms of exclusion and oppression for what they are. Since addressing such inequality of power is central to addressing the general question of identity imposition, I leave off discussion of it until later, but it is worth noting at this juncture that the kind of remedies suggested above (affirmative action, "protective" legislation) should be seen as working to effect such shifts in the distribution of power in part by putting the power of the state to work on behalf of those who are disadvantaged in the distribution of social power as it currently stands.

6.5. Social Exclusion II: Treating "Them" Just Like "Us"

Not all social exclusion involves the imposition of a demeaning identity. Reasonable political deliberation is also undermined when a group of people has a supposedly ennobling identity imposed on them. We can break down the imposition of an identity into three aspects. First of all, imposing an identity on someone involves determining when that identity is relevant. Second, imposing an identity on someone means determining, at least in certain circumstances, which claims have normative authority for them, regardless of whether they themselves see these claims as having authority.

25. MacKinnon, for example, argues that the emancipatory power of consciousness-raising lies precisely here: "It is validating to comprehend oneself as devalidated rather than invalid." MacKinnon, *Towards a Feminist Theory of the State* (Cambridge: Harvard University Press, 1989), 100.

26. On the general importance of active and respectful listening for reasonable political deliberation and the ways in which oppressive power structures undermine or distort that capacity, see Susan Bickford, *The Dissonance of Democracy*.

Third, imposing an identity on someone makes it impossible to see them except through the screen on which we have projected the imposed identity, and thus denies them their individuality and their independence from us. This further prevents us from regarding them as free. Note also that the imposition of an identity prevents the formation of the political relation of citizenship in two ways. First, it prevents the imposers from seeing the imposed upon as self-determining and thus free. Second, it is also expressive of our failure to regard them as equals, as coauthors with us of the nature of our political relationship.

A common and familiar form of the imposition of nondemeaning identities in our society involves people in positions of power ascribing to others an identity "just like us." This sort of ascription is what has gone wrong where people in positions of privilege are accused of failing to "get it" despite what they claim are their good intentions. Think, for example, of the members of the Senate Judiciary Committee with regard to the harm of sexual harassment in the Anita Hill/Clarence Thomas hearings. (Such charges are also often made by women of color, lesbians, and others who charge that they are excluded from the discourse of mainstream feminism.)[27] In the case of the Senate hearings, senators failed to believe Hill's claims because they could not imagine being in her shoes and having put up with what she alleged Thomas had done to her and yet staying quiet, following Thomas to another job, and so forth. That is, they ascribed to her an identity as being just like them. Perhaps they did this under some ideal of equality, of treating everyone similarly. Because the reasons she alleged motivated her would not have motivated them, they failed to take them up as valid reasons for action, and so assumed that she must not be telling the whole truth of what happened. What on the surface looked as if it would be a forum in which an exchange of reasons would lead to a shared view of what had happened and of its social and legal significance failed to produce that shared view because the senators could not see Hill's reasons as reasons as a result of their ascribing a particular identity to her.

What are often thought to be standard liberal remedies to discrimination involve imposing an identity on the oppressed as being just like us. On such

27. For a discussion of the Hill/Thomas hearings as an example of this point, see Iris Marion Young, "Asymmetrical Reciprocity: On Moral Respect, Wonder, and Enlarged Thought," *Constellations* 3 (1997): 340–363. On the charge of exclusion in feminist theory, see María Lugones and Elizabeth Spelman, "Have We Got a Theory for You!" in *Hypatia Reborn*, eds. Azizah al-Hibri and Margaret Simons (Bloomington: Indiana University Press, 1990); Marilyn Frye, "On Being White: Towards a Feminist Understanding Of Race And Race Supremacy" in *The Politics of Reality*; and bell hooks, "Sisterhood: Political Solidarity between Women," in *Feminist Social Thought*, ed. Meyers.

a view, men are thought to stop being sexist when they treat women just like men, and whites to stop being racist by treating people of color as just like them. Arguments for "color-blindness" over affirmative action are grounded on such practices, as are the various parts of what MacKinnon calls the difference approach to sex equality in the law.[28] The considerations adduced above help to show where they go wrong. By imposing a new identity on the oppressed group rather than providing that group with the wherewithal to define itself, they continue the oppression, albeit in another form.

It might be suggested at this point that deliberative liberalism is no less sectarian in holding out an ideal of sharing an identity as citizens. There is, however, a fundamental difference between struggling to construct together a shared identity across our differences and taking a given identity and saying to those who do not yet take it as theirs that they will from here on in be regarded as having that identity, as is. In the latter case, we start from a prior theoretical commitment to a conception of citizenship that is, as it were, etched in stone, and then go around applying it to everyone in the spirit of inclusion and equality. Deliberative liberalism takes the former route. It derives the form of a conception of citizenship backward from the end of making possible reasonable political deliberation among a deeply diverse population, and leaves the content of citizenship otherwise open to deliberative construction. The content of our identity as citizens is thus always up for reformulation in the light of political deliberation.[29]

This distinction is of central importance in grasping the radical nature of political liberalism generally. Many interpreters have read Rawls as merely shifting liberalism's prior theoretical commitments from the person (as in comprehensive liberalism) to the citizen. Were that true, political liberalism would involve the imposition of a particular political identity. As I read Rawls, however, he is committed to the approach by which we together construct our identity as citizens.

Before asking what can be done to make possible such joint construction of our political identity, we need to consider an objection. It might be claimed that in focusing on identity imposition I have cast my net too wide. The worry is that the elimination of imposed identities would eliminate means of identity formation that are valuable and not oppressive. It is important to note, however, that not all identities that are unchosen are

---

28. See MacKinnon, "On Difference and Dominance," in *Feminism Unmodified*.

29. I will have more to say about how deliberative liberalism avoids imposing the identity of citizen when I discuss assimilation in chapter 7. Notice for the moment, however, that in seeing the latter sort of practice as a form of social oppression, deliberative liberalism agrees with Tully that the insistence on an authoritative, predetermined language of deliberation is imperial.

thereby imposed. In at least some parts of U.S. society today, much of the meaning of being Jewish is determined by Jews themselves. Jews, that is, do not have their religious identity imposed on them by non-Jews.[30] From the perspective of an individual Jew, however, the meaning of his religious identity may not be something over which he has much control. Perhaps he has come to it through being brought up with the beliefs and positions of his parents. Perhaps he takes religious identity to be strongly tied to tradition and religious authorities and not a matter of individual conscience. These sorts of facts make his identity as a Jew neither freely chosen nor wholly self-determined. Nevertheless, non-Jews do not by and large assume that they know what it is to be a Jew, and so when they offer reasons to Jews, they take actual acceptance to matter—i.e., they actually listen to see if these reasons can be and are accepted. For these reasons, a Jew's identity as a Jew is not imposed on him. As a result, his religious identity does not stand in the way of his forming a political relationship with others that is characterized by freedom and equality.[31]

Insofar as we come to have many of the identities we do through our upbringing, and as this rarely involves conscious choice on our part of which identities to take up, we need to be able to distinguish between education and identity imposition. For me the central difference is that education, at least good education, has as its overall aim the creation of a person who can reflect on her various identities, and thus come to take them up herself. Education, then, establishes the preconditions necessary for our coming to affirm any aspect of our identity reflectively. Identity imposition, on the other hand, aims merely at implanting a particular identity on its objects, and is concerned with their affirming this identity (if at all) merely for ease of enforcement or psychological comfort.

---

30. My claim that Jews here and now do not have their identity imposed on them should not be taken to deny either that Jews throughout most of history in most places have had their identities imposed on them, or that Jewish identity in the United States now is not in some deep and important ways shaped by the fact that the country as a whole is deeply Christian. The possible content of an identity can have been shaped to a very large degree by its encounter with a related dominant identity without the less powerful identity having been imposed on its members in the sense I am discussing here. I am grateful to Sam Fleischacker for pushing me to think more clearly about the status of Jewish identity.

31. The point here has to do with the social position his religious identity places him in (as a result of it not being imposed) rather than the content of the religion itself. It is certainly possible that in virtue of the content of an identity not externally imposed that someone would be unwilling or unable to form relationships of equality with certain others. This failure to take up citizenship is not a result of exclusion, however.

6.6. Exclusion and Constructive Social Power

Exclusion, whether legal, economic or social, renders impossible the reasonable political deliberation of citizens. It thus requires corrective regulation. In this section, I argue that constructive social power, and in particular its asymmetrical distribution, is necessary for the establishment and maintenance of all four forms of exclusion.[32] By tracing the possibility of exclusion to the distribution of social power, we can then formulate remedies to exclusion that will remain liberal.

The theory of constructive social power on which I rely is derived from the work of Catharine MacKinnon, though it is not unique to her.[33] A similar account of power can be found in at least some of the work of Michel Foucault.[34] According to this theory, constructive social power constructs social categories and thus shapes our view of the world, of what is natural and what exceptional. It thus serves to structure the world in which we come to take up particular practical identities. In doing so, it plays two roles in our coming to have the identities we do.

First, constructive social power determines the range of possible meaningful identities. In order for my practical identity to have social relevance, others will have to be able to recognize its contours as fitting some recognizable social categories. I can meaningfully and helpfully describe myself as a man or a woman, as a member of a religious or ethnic group or a profession or club, because all of these categories are considered meaningful in our society. As a result, I can cite such identities to support my rejection or acceptance of reasons in deliberation. I cannot, by contrast, describe myself seriously as someone who regards as authoritative all and only reasons that contain an even number of letters in English, or who only finds the prospect of future pain to be a reason to avoid something when the pain will be inflicted on alternate Tuesdays. Unlike the first set of identities, these can't be regarded as anything more than jokes, or perhaps parts of philosophical thought experiments. Were someone to justify her behavior by citing one of

32. Throughout this section, I use the terms "constructive social power" and "social power" interchangeably. I use "constructive social power" when it seems important to highlight its constructive role.

33. I discuss MacKinnon's theory of power and its possible implications for Rawls's political liberalism at greater length in my "Radical Liberals, Reasonable Feminists: Reason, Objectivity, and Power in the work of Rawls and MacKinnon" (Unpublished manuscript, University of Illinois at Chicago, 2000).

34. See, for instance, his *Discipline and Punish: The Birth of the Prison* (New York: Random House, 1975), *Power/Knowledge*, ed. Colin Gordon (New York: Random House, 1980), and "The Subject and Power," in *Michel Foucault: Beyond Structuralism and Hermeneutics*, 2d. ed., eds. Herbert Dreyfus and Paul Rabinow (Chicago: University of Chicago Press, 1983).

these as her identity, we would be moved to respond that she does not understand the meaning of our words or that we do not understand the meaning of her words. The reason for this reaction, I suggest, is that these are not socially relevant categories of identity.

But social power does more than set out the range of possibility for practical identity. It also ties many of those identities to objective facts. In our society, being a woman is not merely one practical identity among many that sets out a particular set of reasons as authoritative. It is an identity that all and only people with certain physical traits must take up. Identities can be assigned in this way precisely because social power can draw certain lines between some (though not all) identities and the objective facts that are claimed to ground them.

We begin to see how constructive social power might play a role in identity imposition. As I argued above, identity imposition consists of two central aspects: neither the content of the imposed identity nor who occupies it is up to those so identified. Since both of these aspects of a practical identity are shaped by constructive social power, constructive social power will play a role in identity imposition. More precisely, asymmetrically distributed constructive social power will make identity imposition possible. To see this, recall the sense in which identity imposition involves a denial of self-determination. As I suggested in distinguishing imposed identities from identities neither imposed nor chosen, what is required for imposition is not that individuals do not choose their identification or its contents, but that the group as a whole does not.

If it is through the wielding of social power that we contribute to the shaping of certain identities and their assignment to certain objectively determined classes of people, then the denial of this collective process of social construction requires that we not have such power. Moreover, it requires that those who do collectively determine the content and assignment of a particular identity do have that power. Since social power is thus wielded by one group and not another with regard to the construction of the latter group's identity, we can say that the latter group's identity can be imposed only when social power is asymmetrically distributed.

Social power is the power to determine for others whether or not certain aspects of their identity can or must be brought into play in certain circumstances and what claims they will authorize. When this power is asymmetrically distributed, then those decisions cannot be effectively resisted by the people on whom they are imposed. Refusal to accept the dictates of one's identity when those with power have declared it relevant will be viewed not as reasonable rejection of identity imposition, but as willfulness, irrationality, or a sign of mental disorder or incomprehension. When constructive social power is reciprocally distributed, such imposition is impossible. Any attempt to impose an identity can be met with effective resistance, with moves to change the categories or their uses or the grounds on which they are applied.

It might be objected at this point that what is needed is not reciprocal distribution of power but the elimination of other-determining power. That is, what is important, for instance, is not that women as much as men have power to determine the content and role of the identity "woman," but that women *and not men* have such power. What we need to strive for, so this argument goes, is that each group be completely self-determining. Such a view misunderstands the nature of group identities and of power. First of all, groups of people who share an identity are not thereby homogenous. In fact this aspect of their identity cannot even be separated out as a standard module.[35] Black women's identity as black women is not just the addition of the identity "woman," which is the same as the gendered identity of white women, to the identity "black," which is the same as the racial identity of black men. There would therefore be no possible way of properly distributing power to realize this ideal of complete self-determination of groups.

Perhaps more significantly, this objection misunderstands the nature of power. It is in the nature of constructive social power that those who wield it wield it over others as well as themselves. This is part of what is involved in it being social. The very act of asserting a particular identity as a man, for instance, carries with it implications for the way in which women can identify themselves. At the very least, it asserts the significance of gender as a social category and claims that it does not include all people. Beyond that, insofar as it implicitly asserts an identity of "woman" as in some sense its counterpart, the particular content I give to the identity "man" will close off ways that "woman" can be defined in the same social universe. The result of this feature of social power is that we are always in the process of determining the social world in which others live as long as we are in the process of determining the social world in which we live. Such determination becomes imposition, however, when it is one-sided. We thus avoid imposing identities on others only if they are also in a position to take part in the determination of the social world. But that is to say that the best we can hope for is that power be reciprocally distributed, so that insofar as I have power to determine the world in which you live and thus the options you have for occupying that social world, you have the same power over me. In such a world, we would all wield together the power that allows us to construct our

---

35. For a clear articulation of this point and its relevance for feminist theorizing, see Elizabeth Spelman, *Inessential Woman* (Boston: Beacon Press, 1988).

social world together. In such a world, and only in such a world, it would be possible for us all to take up together the political identity of citizens, and to engage together in reasonable political deliberation.

Asymmetrical distributions of constructive power also help support legal and economic exclusion. The conditions that make possible economic exclusion, from economic inequality to poverty, whether economic or deliberative, can serve to reinforce or support asymmetrical distributions of social power on the one hand, and be supported and reinforced by such distributions on the other. Thus, one of the effects of wielding social power asymmetrically is the ability to impose an identity on others that will increase the likelihood of their economic dependence. One of the reasons women continue to earn less than men in the United States, more than thirty years after the federal government outlawed pay discrimination, is because jobs that are seen as appropriate for women are lower-paying. Thus, being forced to identify oneself as a woman has negative effects on one's earning potential.

Insofar as these effects contribute to women's economic dependence on men, and thus on their economic exclusion, women's economic exclusion turns out to depend on their social exclusion. In other cases, it is in part as a result of economic exclusion that a group is locked into social exclusion. Insofar as combating the imposition of an identity requires the wherewithal to provide public responses and challenges to the stereotypes that define one's imposed identity, it will be harder for those who are impoverished or lack the necessary means and capacities to offer such resistance. In either case, an explicit commitment to reciprocal levels of social power will bring with it a commitment to end economic exclusion. Where economic exclusion is supported by social exclusion, it will presumably be undermined by measures designed to eliminate social exclusion. Where it supports social exclusion, then measures that aim to eliminate social exclusion will have to include remedies directed at economic exclusion, such as those discussed in section 6.3.

Similar arguments can be made about the relation of social and legal exclusion. As I suggested in my discussion of legal exclusion, it goes unchallenged when it is accompanied by parallel social exclusion. Once we come to regard other members of our society as cooperating with us in the determination of the social world we inhabit together, and as having a claim to such a place, it is hard to justify legally excluding them from political participation. What reasons could be given for such exclusion, other than those that would justify the temporary exclusion of recent immigrants and children? Once again, the connections go both ways. Thus, even if ending the legal exclusion of nonwhites and women in the United States has not on its own ended their social exclusion, it has presumably made some difference. More importantly, however, insofar as there is any movement toward merely replacing *de jure* legal exclusion with a *de facto* variety, it would be undermined by addressing the social exclusion of the targeted group. As the distribution of social power becomes more reciprocal, groups in danger of legal exclusion will be in a better position to challenge this and all other forms of exclusion effectively.

6.7. An Inclusive Liberalism

What, exactly, is required of a state committed to eliminating exclusion by bringing about reciprocal levels of constructive social power? I characterize the state's role as reactive but ongoing. That is, a commitment to reciprocal levels of social power, if understood within the context of liberalism, can only require the state to act to reduce instances of asymmetrical distribution of social power when and as these are brought to its attention. In this sense, neither the state nor those theorists trying to describe what the state should be like need to have a developed account of what a fully reciprocal distribution of power would look like, or of the content of our identity as citizens. For instance, a commitment to reciprocal levels of social power, enshrined within a constitution, could lead a supreme court to overturn a given piece of legislation on the grounds that it supported or created an asymmetrical distribution of social power. Arguments in favor of certain affirmative action programs, or reforms in family law that would serve to make couples more egalitarian, could all be grounded and thus find strong support in such a commitment.

Recall that the point of articulating abstract ideals is to help us here and now organize our thoughts and provide a compelling framework within which we can offer public reason arguments for various and sundry policies and laws. The arguments presented in this chapter point toward a way of arguing against policies that support or produce various forms of exclusion. Furthermore, since reciprocity of power is a precondition for the possibility of reasonable political deliberation, these arguments will take priority over arguments that take place within reasonable deliberation.

Take, for instance, current debates between advocates of affirmative action and advocates of replacing such programs with purely color- or gender-blind standards. A particularly powerful argument in favor of affirmative action points to the ongoing asymmetry of power between whites and people of color, or between men and women. It goes on to claim that it is necessary to give explicitly preferential treatment to women and minorities in order to offer even the hope of a level playing field in which norms of reasonableness can function properly. The argument for abandoning such policies is that they appear to violate a straightforward application of an ideal of reasonableness: they ask of some people that they recognize certain characteristics of others, which even the others admit are irrelevant to the performance of the job in question, as having a positive weight in standards of hiring or admission. In the absence of considerations of the distribution of power it appears that affirmative action policies require white men to accept a devaluation of their own identities, and are for this reason unreasonable.

If we understand that reciprocal distribution of social power is a necessary precondition for reasonable political deliberation, then we can respond to this argument against affirmative action. Current distributions of power make reasonable political deliberation impossible, so we have to address that distribution before adopting standards such as color-blindness that would be required by norms of reasonableness in the presence of reciprocal levels of social power. Thus, we must act here and now to correct these asymmetries of power, *even if* accomplishing such a redistribution requires supporting policies that themselves would not appear reasonable given reciprocal levels of power. Furthermore, we must do this precisely to uphold the ideal of reasonableness that stands behind the norms being invoked by the opponents of affirmative action.

Finally, since constructive power is a necessary condition of human social existence, giving the state a reactive role with regard to establishing reciprocal levels of social power clarifies how the state can serve as an ongoing spur to change. A positive principle that laid out a set of acceptable nonpolitical identities citizens could take on and took its work to be done when such identities were the only ones in society might leave uncovered some forms of oppression because they either were not then visible or came about as a result of other reforms.[36] Giving the state a reactive role will avoid this problem. We need not spell out in advance which identities imposed by which asymmetries of power the state must address.

The point of articulating deliberative liberalism was to show the possibility of democratic legitimacy in the face of deep diversity. This chapter has shown that such legitimacy is only possible when social power is reciprocally distributed. Seeing that gives us a way to make a public reason argument, and a rather forceful one at that, for adopting policies that would lead to the establishment of (more) reciprocal distributions of social power. In addition, it gives us reasons to work to achieve such distributions through reasonable

---

36. It would, of course, also violate the ideal of citizens coming to form a shared will themselves through processes of reasonable deliberation, not to mention being rather illiberal.

political deliberation, rather than to see the entrenchment of asymmetrical distributions of social power as a reason to give up on democratic or liberal politics. Given those aims, a reactive but ongoing commitment provides precisely what is needed.

In closing this chapter, I note that by working to eliminate exclusion, deliberative liberalism fully realizes the first of Hegel's three criteria of legitimacy. We saw in chapter 5 that we could think of the reasonable political deliberation of citizens as embodying their shared will. This chapter has asked whether in fact all citizens can and do share in that will. The possibility of exclusion throws that into doubt. We have seen, however, that deliberative liberalism can and must be committed to preventing exclusion and that this requires a further commitment to reciprocal levels of social power. Such commitments ensure that in a deliberatively liberal state, the will citizens share is truly shared by all.

7

Assimilation

For any political system whose legitimacy rests on the universal consent of citizens, assimilation is always a temptation. It becomes all the more so if exclusion is ruled out as a means of forging unanimity. Liberals have certainly succumbed to this temptation. Advocates of a politics of identity and other self-described friends of diversity often claim that such reliance on assimilation is not merely the result of a set of individual failings of liberal theorists or politicians, but is symptomatic of a deeper problem within the structure of liberal theory itself. This chapter explores such criticisms, describes their impact on a deliberative liberal account of legitimacy, and suggests the resources deliberative liberalism has for responding to them.

7.1. Liberal Impositions

Two aspects of liberal theory come under the most sustained attack. Many critics point to liberalism's reliance on norms of reason to ground claims to legitimacy as unfairly preventing some people from participating in political deliberation on their own terms. Others point to the equation of equality with similarity, which, they claim, is the central move in liberalism's path to universality and which serves to undermine the ability of some to be both equal and different.

Some critics of liberalism claim that norms of reason provide cover for the strategic machinations of those in power. In a particularly forceful

159

example of this criticism, Stanley Fish accuses Dennis Thompson and Amy Guttman of defining "rational" so as "to make it congruent with the ways of thinking you and those who agree with you customarily deploy."[1] Norms of reason are not, this criticism claims, general and universal, but always the norms of some particular group. If this is true, then insisting that citizens engage one another and their government in reasonable deliberation will require them to assimilate to a particular way of conceiving of themselves, their beliefs, and their place in the world.

A slightly more restricted form of criticism, often deployed by people who are rejecting not the liberal project but its current political instantiations, points to the danger that upholding norms of reason may serve to support an unjust status quo. Cass Sunstein argues that such support rests on the doctrine of what he calls "status quo neutrality": the assumption that the status quo is itself somehow neutral or natural, not itself supported by, for instance, a set of government and legal regulations, prohibitions, and protections.[2] Under the assumption of status quo neutrality, people who chafe under the status quo may find the insistence that they offer overriding reasons for change an unfairly high bar to clear, as it will require them to assume the acceptability of much that they are attempting to change. Many progressive and left-wing critics of current U.S. policies express frustration with a rhetoric of reasonableness that pushes demands for radical or fundamental change off the agenda by fiat.[3] The liberal insistence on reasonableness, these critics charge, unleashes assimilationist pressures because in order to be a full-fledged citizen, someone whose voice must be listened to in political deliberation, everyone must shape her participation according to standards that are not hers and may require her to misrepresent her demands.

As many people have said, it is difficult to read these charges—even in their more radical versions—as all-out assaults on all norms of reason.[4] The problem is that these charges generally rely on arguments that other arguments fail in some way or another. But such arguments themselves must appeal to some norms of what makes a good argument or what makes a just

1. Stanley Fish, "Mutual Respect as a Device of Exclusion," in *Deliberative Politics: Essays on Democracy and Disagreement*, ed. Stephen Macedo (Oxford: Oxford University Press, 1999), 94–95. James Tully makes a similar point with reference to historical forms of what he calls "modern constitutionalism" for imposing an "empire of reason," in his *Strange Multiplicity: Constitutionalism in an Age of Diversity* (Cambridge: Cambridge University Press, 1995).

2. Cass Sunstein, *The Partial Constitution* (Cambridge: Harvard University Press, 1993).

3. See, for instance, Greider, *Who Will Tell the People?* (New York: Simon and Schuster, 1992), 216.

4. See, for instance, Guttman and Thompson's reply to Fish, in their "Democratic Disagreement," in *Deliberative Politics*, 258–259.

or legitimate regime. If this is right, then we need to understand such arguments not as advocating the abandonment of norms of reason *tout court*, but rather as claiming that the norms of reason on which liberalism relies be broadened or shifted to be more inclusive of various forms of difference, to be less assimilationist. In the language I developed in chapter 5, we can say that liberalism has a tendency to fail to acknowledge the plurality of public reason, and that in doing so it succumbs to one form of the temptation to assimilation. One aim of this chapter is to bring out just how deliberative liberalism affirms the plurality of public reason, and how this gives it the tools to resist assimilation.

According to a second line of criticism, liberalism achieves universality by assuming and then imposing similarity as a sort of proxy for universal equality.[5] Historically, liberal theories have rested their arguments for universality and equality on theories of human nature, and this reliance has led them to be assimilationist in this manner. One of the motivations for developing deliberative liberalism is to avoid just such a temptation. Nevertheless, some might worry that in responding to concerns about exclusion, deliberative liberalism succumbs to this problem in a slightly different form.

Deliberative liberalism resists exclusion by securing to citizens the ability to reject imposed identities on the grounds that identity imposition conflicts with two necessary characteristics of the identity of citizen: freedom and equality. If, however, the freedom and equality of citizens is fixed in advance, is not open to deliberative challenge, then the identity of citizen looks very much like an imposed identity. Thus, the identity of citizen is poised to do precisely the work of assimilation that in older theories was done by a theory of human nature. It looks as if people who affirm nonpolitical identities that are inconsistent with this particular conception of citizenship will not be allowed to reject their political identities. Deliberative liberalism thus appears to demand assimilation. I argue here that deliberative liberalism does not impose a predetermined identity of citizen on those who would not accept it. In order to make this argument, I rely on the distinction between form and content features of an identity developed in chapter 5. I suggest that liberalism is driven to adopt assimilationist practices as a result of certain commitments it ought not abandon, and I argue that a liberal theory can make good on those commitments while resisting assimilation by relying on a political conception of citizenship as deliberative liberalism does. The key is to interpret the fixed qualities of our identity as citizen as form

5. See, for instance, Catharine MacKinnon, "On Difference and Dominance," in *Feminism Unmodified* (Cambridge: Harvard University Press, 1987); Iris Marion Young, *Justice and the Politics of Difference* (Princeton, N.J.: Princeton University Press, 1990).

rather than content features of that identity. Doing so also ensures that deliberative liberalism will respect the plurality of public reason, in large measure by accepting a set of arguments I will refer to as arguments from burdensomeness. Such arguments allow people to invoke features of their nonpolitical identities in public reason arguments, and thus to call attention to and resist deliberative liberalism's unintended assimilationist pressures.

Of course, some complaints made in the vocabulary of resistance to assimilation will not be reasonable, and thus it will be appropriate to reject them. What deliberative liberalism will require of citizens in the face of these demands is that they be taken seriously and rejected on the basis of well-articulated reasons that rest on the necessity of adopting this shared project of together working out legitimate political principles, not rejected on the basis of comprehensive theoretical commitments to the good of a certain kind of political arrangement. Such reasons may not be any more compelling to those to whom they are offered than more comprehensive ones (though we might hope that they will be); rather, if even these premises are rejected, then we can conclude that the problem between us is of a very different sort, and one for which deliberative liberalism (or any other polit-ical theory, for that matter), may not be the appropriate place to look for guidance. That is, if a group of people living in a society take it to be of no interest or importance that they jointly work out with their co-residents principles that can guide their interactions and to which they can all agree, then no amount of argument or talk is going to bring them to consent freely to a set of jointly workable principles on the ground that they are jointly acceptable. These people therefore present a very different set of issues than are presented by the kinds of people I take to be the primary concern of deliberative liberalism—those who are interested in jointly working out jointly acceptable political principles, but who do not necessarily begin with a view that liberal principles will be the best sort to adopt. This admission of the limited ambition of deliberative liberalism is no cause for shame, how-ever. Accepting that no political theory, and certainly not deliberative liber-alism, will be acceptable to everyone does not render this sort of project circular or somehow an exercise in self-congratulation. To say that there are limits to what philosophy can accomplish politically is not to say that it can do nothing, or even nothing important or interesting, at all.

7.2. Resistance to Assimilation: Some Examples

I turn first to some concrete examples of assimilationist pressures and demands to resist them. Attention to concrete cases is important here, because much of the antiliberal rhetoric tends to underestimate the basic reasonableness of those resisting assimilation and their arguments. One point of the following survey, then, is to show that within the domain of even reasonable pluralism, there is a lot more difference and dissension than critics like Fish tend to acknowledge.[6] Another is to provide us with examples on which to test the arguments that follow. The various sorts of claims I catalogue all demand what Will Kymlicka calls "group-differentiated citizenship."[7] I suggest that a failure to grant (or at least take seriously) such claims reveals that the society is imposing a political identity on the plaintiffs that conflicts with some other aspect of their identity.[8]

Native peoples in North America have claimed special status with regard to federal, state, and provincial laws in the United States and Canada on the basis of their membership in a particular tribe. The Musqueam nation inhabits lands on the Pacific coast of Canada. They demanded exclusive rights to fish a region of coastal waters on the grounds that fishing those particular waters was in part constitutive of their cultural identity. On these grounds they sought in the Canadian courts the right to exclude non-aboriginal fishermen from fishing those waters. The court granted them this power, but insisted that in fishing those coastal waters they nevertheless obey certain federal restrictions aimed at conservation.[9]

Ojibwe tribes in the Great Lakes region of the United States claim unrestricted access to fish the small lakes that dot the region, including those that are off-reservation. They claim exemptions from state regula-

6. I do not mean to deny here that many liberal theorists define reasonable pluralism far too narrowly. My point is twofold: that the circle of reasonable pluralism can be rather large, and that in making it so, we leave room for a lot of the committed antiliberals whom Fish sees himself as defending. The further question of how to treat those who still fall outside even this wider circle of reasonableness is not one I take up in this book. It is one for which I doubt philosophy is the appropriate tool.

7. Will Kymlicka, *Multicultural Citizenship* (Oxford: Oxford University Press, 1995). The book as a whole argues that there is room within liberalism for group-differentiated citizenship. In that sense, Kymlicka's project and mine are quite similar. Nevertheless, there are important differences in our projects. These manifest themselves in our intended audiences. Kymlicka is addressing liberals and arguing that they have reason to take multicultural claims seriously. While I am addressing liberals in a similar fashion, I am also addressing advocates of a politics of identity who would not describe themselves as liberal and arguing that they have a reason to take liberalism—at least a form of political liberalism such as deliberative liberalism—seriously.

8. As will become clear, taking such claims seriously is not the same as always regarding them as valid. Rather, it is sufficient for deliberative liberalism to regard them as *prima facie* reasonable, and thus to be taken seriously, and to have what the claimants themselves can regard as reasonable criteria for determining how and whether they are to be addressed through the establishment of policies or exemptions as requested.

9. *Regina v. Sparrow*, 1990, 3, *Canadian Native Law Reporter* (Supreme Court of Canada), 160–188, discussed in Tully, *Strange Multiplicity*, 173.

tion of fishing in those lakes on the grounds that they were granted these rights in exchange for land in treaties with the U.S. government. These claims were recently recognized by the U.S. Supreme Court, but they have stirred up controversy and are resisted by local non-aboriginal fishermen and landowners.[10]

In both cases, and in other similar cases involving claims to land that has special historical or spiritual significance to a particular tribe, aboriginal peoples demand sets of property rights unlike those afforded other citizens. Even when the basis of such claims is contractual rather that the content of a tribal identity, what is demanded is a specifically mediated relationship to the state (other groups of citizens cannot, for instance, sign treaties with their federal government). It is in virtue of our citizenship that we are thought to have a certain bundle of rights, and the equality of citizens is generally thought to be manifested in citizens having equally protected equal bundles of such rights, including property rights. The demands of native peoples to different bundles of property rights thus involve a demand for a different sort of citizenship.

To take a third sort of example, when a tribe claims title to the land on which it lives as tribal land, it is claiming that it is the tribe and not individual members of the tribe who should have the rights normally associated with property ownership: the rights to sell, to restrict access, and to determine what activities can be performed on the land. It thus claims the authority to determine how individual tribal members who live on the land in question will use it. Such claims involve two sorts of departures from the content of citizenship of those who are not members of the tribe. First, it limits the rights of individual tribal members beyond the ways these rights are limited by their citizenship. The tribe may prohibit them from opening certain businesses on their parcel of tribal land, or from selling it to outsiders. Second, it gives to the tribal authorities powers that otherwise belong to the state, such as the power to determine what sorts of activities are permissible on and with the land.

These demands are increasingly being recognized as legitimate, but they are still controversial. Furthermore, when they are rejected, it is often in the name of liberal ideals of equality and autonomy.[11] Part of the resistance to

10. *Minnesota v. Mille Lacs Band of Chippewa Indians*, 526 U.S. 172 (1999). The decision was 5–4. The treaty in question dates to 1838, before Minnesota became a state, and the state argued that its statehood abrogated the treaty rights. While the details of the case turn on fine points of interpretation of executive power and the relative priority of acts of government, the general point I am interested in here is accepted by all the justices and is established constitutional law (at least in theory): members of native tribes are in part governed in their dealings with the state by treaties signed between the tribe and the state rather than directly as individuals under the law.

them stems from the sense that they involve a demand for a special status and thus undermine the equality of citizens. What supports the legitimacy of such claims, however, is the counterargument that their rejection would amount to assimilation, to the requirement that native peoples conform their relationship to the state to norms and ideals that were not developed with their way of life in mind.[12]

To take a different sort of example, many members of fundamentalist religious groups in the United States object to mandatory forms of primary education on the grounds that they undermine parents' ability to inculcate their religious values in their children or are otherwise detrimental to the survival of their community. Fundamentalists in Tennessee objected to a required reading course on the grounds that the curriculum denigrated their religious views, in part by its attempt to present a wide variety of religious views in a nonjudgmental manner.[13] Old Order Amish in Wisconsin demanded and were granted an exemption from the state requirement that all children attend school to age sixteen on the grounds that the last two years of schooling interfere with the practical and religious training the community requires of its members and expose the community's youth to a wide variety of alternative lifestyles at an impressionable age.[14] In other cases, members of minority religions demand some sort of official recognition of their holidays, or accommodation of their traditional ways of dress or dietary rules. Sikh barristers in Britain have been exempted from the requirement to wear a wig in court, and Sikhs elsewhere have been

11. See for instance the discussion of the 1969 Indian Act in Canada in Kymlicka, *Multicultural Citizenship*, 59. The Indian Act was passed by the liberal government of Pierre Trudeau and was supported by the liberal thought that the proper way to treat the native peoples of Canada was like everyone else.

12. One might make the case even more strongly by pointing out that the norms of citizenship, especially with regard to property rights, were arguably designed not in ignorance of Native American relations to the land, but in an effort to delegitimize that relationship in order to justify imperial conquest. For a version of this argument, with regard to Locke's theory of property, see Tully, *Strange Multiplicity*, 70–78.

13. *Mozert v. Hawkins County Board of Education*, 827 F. 2nd 1058 (5th Cir. 1987). The court upheld the school board's decision to make the course mandatory, arguing in part that exposure did not amount to indoctrination. The implications of *Mozert* for liberal justifications of civic education have been much discussed in the literature. A sampling of the different positions can be found in the following articles: Stephen Macedo, "Liberal Civic Education and Religious Fundamentalism: The Case of God v. John Rawls?" *Ethics* 105 (1995): 468–496; Fish, "Mutual Respect"; William Galston, "Diversity, Toleration, and Deliberative Democracy: Religious Minorities and Public Schooling," in *Deliberative Politics*, ed. Macedo; Nomi Stolzenberg, "He Drew a Circle that Shut Me Out: Assimilation, Indoctrination, and the Paradox of Liberal Education," *Harvard Law Review* 106 (1993): 581–667; Eamonn Callan, *Creating Citizens* (Oxford: Oxford University Press, 1997).

14. See *Wisconsin v. Yoder*, 406 U.S. 205 (1971).

exempted from motorcycle helmet laws. As I discussed in chapter 5, Muslim girls in France have demanded the right to wear head coverings in class despite laws that prohibit the ostentatious display of religion in the schools. These sorts of cases vary along a number of dimensions. First, they differ as to the centrality of the requirement being challenged to an ideal of citizenship. Second, they differ as to whether the person making the demand is seeking an exemption on her own behalf or for her children, who might not yet be in a position to know where their allegiances would lie in such a conflict.[15] Nevertheless, all the demands listed above involve contesting some aspect of citizenship on the grounds that it conflicts with an obligation grounded in a religious or other nonpolitical identity. And, once again, rejecting any of them will leave a society open to the charge of assimilation. That is, for the state to deny any of these objections on the grounds of a conception of citizenship that authorizes the practices being questioned is to demand that its members conform their nonpolitical identities within certain boundaries circumscribed by a conception of citizenship to which they object.[16]

A third sort of case involves the claims of linguistic and ethnic minorities to be able to conduct certain aspects of their lives in their own language and in accordance with their own customs. Some native tribes and Spanish-speaking populations in the southwestern United States demand publicly funded schooling in their own languages rather than in English. Similar demands are made on behalf of linguistic minorities throughout the world, from the Kosovar Albanians to Catalonians in Spain to nonwhite linguistic groups in South Africa under apartheid to Tibetans in China.[17] Similarly, linguistic minorities often demand government services in their own language, or that the government provide translators for such encounters with the state as trials and hearings. Once again, a claim is being made that the content of citizens' rights be dependent on some particular aspect of their nonpolitical identity, such as their native language. And once again, failure to see the reasonableness of these claims means that a state is assimilationist,

15. Cases involving the education of children are particularly difficult, as they may sometimes involve raising children (and especially girls) to subordinate roles, imposing on them an identity that conflicts with their identity as citizens. Such cases thus lie in the intersection of the worries about exclusion and assimilation. I look at such cases briefly at the beginning of chapter 8.

16. It may turn out that not all of these demands should be acceded to. What is important for the question of assimilation, I want to maintain, is the way they are treated, and the grounds on which they are rejected or accepted, rather than the ultimate fate of the particular demands.

17. My placement of these cases in the same list should not be taken as a denial of their very different historical and political contexts and the relevance of those contexts to the justice of the demands being made.

insofar as it demands that people interact as citizens in a particular language, or within the framework of particular cultural practices.

A final sort of case involves demands for diverse federalism, a system where different groups stand in different relationships to a federal system, whereby the rights and obligations of citizenship are differentiated according to group membership or place of residence. What differentiates these claims from those just mentioned is that they involve claims to forms of collective self-government. In the cases above, what is at stake is the range of services, as it were, available to people of a particular group. Demands for diverse federalism involve demands for control over the provision of those services as well. For example, the residents of Quebec have collective powers that members of other Canadian provinces do not have, such as control over immigration into the province from outside Canada, greater control over tax dollars, and a provincial rather than a federal pension fund. Some moderate Quebec nationalists merely demand further autonomy within an even more diverse Canadian federation. Aboriginal tribes in Canada claim varying degrees of self-government. The Inuit now have their own territory, the Mohawk claim the status of a sovereign nation, and other tribes claim statuses more like municipalities. As with the other demands against assimilationist norms, demands for diverse federalism involve demands that the content of our identity as citizens of the same polity vary according to some nonpolitical aspect of our identity, and the argument made in support of such policies is that failure to implement them is tantamount to requiring everyone to uphold a conception of citizenship that is well-suited to only some members of the society.

7.3. The Dilemma of Liberal Assimilation

In the cases described in the previous section, the groups making demands are all, in one way or another, rejecting a particular conception of citizenship. Treating such demands as reasonable, as legitimate moves in reasonable political deliberation, however, means regarding them as also grounded in a conception of universally shareable citizenship. It might seem then that from within the framework of a liberal theory based on an idea of universally shareable citizenship, we cannot possibly appreciate and adequately respond to these demands. On the one hand, if we treat them as reasonable, we appear to undermine their force, regarding them as grounded in the plaintiff's political identity as citizen, and thus ultimately not challenging that identity. On the other hand, if we accept them at face value as mounting a challenge to our conception of citizenship, then they must be mounting that challenge from some nonpolitical identity and doing so will seem to count as unreasonable according to the principle of public reason. We might call this the dilemma of liberal assimilation. I argue here that this dilemma is real. That is, it results from countervailing pressures neither of which should be dismissed. In the following sections, I argue that deliberative liberalism solves this dilemma through its political conception of citizenship, which fixes its form features while leaving its content features open to deliberative construction.

We can restate the dilemma of liberal assimilation in terms of demands on the identity of citizen. On the one hand, it must be fixed; on the other, it must be open to deliberative challenge. Neither of these desiderata should be abandoned. It is precisely the fixed quality of the identity of citizen that allows it to serve as the fulcrum by which citizens can resist their exclusion through identity imposition without appealing to a comprehensive doctrine such as a theory of human nature. Deliberative liberalism regards identity imposition as a threat to democratic legitimacy precisely because it undermines certain fixed features of citizenship: freedom and equality. Thus, deliberative liberals ought not to abandon a commitment to the freedom and equality of citizens, for such a commitment provides the basis for deliberative liberalism's inclusiveness.

Similarly, there are good reasons to insist that overridingness and obligatoriness remain fixed features of citizenship. Citizenship is obligatory in two senses, according to liberalism. First, it is in general not an optional role for most residents of the territory of the state. If you are born in the United States, you are a citizen of the United States, and it takes extraordinary measures to change that status. Even though liberals insist that it is a condition of justice that there be no legal barriers to emigration, they do not take the lack of such barriers to be sufficient to show that citizenship is freely accepted. Thus, for instance, Rawls assumes that a political society is a closed system, entered only by birth, and left only by death.[18] Because citizenship is obligatory in this sense, the argument that it is a status to which we must freely consent if it is to be legitimate must conceive of that free consent as something other than the failure to emigrate in the face of its legal possibility.

Citizenship is also obligatory in the sense that, from the state's point of view, being a citizen means being subject to the laws of the state, and being legitimately subject to the coercive force of the state in enforcing those laws. My objection to a particular legitimately enacted law, and even my active resistance to it, does not free me from the obligation to obey it nor

18. John Rawls, *Political Liberalism* (New York: Columbia University Press, 1996), 12, 18.

prevent the state from legitimately enforcing my obedience to it. Thus, although there is an important sense in which I consent to the political and legal system that has this power over me (at least in a legitimate democratic system), I may not consent to each law individually, and my consent in this form is not a necessary condition of my obligation to obey the law in question.

Liberal citizenship is overriding in the sense that, at least in the political domain, liberal citizens are to be guided by their political rather than their nonpolitical identities in determining their position about a given policy or political principle. Liberalism thus asks us to approach political questions as citizens, rather than as religious believers or members of particular groups or classes. This requirement lies at the heart of the principle of public reason.

We can think of the combined requirements of obligatoriness and overridingness as required by the need for some sort of unity within a coherent political society, especially one otherwise characterized by deep diversity. Obligatoriness ensures that all members of the society will have one identity that they share, and that can thus be the basis of their unification into a single (albeit diverse and heterogeneous) society. Overridingness ensures that it is this shared identity that serves as the foundation of the general organization of the society. As we saw in the discussion of Hegel, in modern societies the state provides the sphere of unity that makes possible the ordering of difference in the other aspects of modern life. It can only do this if it is the final authority in its own domain, and it can only manage to be that sort of authority if citizens' political identities override their nonpolitical identities on political questions. This connection with the unity of political society ensures that liberalism cannot just abandon its commitment to these features of citizenship.[19]

Requiring that these features of citizenship be fixed, however, seems to leave citizenship closed to deliberative challenge. The tendency to ignore such challenges, however, is what renders liberalism hopelessly and irredeemably assimilationist in the eyes of many of its critics. Many of the demands I catalogued in the previous section could be phrased as a rejection of a comprehensive liberal view of citizens as autonomous agents, unhindered by substantive ties to particular languages, parcels of land, or religious

19. An anarchist will, of course, reject these aspects of citizenship, and perhaps the very idea of our sharing a political identity at all. The remarks above are not meant to provide an argument for liberalism over anarchism, though they do endorse these liberal commitments that anarchism rejects. My point here is rather limited. I want to mark the boundaries beyond which liberal theory, if it is to remain liberal, cannot go in addressing assimilationist tendencies. Whether or not we should respect those boundaries and thus endorse or reject liberal commitments will in part depend on what can be done within them. It is that question I pursue in the rest of the chapter. I am grateful to Bill Hart for pushing me to think about these matters.

obligation.[20] If it is precisely the freedom or equality of citizens that is being called into question, then the ground from which this is being questioned cannot itself be the freedom and equality of citizens.

The problem of taking certain features of citizenship as fixed may appear even more serious with respect to overridingness and obligatoriness. If citizenship is obligatory in the two senses I described above, then its authority is inescapable. Thus, those who chafe under that authority have no plausible exit strategy—they cannot leave, and they cannot stay and yet opt out of compliance with the law. Moreover, a society whose only response to such people is "love it or leave it" would not be just by even traditional liberal standards.

What is left for such people is to work to change the law so that it is less of a burden on their occupation of their nonpolitical identities. That is, they might try to engage politically from the perspective of their nonpolitical identities, precisely on those issues where their nonpolitical identities conflicted with their identities as citizens. The overridingness requirement, however, would appear to prevent precisely such activity, and so it may seem that a society in which citizenship is overriding and obligatory will fail to recognize precisely the sorts of claims for differentiated citizenship or laws sensitive to certain nonpolitical identities that I identified in section 7.2.

7.4. Fixing Form, Challenging Content

Deliberative liberalism resolves this dilemma by holding the form features of citizenship more or less fixed and yet leaving the content features open to deliberative challenge.[21] In this section, I show how attention to the distinction between form and content features of citizenship allows deliberative liberalism to insist on a fixed conception of citizenship without becoming assimilationist. I start by discussing freedom and equality, and then move to overridingness and obligatoriness.

I submit that what is being called into question in the demands discussed in section 7.2 is a particular conception of freedom or equality making up part of the content of citizenship. Such demands can be made consistent

20. Such charges are familiar in "communitarian" critics of liberalism. See, for example, Michael Sandel, *Liberalism and the Limits of Justice* (Cambridge: Cambridge University Press, 1982). See also Fish, "Mutual Respect," 95.

21. Even the form features are only more or less fixed since they, too, must ultimately meet with citizens' deliberative endorsement. The possibility that they do not meet with such endorsement generates the problem of stability, which is discussed in detail in chapter 8.

with an affirmation of freedom and equality as form features of citizenship. In fact, as I argue below, it is in part on the basis of its commitment to a conception of citizenship with these form features that deliberative liberalism has the resources to address such demands.

As I argued in chapter 5, deliberative liberalism understands citizens as free and equal because it understands them as participants in a joint activity of reasonable political deliberation that serves to generate and support legitimate political principles. These form characteristics constrain acceptable content characteristics of citizenship. Citizens, for instance, cannot be differentiated into hierarchical classes. At the same time, these form characteristics do not uniquely determine the content of citizenship. In fact, freedom, considered as a form characteristic of citizenship, supports the content of citizenship being deliberatively constructed. By maintaining that the form of citizenship contains certain fixed features that in part mandate that the content of citizenship be constructed through deliberation, deliberative liberalism provides the resources to resist both exclusion and assimilation. The fact that freedom and equality are essential form characteristics of citizenship does not imply among the content characteristics of citizenship any particular conception of freedom and equality.

In fact, making freedom and equality necessary form characteristics rules out any particular conception of freedom and equality as necessary content characteristics, if these are grounded theoretically rather than deliberatively constructed. That is, were a political theory to determine that part of the content of citizenship was that citizens were equal in the sense that they had equal worth before God, or an equal claim, qua individuals, to the productive surplus of the society, or that they were autonomous in either the Millian or the Kantian sense, and then to instill such a conception of citizenship in law based solely on this theoretical determination, the theory would be imposing a content on citizenship not supported by its form. Since citizenship has the form characteristics of freedom and equality, it must always be open to citizens to reject any particular content characteristic of citizenship in political deliberation. And this must include the possibility of rejecting a theoretically derived content characteristic of freedom or equality.

Similarly, deliberative liberalism's insistence that citizenship include the features of overridingness and obligatoriness will only lead it into the dilemma of liberal assimilation if these features are regarded as content rather than form features of citizenship. The argument above from the centrality of these features of citizenship to liberalism being assimilationist works as follows: first, the obligatory quality of citizenship locked people into a particular system; then, the overriding quality of citizenship forced them into a particular mold. If this argument involves content characteristics of citizenship, then it is an argument about what constitutes the set of reasons whose authority derives from the identity of citizen. It is thus an argument about the content of public reason. As I said at the beginning of this chapter, assimilation involves the denial of the plurality of public reason. Since the combination of obligatoriness and overridingness considered as content characteristics of citizenship is to place unifying pressure on the content of public reason, these features can be seen as contributing to, if not being wholly responsible for, the assimilationist quality of traditional liberalism.

When we understand these features as form characteristics, however, they work together in a rather different manner. It is this possibility that allows deliberative liberalism to affirm the centrality of these two features to its conception of citizenship without thereby being assimilationist. As I argue in chapter 5, overridingness and obligatoriness, understood as form characteristics, do not determine the content of public reason. Instead, they lead to the principle of public reason itself. Recall from that discussion that the very need to restrict political deliberation to public reason was the fact that citizenship was obligatory: that it was not an identity freely adopted or easily abandoned, and it was an identity the state took you to have whether or not you came to affirm its reasons for action. Together, the two sides of obligatoriness thus led to the requirement that political deliberation invoke public reasons if such deliberation was to yield political principles that could meet a consent-based test for legitimacy.

Similarly, overridingness can be seen as the form the principle of public reason takes within deliberative liberalism. It involves the requirement that when acting in the political domain, I act as a citizen, rather than solely as dictated by some other aspect of my identity. But this just requires that I offer and act on public reasons when involved in political deliberation, rather than insisting on the whole truth as I see it, if that is not supported by the balance of public reasons. Thus, considered as a form characteristic, overridingness does not single out a set of public reasons; instead, it merely tells us to argue only on the basis of public reasons when engaged in political deliberation.

Such a requirement does not lead to a denial of the plurality of public reason. I am not in violation of this requirement if what I take in good faith to be public reasons turn out to be reasons you cannot accept as a citizen. All the requirement of overridingness demands is that I first make political arguments in terms of what I regard in good faith to be public reasons, and then take seriously your rejection of my reasons if they turn out to be reasons you cannot affirm. We can thus see the fact that citizenship is overriding within the political domain as nothing more than the requirement that citizens follow the principle of public reason, understood to include not only a requirement that we make only public reason claims within political deliberation, but also that we respond appropriately to the claims of others, and to their responses to our claims.

In the next section, I discuss one important means of bringing nonpolitical identities to bear within public reason arguments. I suggest that we can understand the demands surveyed in section 7.2 as making arguments from what I call the burdensomeness of citizenship. Because such arguments challenge the current content features of citizenship while resting on facts about the plaintiffs' nonpolitical identities, they are truly challenges to the political order. Because they nevertheless adhere to the principle of public reason, they are fully admissible within deliberative liberalism. Thus, deliberative liberalism provides a way of understanding these demands that escapes the trap set by the dilemma of liberal assimilation. It is important to note, however, that such demands take on special force within reasonable political deliberation precisely because they rest on deliberative liberalism's insistence that overridingness is an essential form feature of citizenship.

7.5. Arguments from Burdensomeness

Within reasonable political deliberation, it must always be open to citizens to object to a particular content feature of citizenship on the grounds that it places an undue burden on them in virtue of some aspect of their nonpolitical identity. All of the complaints I discussed in section 7.2 could be made in this form. In this section, I discuss such arguments in some detail, focusing on how a state in which such arguments are taken seriously will prevent citizenship from being an imposed identity, and how phrasing different demands for group-differentiated citizenship in terms of burdensomeness helps to evaluate their force.

It is important to distinguish the sort of burdensomeness these arguments criticize from mere difficulty or fear of change as such. Arguments from burdensomeness do not merely suggest that a certain conception of citizenship would require effort or even sacrifice. Progressive taxation schemes, for instance, are not going to count as burdensome. Rather, we can think of burdensomeness as addressing the issue of what Tully calls "self-rule." Tully argues that claims to self-rule are always claims people make to be able to rule themselves in accordance with their own customs and ways.[22] The demand for self-rule takes all sorts of forms, according to Tully. It need not

22. Tully, *Strange Multiplicity*, 4.

only stem from a homogenous group that demands its own institutions (although this can be one source of the demand). Nor are such demands necessarily demands for autonomy in the standard liberal sense. When fundamentalists demand the right to live in accordance with their religious beliefs, they are demanding not liberal autonomy but protection from critical forces that might engender such autonomy. Nevertheless, they are demanding a sort of self-rule—the ability to order their lives in what they regard to be the right way. Demands for self-rule are thus demands for the right to be different and for that difference not to be the grounds of exclusion. We can say, then, using this language, that the burdensomeness of citizenship rests in its standing in the way of this form of self-rule. The fundamentalist, for instance, can make her case for an exemption from the requirement that her children's education include certain courses in terms of burdensomeness. She can maintain that without such exemptions, citizenship is burdensome to her because as a result of educational policies she must accept *qua* citizen as it is currently determined, the culture that makes it possible for her to live her life according to her customs and ways is threatened with destruction. As a result, the form of self-rule she achieves as a citizen of a democratic society costs her the ability to order her life according to practices she takes to be more fully hers. It is thus burdensome in the relevant sense. Similarly, the demand for a certain degree of autonomy on behalf of a national minority is a demand for self-rule and will have force to the extent that such self-rule is rendered difficult or impossible in a more centralized state.

Having isolated the domain in which burdensomeness occurs, we might still ask what degree of strain is too great. Must it be the case that occupying the identity of liberal citizenship makes it absolutely impossible to rule myself in accordance with my customs and ways, or is there some lower bar that ought not be crossed? The question is relevant because people are capable of a certain degree of psychic disconnection. From the point of view of my identity as citizen, perhaps I am led to see my religious identity and the practices it authorizes as barbaric or just arbitrary. From the point of view of my religious identity I might regard the fact that I am also a citizen and thus bound by the laws of a liberal, secular state to be a form of impurity. It represents a necessary but unwelcome compromise with the modern world and its godless, sinful ways.

Nevertheless, I might be able to take up both identities fully, and to move between them as needed. Conflicts of this sort will not necessarily require me to abandon one or the other identity or relegate one of them to a permanently subordinate status. Finding oneself in such a condition is, it seems to me, one of the difficult, but not necessarily deplorable, facts of modern life. At the same time, concluding that arguments from burdensomeness can only be made where dual identity is rendered impossible sets the bar too high. There may be times when it is possible to take on both identities, and yet there is nonetheless a burden in doing so that a liberal theory ought to be concerned about.

An alternative would be to say that citizenship is burdensome when it is impossible for me to take up a nonpolitical identity with integrity. Such a formulation seems in accordance with Rawls's means of covering similar ground. In *Political Liberalism*, Rawls argues that legitimate political principles must be endorsed by an "overlapping consensus" of the population. The idea is that people may have different sorts of grounds for coming to endorse a given set of political principles. What is important is not that they agree all the way down (this possibility is ruled out by the fact of reasonable pluralism), but that the range of principles they would endorse overlaps, so that there are some principles they could all endorse, albeit for different reasons. For the overlapping consensus to do the work Rawls requires of it, all (or nearly all) citizens must come to fit the political conception of justice into their comprehensive views. In some cases these comprehensive views will be pluralist, and then the issue of integrity might not rise to the surface. In the cases where comprehensive doctrines are unified (what Rawls calls fully and generally comprehensive),[23] their adherents will have to find a means of adopting the political conception from within the framework provided by their comprehensive doctrines. But that is just to require that they can affirm their citizenship with integrity, within the confines of a unified doctrine that informs their way of life.

While the integrity test strikes me as in general a more appropriate one to invoke, it may do too much work. In the end, determining what will count as sufficiently burdensome needs to be left somewhat open. It will depend on what else is at stake. For instance, any burden placed on a group's ability to govern itself in accordance with its customs and ways may be unacceptable when the issue only concerns adult members of the group and does not in any way render citizenship burdensome to nonmembers. Close to this pole are cases involving certain aboriginal land claims or aboriginal demands to place certain, reasonably mild restrictions on the alienability of aboriginal land.[24]

---

23. See Rawls, *Political Liberalism*, 13 for a discussion of full and general comprehensiveness.

24. Some of the first sort of case I discussed in section 7.2 fit this description—in particular, the Musqueam Nation's demand for exclusive rights to fish certain waters, and some of the land claims Kymlicka discusses. These involve restriction on the alienability of certain land claims imposed by aboriginal communities as a means of making sure that they are not "taken over" by non-aboriginals. See also Will Kymlicka, *Liberalism, Community, and Culture* (Oxford: Clarendon Press, 1989), 146.

In other cases, where protecting a group's ability to govern itself and thus to live according to its own customs and ways will require greater sacrifice on the part of other citizens or future citizens, the threshold of burdensomeness ought to be raised. For instance, it might be that the fundamentalist, in order to oppose the education policy, will have to show that the effects on her ability to take up the identity of both a citizen and a religious believer are particularly severe, since exempting her community from the educational requirements requires restricting the rights of her children in an important sense. How high the threshold would need to be placed will vary from case to case. In general, however, we should be guided in the first instance by the ideal of reasonable political deliberation and, where relevant, concerns about the asymmetrical distribution of power and the burdensomeness of citizenship. There is probably no formula that will tell us how to balance the competing concerns that arise here. Nevertheless, the fact that the rights and liberties to be restricted in order to unburden members of a particular culture are themselves in part grounded by the same features that support those restrictions should make working out the details of particular cases more straightforward. All sides are appealing to the same basic principles, and this underlying agreement is already a big step toward resolution of conflict in attitudes of mutual recognition and respect.

Even if we cannot adduce particular formulas for resolving these issues, there are some further comments to be made on the subject. It will never be sufficient to say that participation in democratic life is burdensome in terms of time or resources consumed, or that it leads individuals and cultures to change in various ways their values, attitudes, and preferences. In the first case, I have in mind someone who, say, rejects the obligations placed on her by a progressive tax scheme because she sees it as an undue financial burden. This fact alone is not sufficient to support a successful argument from burdensomeness. Since her earnings and wealth are hers as a result of the continued functioning of a set of political and economic institutions that entitle her to certain earnings and so forth, she has no absolute right to them. Some taxation schemes may be better supported by the balance of public reasons as she understands them, and she can certainly argue for or against various tax schemes on that basis. Financial burden, however, will only translate into the sorts of cultural burden that support arguments from burdensomeness if it is so extreme as to preclude her from pursuing certain activities bound up with her nonpolitical identities. Within a progressive tax scheme, however, those most financially burdened by taxation are likely to be the least culturally burdened, as even after redistribution they are still better off than their fellow citizens and so have greater all-purpose means to pursue activities constitutive of their identity.[25]

The second case involves someone who objects to his culture's full participation in the political life of the society on the grounds that such participation would alter the particular content of his culture. Here it is necessary to distinguish someone who is complaining about the possibility of any change at all from someone who is worried that his culture will be rendered unrecognizable. The first person has no grounds for complaint, it seems to me. It is the nature of cultures to change, and to do so through their interaction with other cultures. It is just a mistaken anthropological picture to see cultures as isolated billiard balls: homogenous, enclosed, and static.[26] Furthermore, it is a mistake to think that the aim of democratic politics is to leave us as we are. Democracy is not, as some social choice theorists would have it, about the amalgamation of static individual preferences; it is not synonymous with majority rule. The effect of democratic and liberal institutions is among other things to foster diversity awareness, and thus to change our attitudes and preferences and values in such a way as to form a basis for ongoing collective action in attitudes of mutual respect.[27] If it is these transformations that are being rejected, then we can only conclude that the culture rejecting them is unreasonable in this regard, as it rejects the very project of finding legitimate political principles in the face of deep diversity in rejecting one of that project's necessary consequences.

In saying this, however, we need to be careful. It is important to distinguish such unreasonableness from something that may look very similar but is not. There are cultures that may not merely undergo transformation of the sorts suggested above by participating in the kind of unifying institutions liberalism generally envisages. Such cultures may become unrecognizable, going from vibrant, life-ordering ways of being in the world to a set of folklore that provides grounds for the formation of an interest group. Here

25. It might be further objected that the rich will be culturally burdened, as their identity as members of the upper classes carries with it particularly expensive pursuits. So, for the Prince of Wales not to maintain a stable of polo ponies might be as burdensome to his cultural identity as not being able to go bowling on Wednesday nights would be to a steelworker. The problem with this objection is that although the Prince might be able to make a public reason argument to this effect, it would be unlikely to win out in reasonable political deliberation. For the difference between the ability to make a public reason argument and the ability to win a public reason argument, see below.

26. For interesting discussion of this point, see Tully, *Strange Multiplicity*; Michael Carrithers, *Why Humans Have Cultures* (Oxford: Oxford University Press, 1992); and Anthony Appiah, *In My Father's House* (Oxford: Oxford University Press, 1992).

27. I discuss in chapter 8 how democratic politics conceived as deliberative liberalism conceives it serves to foster diversity awareness, when I discuss the educational role played by reasonable political deliberation.

we can think once again of aboriginal nations within the United States and Canada. Since a large part of their cultural identity, at least that part that enters into disputes with the U.S. or Canadian governments, involves their claims to be sovereign peoples, even the act of entering into the political system on the same terms as everyone else would be giving up a significant aspect of their cultural identity. Such a transformation, I take it, would and should count as burdensome. Demands for such diverse federalism are, in these and other similar cases, fully reasonable, and would involve making arguments from burdensomeness.

I turn now to the way arguments from burdensomeness might work in practice. The foregoing arguments may lead some liberal skeptics to think that I have drawn the line of cultural protection too boldly, that the upshot of authorizing arguments from burdensomeness will be the weakening of liberal principles and ideals to the point that they are unrecognizable. This is not the case. Notice that the effect of these arguments is mitigated by their placement within the theory of deliberative liberalism as a whole. Here I draw attention to the distinction between making a public reason argument and winning one. That arguments from burdensomeness can be made in public reason and that other citizens are thus obligated to take them up ensures that certain claims to cultural recognition (as well as other sorts of liberty claims) can be made within deliberative liberalism.

Nevertheless, the mere fact that I can make a public reason argument is no guarantee that the result of reasonable deliberation will be policies or principles that my argument supports. Others may advance countervailing public reason arguments, and these may turn out to have more force. They may appeal to more fundamental values or they may suggest why there is an alternative that upholds the values in question more thoroughly and equitably than my proposal does. At stake here is not whether my argument is sufficiently popular, but whether my fellow citizens, upon reflection, find it conclusive. The fact that certain forms of cultural protection will require abrogating fundamental liberties of some individuals supports a public reason argument against granting such protection. The point of allowing as wide an array of arguments from burdensomeness as I have is that we need not say that demands for cultural recognition of this sort are incoherent from the point of view of public reason, but we can nevertheless sometimes conclude that they are not ultimately compelling. Being able to say that allows a certain form of recognition to take place even in cases where a liberal society will not support special measures for the protection of the culture.[28]

28. The question of whether or not such recognition is sufficient from the point of view of those whose arguments lose is taken up in chapter 8.

Note also that deliberative liberalism's ability to regard arguments from burdensomeness as public reason arguments allows it to respond to concerns about assimilation without requiring the appointment, implicit or explicit, of an Identity Commissar.[29] It does so in the same way that the concern with reciprocal levels of constructive social power does, by functioning in a purely reactive manner. A deliberative state might thus include in its constitution an article to the effect that citizens cannot be unduly burdened in their capacity to live according to the dictates of their nonpolitical identities. Doing so opens up room for courts and legislatures to hear from those who find liberalism itself a source of oppression. It provides a means for a government to ensure continually that the content of citizenship does not make the government assimilationist. Such reform requires, however, that someone who actually is burdened or stands to be burdened by a given policy or principle come forward to lodge the complaint. The state does not need to appoint agents who determine which cases should be brought on whose behalf. Thus, there is no worry that such a principle would lead to the imposition of certain "authentic" identities on people who do not affirm them.

I think the case of Quebec is instructive here. The 1982 Canadian Constitution is the *bête noire* of Quebec nationalists. Very little nationalist rhetoric fails to touch on the injustice of the Charter's imposition on Quebec over that province's express dissent. In separatist campaigns, it is common to hear Quebeckers who advocate secession claim that, in fact, it was Canada that seceded from Quebec in 1982 through the imposition of the constitution.

The language I develop in this chapter gives us a way of making sense of these claims, and of the sense of injustice that underlies them. For the most part, Quebec nationalists do not reject the idea of sharing an identity as citizens with others from whom they differ. This is true with respect to both non-francophone Quebeckers and non-Quebec Canadians. That is, their complaint does not arise out of an insistence that their national identity (as Quebeckers) be equivalent to either their ethnic identity (as francophones) or their political identity (currently as Canadians). Thus, francophone nationalists do not argue in favor of a uni-ethnic or even uni-cultural state, nor do they reject the creation of a new confederal system that would re-link

---

29. I owe this term to Stephen Warner. I am grateful to him and to other fellows at the Humanities Institute at the University of Illinois at Chicago for discussion of this point. I think liberalism, whether concerned with identity politics or not, is often misread as requiring an Identity Commissar (or perhaps critics assume that the philosopher writing the theory plays such a role). Where these charges go wrong is in failing to see that liberal principles are meant to open up room for individual citizens (or groups of citizens) to raise their own complaints on their own behalf and to have these demands make a difference in the course the political deliberation takes. They are not meant to determine ahead of time the results of such deliberation.

Quebec with the other Canadian provinces, either directly or through the other provinces' continued allegiance to the federal government.

Rather, their complaint is that the conception of citizenship constructed by the 1982 constitution leaves no room for Quebeckers (at least) to take up their national identity as Quebeckers alongside their political identity as Canadians, and that this threatens their linguistic identity as francophones. Unlike the earlier form of confederation, which provided room for these sorts of multiple affiliations, the 1982 constitution imposes too uniform a political identity on all Canadians. Thus, the underlying claim made by the Quebec nationalists appeals to the burdensomeness of their identity as Canadian citizens. It is thus one that deliberative liberalism, unlike the liberalism currently serving as the ruling ideology of Canada, could hear and be sensitive to. At the same time, deliberative liberalism would insist that to be just, the nationalist project ought not itself rest on an identification of political with national, ethnic, or linguistic identity.

Finally, note that arguments from burdensomeness will also have the effect of supporting standard liberal features of citizenship and the state, such as those that place limits on the domain of the political and resist the incursion of the state into nonpolitical aspects of our identities (except in those cases where such an incursion is necessary to preserve the form of citizenship as characterized by freedom and equality). The general idea is that in considering just how to shape the contours of our identities as citizens, given the fact of deep diversity, we will be led to restrict the ways in which our being citizens determines what we must do in an effort to make sure that the combined obligatoriness and overridingness of citizenship will not place too great a burden on our ability to affirm our various nonpolitical identities. We will thus have reason to endorse, as citizens, such basic liberal measures as a guarantee of freedom of speech and liberty of conscience, and to grant people rather wide latitude to organize their nonpolitical lives as they see fit. Failures to protect the basic liberties of all citizens will result in some citizens finding themselves burdened by their political identity, an identity they cannot opt out of that overrides their nonpolitical identities in political deliberation. Thus, deliberative liberalism's political conception of citizenship supports recognizably liberal protections of basic liberties without at the same time supporting the assimilationist implications of similar policies adopted by comprehensive liberals.

7.6. Hegel's Second Criterion: Individual Self-Determination

Recall that Hegel's second criterion of legitimacy required that a modern society leave room for robust forms of individual choice and self-fashioning, and comprised three interrelated elements. First, the institutions of a legiti-mate social system must provide room for us to occupy a number of differ-ent roles. Second, at least some of these roles must include room for a robust form of self-fashioning. Third, we must be able to step back from any of our social roles to reflect critically on them in order to see for ourselves that they are worthy of allegiance.

The main work of this chapter has been to show that a deliberatively lib-eral state leaves room for its citizens to occupy other roles. The ability to make arguments from burdensomeness within reasonable political delibera-tion ensures that citizens have a strong ground for criticizing state policies that infringe on this ability. Nevertheless, to meet this aspect of Hegel's cri-terion fully, the other institutions in such a state must leave similar sorts of room. Nothing in my discussion to this point would seem to rule out the possibility of at least some citizens belonging to, say, a religious organiza-tion that prevented them from taking up multiple roles within society, other than those set out by the religion and that of citizen. It might, for instance, be the case that members of this group are assigned spouses and professions by the authorities within the group. Members of such a group will have a great deal less room for individual self-determination than other citizens of a modern state. So we need to ask whether the presence of such groups is acceptable to deliberative liberalism, and if it is, whether the relative lack of autonomy on the part of the members of the group is a sign that deliberative liberalism cannot meet Hegel's second criterion.

Deliberative liberalism regards citizenship as obligatory and overriding, free and equal. One consequence of this conception of citizenship is that deliberative liberalism requires groups in the society to accept that their members are also citizens, and that they have certain rights and duties that derive from their identity as citizens. For the most part, their political duties center around the requirement that they offer public reasons when engaged in political deliberation and their political rights include such things as free-dom of conscience and freedom of expression. Thus, we can make a distinc-tion for the kinds of groups in question between those who accept that their members are citizens but beyond this limit their choices about their lives in line with religious practice or doctrine, and those who prevent their mem-bers from actively taking up the role of citizen.

If the group accepts that its members are also citizens, and thus does not restrict their participation in political deliberation, prevent their assertion of their rights (including the right to leave the group), or interfere with their recognition of the four essential form characteristics of citizenship, then deliberative liberalism has no grounds for objecting to it. Notice, however, that members of such groups do occupy two rather different identities. Furthermore (and here deliberative liberalism departs from Hegel), for such citizens the identity that affords them a robust form of self-determination is their identity as citizens. Here it is significant that deliberative liberalism is a democratic theory. As such, it makes citizenship itself a robustly self-determining role, insofar as citizens have wide collective latitude to determine the precise duties and rights that citizens have.

What is still lacking for such people, however, is a wide range of choice over significant aspects of their lives. They have no choice but to be citizens, and the other major relationships of their lives are determined by religious authorities. How much does this matter? It will depend on the relationship individual members bear to this group. That is, to the extent their membership in this group resembles freely endorsed participation, their further lack of choice does not undermine the legitimacy of a deliberatively liberal state. Of course, insofar as growing up within such a community will no doubt lead many of its members to adopt its precepts willingly, it may look as if their allegiance to the group does not resemble a free choice.

Here I think we can rely on the other aspects of deliberative liberalism to play a role. First of all, to the extent that the identity of group members is not reflectively endorsed, it is imposed, and members who object to their lives being determined as the group determines them therefore have grounds for complaint due to identity imposition. To ensure that such a possibility is truly open, the state may have grounds for insisting that group members not only formally have the identity of citizen, but are taught what this means through mandatory civics education.[30] The point of such education would not be to instill liberal values in the children of the religious group (which would be assimilationist, and thus vulnerable to challenge as unduly burdensome), but rather to ensure the multiplicity of their identities, from which members of the group could truly affirm their membership in this group. Groups that permitted such reflection would thus be providing their members with an important (albeit limited) form of free choice, and would not undermine the sense in which deliberative liberalism meets this aspect of the second criterion.

It is worth noting at this point that such a category of what might be called reasonable fundamentalists is not by any means empty. In fact, I would maintain, many fundamentalists within the United States fit into this category. Certainly the plaintiffs in the *Mozert* case do, as they worked to find a compromise with the school officials and, when that broke down, followed political and legal means of redress, and furthermore accepted the

---

30. Rawls argues that political liberalism can have recourse to such education. See Rawls, *Political Liberalism*, 199–200. I discuss this issue further at the beginning of chapter 8.

judgments of the courts. They thus acted as citizens who wanted their citizenship to be compatible with their identity as fundamentalist Christians rather than as religious believers who rejected any identity as citizen that required compromise.

This leaves groups who prevent their members from taking up the role of citizen. I leave aside groups who advocate that their members violate the law and focus on more moderate groups who prevent their members from actively taking up their identities as citizens, from participating in political deliberation, and from reflecting on their religious identities from the point of view of their political identities. Such groups reject deliberative liberalism's insistence that citizenship have the form characteristics of being obligatory and overriding. Note that they do more than merely reject certain content characteristics: that level of rejection would accept that their members could participate in political deliberation as citizens, which is precisely what the group currently under consideration rejects.

Members of such a group may indeed lack the sort of opportunity for robust forms of individual choice and self-determination required by the second criterion. But deliberative liberalism has grounds for insisting that such a group permit its members to take up their identities as citizens and thus become more like the second group. These grounds, once again, lie in the way imposed identities undermine the essential form features of citizenship and thus the possibility of reasonable deliberation.

Such groups pose genuinely difficult problems for deliberative liberalism, as they pit its means for addressing exclusion and assimilation against one another. The group can make an argument from burdensomeness to be exempted from the sort of mandatory civics education and other measures designed to ensure that all its members are citizens, while members of the group who reject its all-encompassing nature can make arguments against allowing the imposition of an identity that prevents them from being citizens. I will look at one such case in more detail at the beginning of chapter 8.

For now, however, I merely conclude that to the extent that a group takes part in political deliberation in good faith, even with the aim of securing certain exemptions that make its way of life possible, it allows its members to be citizens and thus allows them to take up a multiplicity of identities. To the extent that it does not do this, then deliberative liberalism has grounds for overriding its directives or otherwise challenging its practices. Thus, we can conclude that deliberative liberalism meets this aspect of Hegel's second criterion.

Moving to the second aspect, that some of the roles citizens occupy include room for a robust form of self-fashioning, I merely expand on a point I made in passing above. What distinguishes deliberative liberalism from Hegel's philosophy of right is that it is a democratic theory. As a result, the identity of citizen itself involves a robust form of self-fashioning. This aspect of citizenship is further enhanced by the fact that deliberative liberalism conceives of the content of citizenship as deliberatively constructed rather than theoretically derived. Finally, the practical effect of citizenship not being burdensome is that most citizens will have a wide range of choice about many of the other nonpolitical identities they take up: being citizens will not, for the most part, prevent them from taking up a wide range of different nonpolitical identities.

The argument that deliberative liberalism meets the third aspect of the criterion also turns on considerations I brought out in discussing the first aspect. The third aspect requires that we be able to step back from any of our particular identities in order to reflect on our allegiance to them. In one important respect, our ability to do this is secured by the elimination of imposed identities. For what identity imposition does is prevent people from effectively reflecting on those identities imposed on them. It is precisely because an identity is imposed on me that I have that identity regardless of my endorsement or rejection of it. Thus, eliminating identity imposition opens up the possibility that reflection on aspects of our identity could matter to our continued occupation of that identity.

To show that deliberative liberalism meets this aspect of the second criterion, it remains for us to show that we have a place from which to engage in such reflection. That, however, is provided by our occupation of multiple identities. That is, the place to which we step back in order to reflect on a particular aspect of our identity need not be some neutral or noumenal self that stands behind all of the particular aspects of our practical identities; it can be any other particular aspect of our practical identities. Thus, for instance, as long as one of our identities is that of citizen, we can always assess the other aspects of our identities from the perspective of our being citizens. Such reflection is what is guaranteed by the remedies to exclusion discussed in chapter 6. Similarly, I can reflect on the precise nature of my identity as citizen from the perspective of my nonpolitical identities. That I have such identities from which to do this, and that such reflection can matter, is the result of the aspects of deliberative liberalism I have discussed in this chapter. It is important to note here that our identity as citizen does not have any general priority within deliberative liberalism. It is, considered generally, just one of the particular identities members of a diverse society have. Its claim to priority extends only over its own domain, and that claim serves as much to restrict the domain as to place limits on our other identities.

The foregoing considerations show that deliberative liberalism can meet all three aspects of Hegel's second criterion of legitimacy. They nevertheless may have a sort of formal quality about them, and thus may fail to convince a skeptical reader that deliberative liberalism does in fact secure room for robust forms of individual choice and self-determination. Some general remarks about why and how it does this are therefore in order. I think one of the problems with arguing that deliberative liberalism meets this criterion is the very obviousness of the fact that it does. After all, this is the criterion liberalism generally takes to be the sole—or at least the primary—criterion of legitimacy.

Within Hegel's theory, there is work to be done to show that what is not straightforwardly a liberal individualist theory can nevertheless account for the sort of freedom liberal individualists take to be fundamental. Deliberative liberalism is, however, very explicitly a liberal theory, so it does not require much argument to show that it will secure this form of freedom. Here it is helpful to recall that as a liberal theory, it secures the basic individual liberties and thus ensures that large areas of life are left up to individual citizens to live as they please or think appropriate. A deliberatively liberal state, for instance, would not tell us what to believe, how to worship, whom to marry, what to do professionally, or how to raise our children, though it might place certain constraints on how we do all of these things. Arguments from burdensomeness support general principles of liberty and thus provide a means within political deliberation to secure our commitment to such individual liberty.

In concluding this chapter, I raise a concern the next chapter primarily addresses: stability. We can now see the form stability takes within deliberative liberalism. There are certain form characteristics of citizenship that are necessary for the possibility of reasonable political deliberation, and thus of legitimate political principles within a democracy marked by deep diversity. At the same time, the ultimate legitimacy of even these form features lies in their continued deliberative affirmation by citizens. Thus, in order to be stable, these features will have to derive their justification not only from the philosophical considerations presented here, but also from the affirmation of deliberating citizens. If we are to have reasonable faith in the possibility of democratic legitimacy in the face of deep diversity, we will need some account of why that is likely to happen. One of the tasks of the next chapter is to provide such an account, which then provides us with the grounds for showing that deliberative liberalism meets Hegel's third and final criterion of legitimacy.

8

Stability

If our faith in the possibility of a legitimate liberal democratic regime under conditions of deep diversity is to be reasonable, we must be able to answer two sorts of questions. First, we need to show that such a regime is a conceptual possibility: that there is a consent-based conception of legitimacy that is realizable under conditions of deep diversity. If we understand consent-based legitimacy as arising from the ongoing reasonable political deliberation of citizens, then nothing about the deep diversity of the population undermines the possibility of such legitimacy. But now we must face the second question. Even if a legitimate liberal democratic regime is conceptually possible, it may turn out to be no more than that. Perhaps, for instance, engaging in reasonable political deliberation in a world like ours undermines the conditions under which it is possible for such deliberation to be truly reasonable and thus truly legitimacy-conferring. If our faith in democratic legitimacy is to be reasonable, and more importantly, if it is to serve as a spur to our participation in and further defense of legitimate democratic politics, then we need to show that liberal democratic legitimacy in the face of deep diversity is a real rather than merely a theoretical possibility. That involves showing that a deliberatively liberal society would be stable.

8.1. Shifting Perspectives

Answering this second question requires that we shift perspective. The stability of a political system depends on how that system functions as a whole

186

over time. It depends on the effects the system has on citizens, as well as the ways in which citizens act within it. Stability, we might say, is a by-product of a legitimate political order, rather than a component of it.

Because stability is a by-product of a legitimate political order, the stability of such a society can be used as evidence of the legitimacy of its political structures. In addition, and more relevant to the work I undertake in this chapter, showing that the theoretical components of a particular conception of legitimacy would together serve to foster stability will be evidence that these components do in fact constitute an adequate conception of legitimacy. Note, however, that while stability is a by-product of a legitimate political order, it is not itself an ideal at which a political society ought to aim directly. That a particular practice or policy would threaten the stability of a society is not itself a reason for rejecting it. Stability thus plays a different functional role in the argument for deliberative liberalism than the components of its account of legitimacy developed in chapters 5, 6, and 7. I stress this point because it is otherwise easy to confuse an insistence that legitimate political principles foster stability with the affirmation of consensus as a necessary component of legitimacy. Such confusion makes the concern with stability seem merely a way to smuggle uniformity and thus exclusion and assimilation into deliberative liberalism through the back door. Since stability is a by-product of political legitimacy, it can only be achieved by avoiding exclusion and assimilation.

As we saw in the earlier discussions of Rousseau and Hegel, stability is largely a matter of a political system generating its own continued support for the conditions under which it can keep functioning. Deliberative liberalism will be stable if reasonable political deliberation fosters in citizens attitudes that bolster their support for the principle of pubic reason and the conditions under which political deliberation can be legitimacy-conferring. In this chapter, I argue that the very process of reasonable political deliberation is likely to foster reasonableness on the part of citizens. The result of citizens being reasonable is that they come to attach independent value to living in a society whose political principles are legitimated through reasonable deliberation, and thus come to support the conditions that make such deliberation legitimacy-conferring. This argument shows that a political regime whose legitimacy rests on the ongoing reasonable political deliberation of its citizens can be self-supporting, and thus reassures citizens who find such a regime attractive that they can participate in reasonable political deliberation in good faith. In addition, showing that deliberative liberalism is stable will serve to confirm that its conception of legitimacy is adequate. Finally, in laying out this argument, I also highlight the ways in which it shows that deliberative liberalism can meet Hegel's third criterion of legitimacy.

By the end of the chapter, then, the argument of the book will be complete. I will have finished the defense of our reasonable faith in the possibility of a legitimate liberal democratic regime under conditions of deep diversity. And I will have shown that deliberative liberalism meets Hegel's three criteria of legitimacy.

8.2. Mandatory Education and Religious Dissent: A Test Case

Arguments about stability have to do with how a state that embodies a given theory would work as a whole. Thus, before investigating the stability of deliberative liberalism, I look at a question that requires us to consider how the various parts of deliberative liberalism fit together into a whole: what, if any, forms of education can a deliberatively liberal state require, and what, if any, grounds do parents have for demanding that their children be exempted from such requirements? My aim in examining this question is not to offer any clear resolution to what is a genuinely hard issue for diverse liberal democracies, but rather to highlight some of the important structural features of deliberative liberalism, in particular the way considerations of the distribution of constructive power and the burdensomeness of citizenship work together within the framework of reasonable political deliberation. I start by laying out the reasons why such cases are genuinely difficult, and then try to suggest how deliberative liberalism offers a helpful way of thinking through them.

Conflicts over state requirements in education have most often, at least in the United States, revolved around issues of religious doctrine.[1] The general form of such cases is typified in *Wisconsin v. Yoder*, the 1971 Supreme Court case that granted a group of Old Order Amish in Wisconsin an exemption from the final two years of a state requirement that children attend school until the age of sixteen on the grounds that it interfered with the traditional practical education within the community. The state imposes some general education requirements on all children. The grounds for these may differ, but I will consider cases where the reasons for the requirement lie in ensuring that children grow up capable of performing their roles as citizens. A religious community then objects to some aspect of the requirement on the ground that it interferes with their ability to raise their children in a manner that will enable them to become full-fledged members of the

---

1. A different sort of debate has occupied center stage in Canada and other multilingual countries, where the primary issue has been the language of instruction.

religious community. The issue becomes particularly tangled if the aspect of religious life that can be preserved only through this exemption is one that undermines the ability of at least some members of the group to take up fully the role of citizen. Imagine, for instance, a religious group for whom a strict gender hierarchy is constitutive of their identity and religious practice. Women in this group are valued and protected, and there is markedly less violence against women in this community than in the wider society.[2] Nevertheless, women are expected to live domestic lives and are not permitted to assume leadership roles within the community (although they are not prevented from voting, serving on juries, etc.). They thus have little or no contact with the wider world, although they are not forcibly restrained from doing so. The community's leaders argue that any form of required education that has the effect of encouraging children to reject this hierarchical arrangement places an undue burden on the community, as it undermines their ability to survive intact as a community over time. The state, and perhaps some female members (or ex-members) of the group itself, argue that the state has an obligation to undermine the imposition of a particular identity on the women in the community by the men in the community.

What should a deliberative liberal say in such a case? Must we either try to balance the opposing pulls of the two arguments, or else argue for a prioritization scheme that would allow one of them to take precedence? Deliberative liberalism provides a more attractive way of conceiving of the problem, but to see how it does so we need to step back and look at how the theory works as a whole. From that perspective, we can see that there is no necessary tension between the two arguments, and thus that there is a way to approach this problem that does not lead us to think that we must either balance or prioritize.[3]

For a political principle or a policy to be legitimate, it must meet with the ongoing endorsement of citizens in the course of their reasonable political deliberation. That endorsement requires that the policy be fully supported by public reasons, reasons that are authoritative for people as citizens. Thus, if we want to know whether a policy is one that deliberative liberalism can support or that it ought to reject, we have to look at the arguments in favor

2. I do not mean to suggest that religious communities that impose subordinate positions on women are always free of violence against them. Subordination itself can be thought of as a form of violence, and it is certainly likely that a group that is systematically subordinated will be more, rather than less, likely to fall victim to further violence by those who subordinate them. I make the assumption I do here in order to think about the implications of the best-case scenario for the religious community's claims.

3. In saying that there is no necessary tension between the principles, I am not claiming that these sorts of problems will admit of solutions without remainder, so to speak. The claim is, rather, that deliberative liberalism allows us to see that remainder in a different, and perhaps more integrated light.

of it and ask whether they are in fact public reason arguments. Since the authority of reasons is grounded in aspects of the deliberators' practical identities, determining this is tantamount to asking whether our identity as citizens supports the reasons offered in favor of the policy. In many cases, this question cannot be answered ahead of time, within the comfortable confines of the theory of deliberative liberalism itself. It must instead be answered by citizens themselves, in the course of their deliberation. As I have argued in the preceding several chapters, the content of the identity we share as citizens is, in large part, up to us to work out collectively. Nevertheless, there are some constraints as to the form that identity can take, constraints that grow out of the role citizens play in legitimating the political system and its policies through reasonable political deliberation. Insofar as a given policy can find support in (or is ruled out by) these formal features of citizenship, we can say ahead of time what deliberative liberalism will have to say on the matter.[4]

I have singled out four formal features of citizenship within deliberative liberalism: freedom, equality, overridingness, and obligatoriness. Insofar as a policy would undermine someone's ability to take up the role of citizen having these four formal features, citizens have overriding reasons to reject it. What then gives special weight to arguments against asymmetrical distributions of constructive social power and the burdensomeness of citizenship is that they rest on these constraints. In the presence of asymmetrical distributions of constructive power, the freedom and equality of citizens is undermined. When citizenship is burdensome, it cannot be overriding and obligatory without undermining citizens' freedom and equality.

From this perspective, then, we can diffuse the apparent tension between the arguments over mandatory civics education. Instead of asking how to balance two apparently competing arguments, we now find ourselves faced with a different set of questions. First, we need to ask whether the four formal features of citizenship are in fact jointly satisfiable. If they are, then there will be a way to take up both kinds of concerns adequately, such that there are no theoretical grounds for rejecting the proposal. Of course, this may not yield a unique proposal, but then we are left with a case where it

---

4. Of course, we say this as political philosophers working out a theory, with all the lack of political or other authority that entails. Even with respect to such issues, their enactment into law will require their ongoing deliberative endorsement by citizens. Nevertheless, it is an important and, to my mind, attractive feature of deliberative liberalism that it provides a way of distinguishing between those issues that are open to determination through political deliberation and those that admit of a kind of prior, theoretical determination because they constitute the preconditions of political deliberation proceeding reasonably. Among other advantages, it gives us a way of clearly conceiving of the problem of stability.

must be left up to the deliberation of actual citizens to resolve the matter in line with the full content of their shared identity as citizens and the particular features of the case.

The case of religious exemptions from education would be particularly worrisome if it indicated that these four features were not in fact jointly satisfiable. Then and (I suggest) only then would the presence of such cases be grounds for doubt about the possibility of democratic legitimacy in the face of deep diversity. Hard cases are not counterexamples. My argument here is meant to show that the question of civics education is merely a hard case and not a counterexample, rather than to offer a way of solving it.

In the case I am imagining, both sides argue for their position within the confines of reasonable political deliberation. Both sides are concerned to make public reason arguments in favor of their position, even if they see the force of those arguments very differently. Since the central feature of being a citizen is an ongoing commitment to participation in reasonable political deliberation, especially when faced with political conflicts, no one in this situation is rejecting the central ideal of deliberative liberalism, or its conception of citizenship. The religious authorities are not claiming that religious law should determine questions of legal status, or that they should be exempt from the broader legal obligations of citizens. They are, rather, acting as citizens in offering a public reason argument in favor of the exemption they desire, an argument that rests on what they claim is an unduly burdensome feature of citizenship.

The state, meanwhile, need not ground its requirement in what I earlier called a theoretically-driven conception of citizenship. It can argue that certain forms of education are necessary if children are to take up a role with the formal features of freedom, equality, overridingness, and obligatoriness that centrally involves participation in reasonable political deliberation. In particular, it can argue that children, as future citizens, cannot be brought up in ignorance of their status as citizens, and of the rights and duties that flow from that status.[5] It can conceivably further argue that they cannot be brought up in a manner that would seriously undermine their capacity to be reasonable.[6] Thus, although there is disagreement about how all four form

5. Rawls makes an argument of this form in support of mandatory civics education in his *Political Liberalism* (New York: Columbia University Press, 1996), 199–200.

6. Stephen Macedo can be read as making this point in support of exposure to diversity in the course of education in his "Liberal Civic Education and Religious Fundamentalism: The Case of God v. John Rawls?" *Ethics* 105 (1995): 468–496. In *Creating Citizens* (Oxford: Oxford University Press, 1997), Eamonn Callan takes a slightly different approach, but also stresses the importance of reasonableness to citizenship as the grounds on which the state can insist on certain mandatory forms of education.

features can be mutually satisfied, both sides are advocating that they be mutually satisfied.

What follows from these considerations? I want to draw two broad lessons. The first is that in working out policies or principles in an effort to avoid either exclusion or assimilation, it is important to be sensitive to the other concern. The second involves the relationship between belief, reasonableness, and toleration. If the state makes certain forms of education mandatory, in part to ensure that children will develop into reasonable citizens capable of interacting with their fellow citizens as free and equal, it must strive to do this as much as possible in a nonburdensome manner. In particular, it must strive to develop policies that will be nonburdensome to those communities that reject the substantive values of freedom and equality for their members. At the same time, it will be incumbent upon such communities to find a way to reproduce their own values in a way that does not infringe on the formal features of the identity of the community members as citizens.

The practical upshot is that the state can only require certain forms of education insofar as it can show that these are necessary to ensure that children can fully take up their identity as citizens. It cannot, for instance, use educational requirements as a means of liberalizing illiberal religious communities. Furthermore, it will have to make exemptions for any group who can make a case that their members' capacities qua citizens are not undermined in the absence of such requirements and that those requirements are themselves burdensome. Finally, it must carefully focus its requirements so that they serve to patch holes that may exist in the effects of more general social forces that foster reasonableness. It is in the nature of a liberal democracy guided by reasonable political deliberation to foster reasonableness in its citizens by exposing them to and encouraging them to take an active part in reasonable political deliberation. Reasonableness is further fostered in a society that takes seriously and is moved to redress asymmetrical distributions of power and the unfair burdening of particular groups. If the reason given for certain education requirements is that they foster reasonableness, then it will also have to be shown that they do so in precisely those cases where the general fostering of reasonableness is unlikely to take hold on its own.[7]

7. One might argue that in the case of rather closed religious communities who prevent their daughters from having any but the most meager contact with the wider world, these women will be insulated from the general effects of deliberative liberalism in fostering reasonableness and thus are a suitable target for mandatory education requirements meant to foster reasonableness. In cases where the religion fosters subservience without isolation, there might be a less strong case to be made for further requirements, on the grounds that the general fostering of reasonableness will have sufficient effect on women in these communities that their occupation of subservient roles will not be the result of religious identity imposition.

On the other side, a community that cannot make sufficiently strong arguments for the burdensomeness of these requirements will have to find ways to limit what they see as the damage of such requirements in ways that do not undermine the capacity of their members to take up their roles as citizens. Groups who cannot shield their children from exposure to heterodox views or members of different cultures because of certain forms of required education will have to instill proper loyalty to the group's beliefs and practices in other ways, through inducement and persuasion. A deliberatively liberal state that ensures that its members can take up their roles as citizens cannot object if they also take up religious roles that see citizenship as a necessary concession to the impurity of worldly existence rather than as an ennobling form of autonomous existence. After all, its goal cannot be the creation of comprehensive liberals; such a goal would be illiberal.

In some cases, of course, groups will be unable to sustain themselves in their present form once their members also grow up with the capacity to become full citizens. Such communities will find that they cannot continue to thrive without undergoing fundamental changes. This fact alone should not give us reason to think that there is nothing to mourn in their passing. No social world has room for all types of life, and every social world will inevitably exclude some worthy forms of life. What deliberative liberalism requires is that the exclusion not be arbitrary, in the sense that it can be justified to those being excluded. Of course, groups whose demise is brought on by the principles of deliberative liberalism cannot be expected to rejoice at the prospect. Nevertheless, the exclusionary consequences of deliberative liberalism will be non-arbitrary if the excluded groups can also see that a deliberatively liberal state is worthy of reconciliation. (For an argument as to why this might be so, see section 8.5.)

I turn now to the second lesson I want to take from this section. It is important to see clearly that reasonableness is consistent with both toleration of and respect for those with whom you disagree and unflinching commitment to the truth and rightness of your own beliefs. Reasonableness requires accepting what Rawls calls the "burdens of judgment," and these amount to accepting that although one's own beliefs and practices are fully supported by reasons, it is nevertheless possible that other people with other beliefs and practices are also fully supported in what they do by good reasons. I discuss this aspect of reasonableness in greater detail in the next section. In closing this section, however, I merely note that the state can adopt as one of its objectives the fostering of reasonableness on the part of its citizens and at the same time respect the strength and depth of their commitment to the absolute truth of their deepest and most important beliefs. It is this possibility that opens up room for deliberative liberalism to resolve apparent conflicts between its inclusive and non-assimilationist aims. It is also, as we shall see in the rest of the chapter, what allows deliberative liberalism to satisfy the stability criterion of legitimacy.

8.3. Reasonable Deliberation as Self-Reproducing

The first aspect of Hegel's stability criterion is that the institutions of the rational state must be self-reproducing. In particular, this requires that people who grow up under these institutions come to form their ends in such a way that they are best satisfied through membership in these very institutions. I have not operated, in my development of deliberative liberalism in this book, at the level of particular institutions. But I think we can nevertheless isolate certain attitudes and ends it might be thought important for citizens to possess if a deliberatively liberal state is to function successfully. We can then ask whether the activity of citizenship itself—that is, the activity of engaging in reasonable political deliberation with one's fellow citizens as a means of resolving political conflicts—fosters these attitudes. In this section, I argue that it does, and thus that deliberative liberalism is self-reproducing.

I focus on the attitude of reasonableness. Rawls describes reasonableness as involving "the willingness to propose and honor fair terms of cooperation" and "the willingness to recognize the burdens of judgment and accept their consequences."[8] Put in political terms, we can think of reasonableness as a willingness to engage in reasonable political deliberation when faced with political conflicts and to abide by the outcome of that deliberation. Reasonable citizens adopt this attitude for more than instrumental reasons. Being reasonable involves more than the mere grudging acceptance that in a liberal democracy it is only by going through the motions of political participation that one has any real chance of getting one's agenda made into law. Rather, accepting the burdens of judgment and their consequences means accepting the fact of deep diversity, and the fact that people can disagree widely about the most important questions and yet all be reasonable in the beliefs they hold. It is to recognize that the only means of treating our fellow citizens with whom we disagree on fundamental questions with the respect they deserve as free and equal citizens is to pursue our political agendas only by means of reasonable political deliberation, only in terms of arguments that can be fully supported by what we in good faith take to be

8. Rawls, *Political Liberalism*, 49 n. 1.

public reasons, even if that means, in the end, that our initial views do not prevail.

At the same time, being reasonable need not involve any lessening of the solidity with which we affirm our own positions. The consequence of accepting the burdens of judgment is the recognition not only that people affirm different comprehensive conceptions, but that they can do so without irrationality, as a result of the full use of their reason. The flip side of this, of course, is that we need not be irrational in holding on to our own beliefs. Thus, being reasonable is consistent with being both tolerant and committed to one's own values, beliefs, and positions.[9]

The reasonableness of citizens is essential to the proper functioning of a deliberatively liberal state. In the absence of widespread reasonableness, political conflicts will divide citizens into warring and irreconcilable camps; they will provide occasions for seeking partisan solutions by any means necessary, rather than opportunities for further collective self-fashioning and determination. Furthermore, it is in virtue of their being reasonable that citizens will be moved to withdraw proposals when they are rejected for fostering identity-imposition or making citizenship unduly burdensome. Thus, if deliberative liberalism is going to be self-reproducing, it must foster reasonableness in citizens.

I want now to argue that the very activity of reasonable political deliberation is likely to foster and maintain the reasonableness of citizens. In doing so, I follow a line of argument that James Tully uses to make a similar point about his own theory of just constitutional negotiation. Tully argues that such negotiation, guided by three norms of mutual respect, serves to transform the "diversity blindness" of citizens into "diversity awareness."[10] For Tully, diversity blindness is to be transcended not by appeal to some unifying "theory" of what makes a constitution just, but rather through an open-ended process of negotiation. In order to open ourselves up to hearing other points of view, we need to come to understand why our point of view is itself a point of view and not an all-encompassing vision of reality. Negotiation, as Tully understands it, provides what might be called the narrative inducement to overcome diversity blindness.

Negotiators come from different cultural backgrounds, and thus are possessed of different visions of what justice entails and what citizenship might require. Negotiations cannot thus proceed by appeal to some universal

9. Ibid., 60.
10. Tully makes the argument I cite here most directly in "Diversity's Gambit Declined," 157–159, but the general themes form the backbone of *Strange Multiplicity: Constitutionalism in an Age of Diversity* (Cambridge: Cambridge University Press, 1995).

principles, because there are no such principles we can automatically assume all will endorse. Rather, negotiators take turns elaborating the stories of their own visions by recounting the stories of their peoples or nations or groups. In doing so, each transforms a vision into a perspective and provides other negotiators with the resources to appreciate and grasp that perspective. Through sharing their own narrative, genealogical accounts and listening to those of others, they perhaps find areas of overlap or means of forging agreement. Negotiation, then, serves not only as a means to agreement, but also as a set of exercises that help to foster diversity awareness. We can helpfully divide these exercises into two sorts: genealogical and intercultural.

Genealogical exercises involve investigating our own backgrounds in order to understand in what ways our own points of view are particular. We ask ourselves how they arise out of our particular histories, cultural practices, and experiences. Such genealogical exercises are invaluable in helping us to see that our view of things might be based on a particular perspective, while at the same time helping others to see how it could nevertheless be reasonable for us to hold such a view.[11]

Intercultural exercises involve coming face to face with people who have different points of view. In doing so, we try to appreciate how they see the world, and how their own view differs from ours without thereby being less worthwhile. These exercises help us to overcome our own diversity blindness by leading us to see that our point of view is just one among many, even if we can adduce good reasons for adopting it. They are also the first step in forging a shared or at least shareable language and a set of reasons in which to deliberate about political and other matters of shared concern. They provide the basis for helping others to see where we are coming from, and they help us to understand where others are coming from.

Within deliberative liberalism, reasonable political deliberation plays a role similar to that played by negotiation in Tully's theory, and it does so in much the same way. Before explicitly drawing the connection between Tully's negotiation and reasonable political deliberation, I highlight a difference between two descriptions of what makes a reason a public reason. In setting out my account of public reason in chapter 5, I relied on Rawls's formula that public reasons were reasons that could be made good to citizens

---

11. I am not claiming here that telling a causal story about belief formation could itself either support or debunk the validity of our beliefs. The point is rather that such genealogical exercises serve as one heuristic to dislodge us from our diversity blindness without necessarily dislodging our beliefs.

generally. In doing so, I eschewed his other formulation of public reason, which ties it to a political conception of justice.

When we focus on the actual deliberation of citizens, and on its role in overcoming diversity blindness, a potential difference between these formulae appears. If we have a fully worked out political conception of justice, then we ought to be able to tell which reasons are public reasons without actually going through the process of deliberation itself. On the other hand, if our sole criterion for determining whether a reason is public is whether it can be made good to citizens generally, then we will actually have to go and see whether it can be by offering it to our fellow citizens and seeing what sorts of responses it brings. Because of this difference, the formulation I adopt makes it easier to draw close ties between an ideal of reasonable deliberation and Tully's ideal negotiation. On my understanding of public reason, we have an ideal of participation in reasonable political debate. To know whether we are truly upholding this ideal, we must actually participate in that deliberation.[12]

Reasonable political deliberation fosters the reasonableness of citizens in the way that Tully's constitutional negotiation does. Taking part in such deliberation will require citizens to undertake both genealogical and intercultural exercises. Imagine that we are taking part in some political deliberation. Doing so requires that we invoke only public reasons for our positions. It may be unclear ahead of time what, precisely, counts as a public reason. This uncertainty, after all, is part of the reason that debate will have to go on, even after we have all agreed to the principle of public reason. Imagine that I defend a certain position with an argument that seems to me to be conclusive. In order to respect the principle of public reason, I first examine the argument and try to determine to what degree it relies on reasons whose authority is grounded not in my identity as a citizen, but rather in other nonpolitical aspects of my identity. Certain things will be easy to excise. I cannot argue in public reason on the basis of the revealed word of God, or on the basis of the increase to my own personal happiness (even though these may be factors in my coming to support the measure at hand). But there might be other aspects of the argument where the line is harder to

12. I think in practice the distance between these two formulations is not as serious as I have made it seem here. Rawls is hesitant about the possibility of ever "finally" working out the details of a political conception of justice. Insofar as we are still in the process of doing so, the two definitions will line up again, as both will require actual political deliberation to determine here and now the content of public reason. Furthermore, as I mentioned in chapter 5, Rawls thinks there will inevitably be a plurality of reasonable political conceptions within any society, and that this then eliminates the possibility of deriving ahead of time which reasons are public and which are not on the basis of a single political conception.

draw. Perhaps the particular use I make of the value of equality is not fully supportable by public reason. Perhaps my argument tacitly rests on a notion of autonomy that can only be given sense by a comprehensive metaphysics of the sort that lies outside the bounds of public reason. At this point both the genealogical and intercultural exercises come into play. I may try to determine what in my life has led me to believe what I do. Is it something everyone in my neighborhood believed? Was it impressed upon me by the rabbis? Such realizations might lead me to scrutinize these aspects of my argument more closely to see if they really are supportable by public reason. Thus, some genealogical work will be of use.[13] Alternatively, I can make my case in the public arena and wait to see what sort of response it brings. If people who do not share aspects of my particular background object to certain premises of my argument and claim that they cannot support them, I may be led to conclude that these premises are not supported by public reasons. In the process I will, at least in part, come face to face with the way the reasons that support my own beliefs are not incontrovertible, and with the sense that people with whom I disagree may be as fully reasonable as I am.

Furthermore, there is a means of making a public reason argument that brings to the fore certain aspects of one's own cultural background. Making such arguments involves making clear to fellow citizens how aspects of your own life are shaped by that culture and making comprehensible to them the sort of harm you would suffer if, through the loss of that cultural background, you were unable to pursue certain projects and plans.

Thus, reasonable political deliberation will expose citizens to the details of their fellow citizens' identities and to the ways they support or rule out certain kinds of claims. In addition, it will lead us to see those details as supporting reasons, and thus will help us to see how others could be reasonable and yet hold views very different from our own. Contrast this with a form of interaction that would teach us about others' lives but would portray them as exotic and weird, as inscrutable and foreign. Such interaction would not have the effect of fostering reasonableness. Reasonable political deliberation will.

Thus, in a plural but well-ordered society, reasonable political deliberation plays precisely the role of Tully's negotiation. Since it is doing the work we do as citizens that fosters the very attitudes we require in order to undertake that work, to see it as having the right sort of point, the institutions that realize reasonable political deliberation and thus make possible our having an identity as citizens will be self-reproducing.

That an institution is self-reproducing is more or less an empirical, psy-

---

13. Such genealogical exercises need not only serve to debunk.

chological question. As a result, it cannot alone be a criterion of legitimacy, which is a normative notion. Thus, it is important to note that the account I have given of the self-reproducing nature of reasonable political deliberation provides the right sort of basis for a further, normative conclusion. What makes reasonable political deliberation self-reproducing is that it fosters an attitude of reasonableness among citizens. That attitude commits citizens not only to following the ideal of reasonable deliberation but to seeing that ideal as capturing an important value of their political society. One result of citizens coming to adopt this attitude, then, is that they come to value not only particular results of such collective determination, but also the activity and the process itself.

The point is not that reasonable political deliberation fosters a kind of civic republicanism, which itself would be a particular comprehensive doctrine. Rather, in fostering reasonableness, political deliberation fosters an attitude that leads citizens to find value in policies with which they disagree but which are nevertheless legitimately enacted. In fact, it can lead them to prefer a society in which policies they do not otherwise support are legitimately adopted to one in which policies they prefer are adopted illegitimately.[14] When citizens are reasonable, we might say, they come to see that they are engaged in a collective endeavor that has its own value, a value not reducible to its results. In addition, as a result of coming to have that attitude, the results such an endeavor can achieve also shift. Differences that are irreconcilable need not prevent civic and political unity, need not undermine the possibility of coming to agreement about political principles. Deep diversity need not undermine our reasonable faith in the possibility of legitimate justice.

8.4. Stability for the Right Reasons

The normative corollary of the self-reproducing nature of reasonable political deliberation is that a deliberatively liberal state will be what Rawls calls "stable for the right reasons." Such stability involves the lack of widespread

14. One could take this attitude and yet still continue to work to change the political consensus so that it eventually adopted one's preferred outcome. Recognizing the great value of legitimately enacted law does not require laying down one's principles in the face of opposing political decisions. Rather, it requires that one's principles include those that lead one to continue to struggle for one's positions within the confines of reasonable political deliberation. If I disagree with policies adopted by the government but recognize their legitimacy, then my reaction should be to obey them in the short term and to keep arguing against them in the longer term.

political alienation. This connection echoes Hegel's connection between stability and freedom. Recall that Hegel argues that the will can only be free insofar as it constitutes itself as a member of stable institutions, because only then does it will itself to be a free will. In the case of stability for the right reasons, a similar connection emerges. When a society is stable for the right reasons, the fact that its members occupy the role of citizen, which has the form features of being obligatory and overriding, is not a barrier to their occupation of other identities, but is properly seen as the best way for members of the society to be secure in their other identities. As a result, they can embrace their political identity, and the burdens it places on them are not a source of alienation.[15]

Rawls sets out the relationship between stability for the right reasons and the justification of justice as fairness in his "Reply to Habermas." My remarks here are merely meant to summarize what he says there.

In *Political Liberalism*, Rawls is concerned to argue for determinate principles of justice in light of the fact of reasonable pluralism. This aim requires offering something like a public reason argument for the political principles he defends. The argument moves through three levels of justification. The first is *pro tanto* justification. At this level, a political conception of justice is argued for without recourse to any comprehensive view. This argument yields what Rawls calls a "freestanding" political account of justice. Because the argument does not rely on any premises particular to any given comprehensive doctrine, it is hoped that all citizens, regardless of their more comprehensive beliefs, will be able to accept it.[16]

Of course, even if citizens can in general accept the freestanding argument in favor of these political principles over various rivals, such acceptance is not sufficient to yield affirmation of a political society guided by such a conception. Insofar as we affirm the political principles Rawls advocates, we are supposed to honor an ideal of public reason that requires us in political matters to give pride of place to our identity as citizens. Affirming the two principles of justice requires that we allow the reasons they authorize to override reasons that only find support in our fuller comprehensive views. Mere acceptance of an argument for political principles need not carry with it that sort of affirmation. I could conceivably accept the argument for the political principles and say that while these are very nice political principles,

---

15. Note here the parallel with Hegel's remark that the modern state's "strength consists in the unity of its universal and ultimate end with the particular interest of individuals, in the fact that they have duties towards the state to the same extent as they also have rights." Hegel, *Elements of the Philosophy of Right*, trans. H. B. Nisbet (Cambridge: Cambridge University Press, 1991), §261, see also §155.

16. Rawls, *Political Liberalism*, 386.

they must yield to my religious or comprehensive moral beliefs wherever these conflict.

In order to avoid this result, each citizen must also be able to embed the political conception of justice within his or her comprehensive conception of the good. Doing so involves fitting its demands and the values it endorses together with those of our deepest nonpolitical beliefs and commitments. This requires what Rawls calls "full individual justification." In reaching full individual justification, each person comes to see the values of the political conception as overriding, at least within its domain, and to endorse that priority as consistent with the demands of her comprehensive conception of the good.[17]

That such a reconciliation between our comprehensive doctrines and our affirmation of the duties and rights of citizenship is possible then makes it plausible that a society can achieve the third level of justification, which Rawls calls "public justification by political society." At this level, all citizens have embedded the political conception within their comprehensive doctrines, and have done so in a manner that takes into account the fact that other citizens are engaged in a similar process. As a result, we can be sure that in offering public reason arguments for political matters, we are offering reasons that are not anathema to our fellow citizens. Public justification tells us that public reasons are reasons supported by the political conception we all share. It also tells us that since everyone has achieved full individual justification, these reasons are thus also supported by their comprehensive conceptions of the good. Citizens can thus offer public reasons to one another in political deliberation without thereby disrespecting each other's religious beliefs. This provides them further reasons for giving the political values special place.[18]

Turning now to deliberative liberalism's related concerns with deep diversity, we can fashion a similar argument about the stability of principles supported by reasonable political deliberation. Any principle that currently finds support in our reasonable political deliberation is supported by the balance of public reasons. Thus, we can make arguments in favor of this principle that do not rely on any reasons whose authority rests only on a particular (set of) nonpolitical identities. Such a policy can then be said to be *pro tanto* justified.

To see that such a principle also passes the level of full justification, recall that among the grounds for rejecting a proposed political principle are that it fosters asymmetrical distributions of social power or that it unduly bur-

17. Ibid., 386–387.
18. Ibid., 387.

dens some people's ability to occupy certain nonpolitical identities. Thus, the fact that a policy or principle currently finds support in reasonable political deliberation means that there is no one who currently has sufficient grounds for rejecting it on the basis of its burdensomeness or because its support rests on an imposed identity. That a principle is not burdensome means, in part, that it can be endorsed without undermining the ability of someone to inhabit any reasonable nonpolitical identity. But this possibility is precisely what is required by full justification. If I can inhabit any given reasonable nonpolitical identity while still taking up the obligatory, overriding identity of citizen that also includes the obligation to obey and uphold the principle in question, then I can embed at least this aspect of the political conception of justice among my nonpolitical identities. Being a citizen does not require me to give up other aspects of who I am, and this compatibility holds even given the requirement that the obligations of citizenship override other obligations within the political domain.

Finally, the very process of ongoing reasonable political deliberation provides the means by which political principles can achieve public justification within deliberative liberalism. Not only do I realize that the principles that govern the political society of which I am a member do not unduly burden my occupation of my particular nonpolitical identities, but I realize that these principles can play a similar role in my fellow citizens' lives, despite the diversity among their nonpolitical identities. That the endorsed principles can play this role for all is a consequence of their legitimacy resting on their emergence from ongoing reasonable political deliberation. Were it not the case that these principles could play such a role in others' lives as well, they would have had grounds for challenging them, or for challenging the ways in which political deliberation is carried out. Thus, it is precisely because these principles and policies find their legitimacy in the ongoing process of political deliberation, and the ongoing endorsement of the conditions that make its reasonableness possible, that they can meet the test of public justification. In addition, the process of reasonable political deliberation itself may also help me to see why my fellow citizens endorse these principles, and thus to secure my trust that their allegiance to them is as solid as my own.

What is necessary for the three levels of justification to realize stability for the right reasons are conditions under which the four form features of citizenship are jointly realizable for all citizens. But these conditions are both the conditions under which the three levels of justification can proceed and also in large part the result of reasonable political deliberation securing these levels of justification. One role that arguments about the distribution of power and the burdensomeness of citizenship play is to lay out the central conditions under which citizenship is fully realizable for all members of political society. At the same time, it is because these arguments can be made within reasonable political deliberation to challenge current social conditions that such deliberation serves to generate stability for the right reasons.[19] The fact that deliberative liberalism achieves stability as it does also provides grounds for thinking that it is worthy of reconciliation.

8.5. Alienation, Recognition, and Reconciliation

Through engaging in the ongoing project of legitimating political principles and policies via reasonable political deliberation, members of a political society come to share an identity as citizens and to give that identity a determinate content, albeit one always open to revision and challenge. In doing this, each of us comes to see that identifying ourselves as citizens in this manner is, given the fact of deep diversity, the best means of acting with integrity with regard to the other aspects of our identities. Since it is because political principles can be supported by public reasons that they can function in this manner, each of us has reasons from within our own complete identity to uphold the ideal of public reasons, and thus to endorse an identity as citizen that is overriding and obligatory, at least in form. Since we endorse that aspect of our identity that gives rise to political obligations, those obligations will not be a source of alienation.

Notice two consequences of this conclusion. The first has to do with the kind of value deliberative liberalism secures in avoiding political alienation. The second involves the ways in which it enables us to recognize our fellow citizens as more than mere rights-bearers without requiring that we somehow eliminate or transcend our differences.

A society not characterized by widespread political alienation is one in which citizens can engage in politics in good faith. Like many of the central values realized by a just society, this one is perhaps only appreciated when it is lacking. A society in which reasonable political deliberation is impossible is one in which any attempts to act collectively will inevitably be regarded by all parties as involving the strategic machinations of those involved. No pro-

19. I do not here provide an argument that reasonable political deliberation will serve to create the conditions in which citizenship is fully realizable for all. Nevertheless, it is my hope that one consequence of seeing the value of deliberative liberalism is that we will be moved to recognize the value of upholding the standards of reasonable political deliberation in our political activity, here and now, in conditions where citizenship is not fully realizable for all, and that as a result of upholding those standards we will be moved to challenge those conditions that stand in the way of the full realization of citizenship for all.

posal will be considered on its merits; proposals will always be scrutinized for the untoward or selfish motives that give rise to them. Deliberation will give way to negotiation, bargaining, and general suspicion. Political activity will come to seem a matter of deal-making in the worst sense, of pressing advantage and battling interest groups. In such a society, good faith political activity will be impossible, because no political activity will be regarded as a good faith effort to fashion a collective solution.

Deliberative liberalism makes possible a kind of good faith politics, by allowing for a form of political activity that is genuinely shared. Good faith participation in reasonable political deliberation involves recognizing the reasonableness of our fellow citizens, even when we differ on many fundamental matters and have irreconcilable differences in nonpolitical domains. In offering public reasons to my fellow citizens I explicitly recognize them as fellow citizens: free and equal, reasonable and rational. Beyond that, however, I also recognize the reasonableness of their nonpolitical identities. I do this in part by being always prepared to withdraw what I take to be public reasons in the face of their rejection on the grounds of burdensomeness.[20]

To understand the value and distinctiveness of such recognition, I compare it with the two forms of recognition that Charles Taylor has suggested liberal regimes must choose between.[21] Taylor argues that we suffer harm if we are not adequately recognized as occupying the central aspects of our practical identities. Such harm is best understood as undermining the conditions of our self-respect. Since liberalism in general regards such harm as significant, it must be concerned to ensure the proper form of recognition. Taylor distinguishes two liberal approaches to affording such recognition and argues that the second achieves what the first does not. I will suggest that deliberative liberalism provides a third means of affording recognition that secures the grounds of our self-respect better than either of the two Taylor suggests.

Liberalism, on Taylor's reading, responds to the fact of deep diversity by eschewing any commitment to a thick set of shared purposes. Liberals take this route on the grounds that the very fact of deep diversity makes it impossible that any such shared purposes could be found. Rather, liberalism attempts to secure the necessary reciprocal recognition by uniting cit-

---

20. Note once again that I need not always end up actually withdrawing my proposal. Rejection may turn out to be unwarranted, or there may be no proposal that is less burdensome than the one I support.

21. Taylor makes these arguments in a number of places, but the basic structure of the argument is most clearly laid out in his essay in *Multiculturalism and The Politics of Recognition*, ed. Amy Guttman (Princeton, N.J.: Princeton University Press, 1992).

izens around a very thin project it assumes can be widely shared. The liberal state is thus organized around a shared project like securing equal basic liberties for all. In so organizing itself, however, the liberal state sets up conditions under which citizens merely recognize each other as rights-holders. Insofar as our self-respect flows from our identifying ourselves merely as rights-holders, this level of reciprocity will be sufficient. That is, in a world where we take pride in our status as bearers of certain rights, the fact that others recognize us as such will be sufficient to ground our self-respect.

Taylor suggests, however, that such a world is not, and should not be, ours. We do not as a matter of course identify ourselves as mere rights-bearers, and we are the better for not doing so. Thus, being recognized by my fellow citizens as a bearer of certain rights may be necessary to secure my self-respect, but it cannot be sufficient. I identify myself in more substantive fashion, as, say, a member of a certain profession, or culture, or linguistic group, and thus require that others recognize these aspects of who I am as well. As a result, this form of liberalism is likely to be guilty of one of two political failures. It can attempt to transform us into the sorts of people who do identify primarily as rights-bearers. In that case, the form of recognition it secures for us will be sufficient. Doing this, however, will require assimilation.

If citizens hold onto their more robust identities, then this form of liberalism is going to fail to take seriously various forms of exclusion that come about when some citizens' recognition as rights-bearers goes hand in hand with publicly expressed contempt for other aspects of their identity. This sort of liberal state regards only the recognition of our status as rights-bearers as politically important. When people are oppressed because others misrecognize nonpolitical aspects of their identity, liberalism will not be able to see this as a matter for political action. As Taylor explains, "We may be 'recognized' in other senses, for example as equal citizens, or rights bearers, or as being entitled to this or that service, and still be unrecognized in our identity. In other words, what is important to us in defining who we are may be quite unacknowledged, may even be condemned in the public life of our society, even though all our citizen's rights are firmly guaranteed."[22] Think here of some of the ways women and nonwhites are excluded in the United States despite being afforded the full spectrum of formal political rights. In such cases, the fact that the state recognizes women, say, as bearers of the same rights as men fails to overcome the imposed shame created when they

---

22. Charles Taylor, "Impediments to a Canadian Future," reprinted in *Reconciling the Solitudes*, ed. Guy LaForest (Montréal: McGill-Queen's University Press, 1993), 190.

are socially devalued through sexual harassment or sexist attitudes that result in their being paid less than a man to do a similar job.[23] Since this social misrecognition imprisons women in a false, distorted, and reduced mode of being, to use Taylor's formulation, it will be the cause of women's self-respect being undermined. Such oppression will be just as devastating as the misrecognition of our political identities through explicitly legal forms of exclusion. If liberalism secures only recognition of citizens qua rights-bearers, then it will only provide sufficient grounds for citizens' self-respect through assimilation or exclusion.

As a result of this argument, Taylor is moved to advocate a second form of liberalism, in which the state endorses a common pursuit broader than the pursuit of justice construed as narrowly as in the first form of liberalism. What makes such a view liberal is that it enshrines protection for minorities and dissenters through constitutional protection of basic liberties. It is unclear, however, that this proposal truly solves the problems of recognition Taylor raises. Even if the rights of those who do not share the society-endorsed common purpose are not threatened, they would seem to receive only the minimal recognition accorded to rights-bearers, and not the full recognition members of the majority culture receive.[24]

Taylor is led to see these as the only options available for liberalism to adopt because he misunderstands what is required for mutual recognition. For Taylor, we can only fully recognize others if we share their projects.[25] I suggest that we can fully recognize others with whom we disagree if we can share an identity as deliberative citizens. We can share an identity as citizens without sharing a project thicker than legitimating the political principles that guide our society through an ongoing commitment to reasonable polit-ical deliberation. Doing so, I now claim, will provide all citizens a form of recognition that secures their self-respect better than either of Taylor's two alternatives.

---

23. See, for instance, Drucilla Cornell, *The Imaginary Domain* (New York: Routledge, 1995), esp. 167–227; Sandra Lee Bartky, "Shame and Gender," in her *Femininity and Domination* (New York: Routledge, 1990).

24. One can see the attempts of various Quebec governments to put into practice Taylor's second form of liberalism by endorsing as a common purpose of Quebec society the protection of French culture in North America. If that is the case, then the widespread disenchantment and alienation felt by non-francophones to such policies, even when their rights, including lan-guage-based rights, are well protected should make us wary of thinking that they are receiving adequate recognition of the sort Taylor champions.

25. Taylor's account of the importance of recognition for securing self-respect owes much to Rousseau and Hegel, and I think his connection between recognition and sharing projects can be traced to a misreading of their understanding of the mutuality necessary to afford adequate recognition. As Taylor reads them, we need to have shared projects. As I read them, we need to share an identity.

We have already seen how participation in reasonable political deliberation can be consistent with a recognition of the reasonableness of the nonpolitical identities of those with whom we disagree. Because deliberative
liberalism explicitly resists assimilation and exclusion, as I argue in chapters
6 and 7, citizens cannot, in recognizing each other as citizens, misrecognize
them in their nonpolitical identities in the ways Taylor suggests they can in
his first form of liberalism. When I participate in reasonable political deliberation with you, I recognize you as a fellow citizen, but in doing so, I also
recognize the reasonableness of your nonpolitical identities, insofar as I take
seriously public reason arguments against burdensome provisions and
imposed identities. At the same time, however, since what we engage in
together is the political project of working out legitimate political principles,
we need not think of citizenship as being a two-tiered identity. All citizens,
no matter what their reasonable nonpolitical projects, will stand in the same
relation to political deliberation, since none of those projects will be the official project of the state. Reasonable political deliberation, then, provides for
the sort of full-blown recognition of people in their deep diversity that Taylor argues is a necessary condition of a just society, but it does so within the
traditional confines of a liberal understanding of what sorts of projects the
state can legitimately adopt as its own.

To say that deliberative liberalism would afford recognition to all citizens
in this manner is tantamount to saying that it is worthy of reconciliation.
Recognition is, we might say, a two-way street. That my fellow citizens recognize me in my full identity, and thus that the state affords me the grounds
of my self-respect as a citizen in a way that bolsters rather than conflicts
with my having self-respect as someone characterized by other nonpolitical
aspects of my identity, is to say that I can regard the political society in
which I live as a home. It is a place where I am given room to be who I am,
and thus a place whose particular structures reflect who I am in important
ways. Being a home in this sense is precisely what makes a society worthy of
reconciliation.[26]

At this point, some may object to the rosy picture I have painted of deliberative liberalism's worthiness. It is inevitable that in a diverse constitutional
regime, some forms of life will not prosper. Furthermore, their failure to

26. Recent works on Hegel's political philosophy by Michael Hardimon and Frederick Neuhouser place a great deal of weight on Hegel's account of why the modern state is worthy of
reconciliation. Both argue that Rawls's political liberalism also takes this as a central concern,
and achieves its result in ways not very different from those relied on by Hegel. One way of
understanding my arguments here is as making this connection explicit in the case of deliberative liberalism. See Neuhouser, *Foundations of Hegel's Social Theory: Actualizing Freedom* (Cambridge: Harvard University Press, 2000); and Hardimon, *Hegel's Social Philosophy: The Project of
Reconciliation* (Cambridge: Cambridge University Press, 1994).

prosper cannot be taken as an indication of either their lack of value or their lack of reasonableness. Finally, there may well be some just social arrangements under which the group in question would prosper. That is, the group does not require the oppression of others or their own hegemony in order to survive under different, more favorable social conditions.[27] How, the objection would then proceed, can I conclude that such people could reconcile themselves to a deliberatively liberal state? And if they cannot, how can I conclude that such a state would be worthy of reconciliation?

Rawls takes up a similar question in his discussion of public reason and of the way in which an ideal of public reason provides the basis of a stronger form of unity than that provided by a mere *modus vivendi*. His answer is rather brief, however, and so after looking at what he says, I will try to offer a somewhat expanded response in the context of deliberative liberalism. In "The Idea of Public Reason Revisited," Rawls argues that upholding an ideal of public reason means that we regard reasonable political deliberation as more than merely the best means of keeping the peace until such time as those who agree with us can seize power. An ideal of public reason is not an expression of a *modus vivendi*. But beyond that, a commitment to the ideal of public reason requires that we remain committed to upholding its strictures even when doing so would not lead to the flourishing of the groups of which we are members. As Rawls says, "while no one is expected to put his or her religious or nonreligious doctrine in danger, we must each give up forever the hope of changing the constitution so as to establish our religion's hegemony, or of qualifying our obligations so as to secure its influence and success. To retain such hopes would be inconsistent with the idea of equal basic liberties for all free and equal citizens."[28]

Rawls suggests that this level of commitment to an ideal of public reason provides the grounds of an answer to the person whose comprehensive doctrine may die out as a result of the adoption of politically liberal principles of justice: "the answer lies in the religious or nonreligious doctrine's understanding and accepting that, except by endorsing a reasonable constitutional

27. Think of a linguistic or national minority in the context of overwhelming economic incentives for younger members of the minority to become bilingual and gradually to move away from the minority culture. Francophones in Canada, and certainly those outside of Quebec, may be in such a position, in that even after the utmost has been done to help them protect their culture and language consistent with the demands of justice, the overwhelming fact of English in North America will mean that over the course of several generations the number of francophone Canadians will continue to diminish. In a different social context, such as the linguistic plurality that characterizes Europe, francophones survive and prosper without special protections or attempts to subvert the demands of justice.

28. Rawls, "The Idea of Public Reason Revisited," 590.

democracy, there is no other way fairly to ensure the liberty of its adherents consistent with the equal liberties of other reasonable free and equal citizens."[29]

Let me now expand on this thought, though with a shift to express its central point in the language of deliberative liberalism. Deliberative liberalism both requires and fosters an attitude of reasonableness among citizens. One consequence of citizens' coming to be reasonable in this way is that they come to attach an intrinsic value to the activity by which legitimate political principles are worked out. As a result, they come to see a value in the legitimacy of political principles over and above any value the principles may have as a result of their content. That citizens come to see such value in legitimate principles is one way of understanding why deliberative liberalism will be stable for the right reasons. Another way of putting this point is to say that members of a deliberatively liberal political society will come to value their political identity as citizens, an identity characterized in part by the four formal features of freedom, equality, overridingness, and obligatoriness.

Now imagine a citizen of such a society some reasonable aspect of whose nonpolitical identity is threatened. By hypothesis, we can imagine that she has offered up public reasons to change the policies that threaten that aspect of her identity on the grounds of burdensomeness, and that her reasons have been overruled by stronger arguments. That is, although the current configuration of political principles burdens her and those who share this aspect of her nonpolitical identity, there is no other configuration of principles that would remove that burden on her without creating even greater injustice somewhere else.

Such a citizen cannot be expected to rejoice at the future that confronts her and those of her community. But what is at stake here is whether she can nevertheless be reconciled to the political society that leaves her in this position. That is, can she continue to affirm its basic principles and ideals, even given the consequences they have for her own life? I argue that she can. First of all, the value she attaches to living in a society governed by legitimate political principles (a result of her being reasonable) is not lost because of the effects of those principles on her ability to live a certain kind of life. As a member of the community that will die out, she is no doubt saddened. As a citizen, however, she would positively recoil at the thought of saving space for her way of life at the expense of her fellow citizens' freedom or equality. She can thus affirm these principles despite their effect because she

29. Ibid.

can recognize them as the only ones, under the circumstances, that are fully consistent with the proper respect for and recognition of her fellow citizens in both their political and their nonpolitical identities. The dismal future of one aspect of her way of life is thus not a result of a failure of respect on the part of her fellow citizens, nor the product of exclusion or assimilation. And while the political society of which she is a part will be a less happy home for her than for others, I think she can still recognize it as a home, one that realizes values with which she identifies—most importantly the values associated with citizenship and collective self-rule—and that demonstrates a proper respect even for those of her values it turns out to undermine. As a result, even for those whose nonpolitical identities may be threatened by the principles adopted by a deliberatively liberal society, such a society will be worthy of reconciliation, a society to which all reasonable members can consent. It will thus be a society that, despite being characterized by a deep diversity that is neither excluded or assimilated away, is legitimate.

8.6. Conclusion

I began this chapter with a consideration of questions about mandatory civics education as a way of highlighting how the conception of citizenship that emerges from deliberative liberalism can be used to think through difficult political issues. That discussion, in turn, set the stage for a consideration of the role played by reasonable deliberation in turning members of a political society into reasonable citizens. We saw that in becoming reasonable, citizens come to attach an independent value to the results of reasonable deliberation. This value then plays a role in explaining why diverse citizens can nevertheless affirm the limitation citizenship places on their nonpolitical identities, even when those limitations are fatal to aspects of their way of life.

We thus have an answer to the second question that grounds doubt about the possibility of a legitimate liberal democratic regime. In a world like ours, marked by burdensome conceptions of citizenship and imposed identities, where not all citizens are committed to reasonable deliberation as the proper ground for political authority, we can still act reasonably in good faith. By engaging in democratic politics according to the principle of public reason and using that engagement to challenge asymmetrical distributions of constructive social power and burdensome conceptions of citizenship, we can be confident that our actions will foster the reasonableness of our fellow citizens and will thus help to bring about a world in which a legitimate liberal democratic regime is a real as well as a theoretical possibility.

If such a regime is possible, then we can reasonably work toward its realization. If we also find such a regime attractive, then we ought to undertake such work. Such work is the work of citizens, however. It must take place primarily in political deliberation with our fellow citizens. It must, that is, go beyond the confines of this, or any other, book.

Bibliography

Affeldt, Steven. "The Force of Freedom." *Political Theory* 27 (1999): 299–333.

Ajzenstadt, Janet. "Decline of Procedural Liberalism: The Slippery Slope to Secession." In *Is Quebec Nationalism Just?*, ed. Joseph Carens. Montréal: McGill-Queen's University Press, 1995.

Appiah, Anthony. *In My Father's House*. Oxford: Oxford University Press, 1992.

Bartky, Sandra Lee. *Femininity and Domination*. New York: Routledge, 1990.

Bell, Derrick. "The Rules of Racial Standing." In *Faces at the Bottom of the Well*. New York: Basic Books, 1992.

Benhabib, Seyla. *Situating the Self*. New York: Routledge, 1992.

——. "Towards a Deliberative Model of Democratic Legitimacy." In *Democracy and Difference*, ed. Seyla Benhabib. Princeton, N.J.: Princeton University Press, 1996.

Benhabib, Seyla, ed. *Democracy and Difference*. Princeton, N.J.: Princeton University Press, 1996.

Bickford, Susan. *The Dissonance of Democracy*. Ithaca, N.Y.: Cornell University Press, 1996.

Bohman, James. *Public Deliberation*. Cambridge, Mass.: MIT Press, 1997.

Bohman, James, and William Rehg, eds. *Deliberative Democracy*. Cambridge, Mass.: MIT Press, 1997.

Bratman, Michael. "Shared Cooperative Activity." *The Philosophical Review* 101 (1992): 327–341.

——. "Shared Intention." *Ethics* 104 (1993): 97–113.

Callan, Eamonn. *Creating Citizens*. Oxford: Oxford University Press, 1997.

Carrithers, Michael. *Why Humans Have Cultures*. Oxford: Oxford University Press, 1992.

Chambers, Simone. *Reasonable Democracy*. Ithaca, N.Y.: Cornell University Press, 1996.

Cohen, Joshua. "Freedom of Expression." *Philosophy and Public Affairs* 22 (1993): 207–263.

Cook, Curtis, ed. *Constitutional Predicament: Canada after the 1992 Referendum*. Montréal: McGill-Queen's University Press, 1994.

Cornell, Drucilla. *The Imaginary Domain*. New York: Routledge, 1995.

——. *At the Heart of Freedom*. Princeton, N.J.: Princeton University Press, 1998.

D'Agostino, Fred. *Free Public Reason: Making It Up as We Go*. New York: Oxford University Press, 1996.

Dent, N.J.H. *Rousseau*. Oxford: Basil Blackwell, 1988.

DuBois, W.E.B. *The Souls of Black Folk*. London: Penguin Classics, 1903.

Dworkin, Andrea. *Pornography: Men Possessing Women*. New York: Perigee, 1981.

Dworkin, Ronald. *Taking Rights Seriously*. Cambridge: Harvard University Press, 1977.

——. "Liberty and Pornography." *The New York Review of Books*, 21 October 1993, 12–15.

Dwyer, Susan, ed. *The Problem of Pornography*. Belmont, Calif.: Wadsworth, 1995.

Ellison, Ralph. *Invisible Man*. 1952. New York: Vintage, 1995.

Elster, Jon, ed. *Rational Choice*. New York: New York University Press, 1986.

Favell, Adrian. *Philosophies of Integration*. New York: St. Martin's Press, 1998.

Fish, Stanley. "Boutique Multiculturalism." In *Multiculturalism and American Democracy*, eds. Arthur M. Melzer, Jerry Weinberger, and M. Richard Zinman. Lawrence: The University Press of Kansas, 1998.

——. "Mutual Respect as a Device of Exclusion." In *Deliberative Politics*, ed. Stephen Macedo. Oxford: Oxford University Press, 1999.

Fleischacker, Samuel. *A Third Concept of Liberty*. Princeton, N.J.: Princeton University Press, 1999.

Foucault, Michel. *Discipline and Punish: The Birth of the Prison*. New York: Random House, 1975.

——. *Power/Knowledge*. Edited by Colin Gordon. New York: Random House, 1980.

——. "The Subject and Power." In *Michel Foucault: Beyond Structuralism and Hermeneutics*, eds. Herbert Dreyfus and Paul Rabinow. 2d ed. Chicago: University of Chicago Press, 1983.

Frye, Marilyn. *The Politics of Reality*. Trumansburg, N.Y.: The Crossing Press, 1983.

Galeotti, Anna Elisabetta. "Citizenship and Equality: The Place for Toleration." *Political Theory* 21 (1993): 585–605.

Galston, William. "Diversity, Toleration, and Deliberative Democracy: Religious Minorities and Public Schooling." In *Deliberative Politics*, ed. Stephen Macedo. Oxford: Oxford University Press, 1999.

Gilbert, Margaret. *On Social Facts*. Princeton, N.J.: Princeton University Press, 1989.

Greenawalt, Kent. *Religious Conviction and Political Choice*. Oxford: Oxford University Press, 1988.

Greider, William. *Who Will Tell The People*. New York: Simon and Schuster, 1992.

Grotius, Hugo. *On the Law of War and Peace*. 1625. Translated by Francis W. Kelsey. Oxford: Oxford University Press, 1925.

Guttman, Amy, and Dennis Thompson. *Democracy and Disagreement*. Cambridge: Harvard University Press, 1996.

——. "Democratic Disagreement." In *Deliberative Politics*, ed. Stephen Macedo. Oxford: Oxford University Press, 1999.

Habermas, Jürgen. *The Structural Transformation of the Public Sphere*. Translated by Thomas Burger. Cambridge, Mass.: MIT Press, 1989.

——. "Reconciliation through the Public Use of Reason: Some Remarks on John Rawls's Political Liberalism." *Journal of Philosophy* 92 (1995): 109–131.

Hardimon, Michael. *Hegel's Social Philosophy: The Project of Reconciliation*. Cambridge: Cambridge University Press, 1994.

Hegel, G.W.F. *Elements of the Philosophy of Right*. 1821. Translated by H. B. Nisbet. Cambridge: Cambridge University Press, 1991.

———. *Lectures on the History of Philosophy*. 1840. Translated by E. S. Haldane and Frances H. Simson. Lincoln: University of Nebraska Press, 1995.

Herman, Barbara. *The Practice of Moral Judgment*. Cambridge: Harvard University Press, 1993.

Hobbes, Thomas. *Leviathan*. 1651. Edited by Richard Tuck. Cambridge: Cambridge University Press, 1991.

Honig, Bonnie. *Political Theory and the Displacement of Politics*. Ithaca, N.Y.: Cornell University Press, 1993.

hooks, bell. "Sisterhood: Political Solidarity between Women." In *Feminist Social Thought*, ed. Diana Tietjens Myers. New York: Routledge, 1997.

Hornsby, Jennifer. "Speech Acts and Pornography." In *The Problem of Pornography*, ed. Susan Dwyer. Belmont, Calif.: Wadsworth, 1995.

Kant, Immanuel. *Critique of Pure Reason*. 1781/1787. Translated by Norman Kemp Smith. New York: St. Martin's Press, 1929.

———. *The Metaphysics of Morals*. 1797. Translated by Mary Gregor. Cambridge: Cambridge University Press, 1991.

Kors, Allan Charles, and Harvey A. Silverglate. *The Shadow University*. New York: The Free Press, 1998.

Korsgaard, Christine. *Creating the Kingdom of Ends*. Cambridge: Cambridge University Press, 1996.

———. *The Sources of Normativity*. Cambridge: Cambridge University Press, 1996.

Kymlicka, Will. *Liberalism, Community, and Culture*. Oxford: Clarendon Press, 1989.

———. *Multicultural Citizenship*. Oxford: Oxford University Press, 1995.

Laden, Anthony Simon. "Outline of a Theory of Reasonable Deliberation." *Canadian Journal of Philosophy* 30 (2000) 551–580.

———. "Radical Liberals, Reasonable Feminists: Reason, Objectivity, and Power in the Work of Rawls and MacKinnon." Unpublished manuscript, University of Illinois at Chicago, 2000.

———. "Republican Moments in Political Liberalism." *Croatian Journal of Philosophy* 3 (fall 2001).

Langton, Rae. "Speech Acts and Unspeakable Acts." *Philosophy and Public Affairs* 22 (1993): 292–330.

Locke, John. *Second Treatise of Government*. 1689. Edited by C. B. MacPherson. Indianapolis: Hackett, 1980.

Lugones, María, and Elizabeth Spelman. "Have We Got a Theory for You!" In *Hypatia Reborn*, eds. Azizah al-Hibri and Margaret Simons. Bloomington: Indiana University Press, 1990.

Macedo, Stephen. "Liberal Civic Education and Religious Fundamentalism: The Case of God v. John Rawls?" *Ethics* 105 (1995): 468–496.

Macedo, Stephen, ed. *Deliberative Politics: Essays on Democracy and Disagreement*. Oxford: Oxford University Press, 1999.

MacKinnon, Catharine. *Feminism Unmodified*. Cambridge: Harvard University Press, 1987.

———. *Towards a Feminist Theory of the State*. Cambridge: Harvard University Press, 1989.

———. *Only Words*. Cambridge: Harvard University Press, 1992.

MacKinnon, Catharine, and Andrea Dworkin, eds. *In Harm's Way: The Pornography Civil Rights Hearings*. Cambridge: Harvard University Press, 1997.

Manin, Bernard. "On Legitimacy and Political Deliberation." *Political Theory* 15 (1987): 338–368.

McCarthy, Thomas. "Kantian Constructivism and Reconstructivism: Rawls and Habermas in Dialogue." *Ethics* 105 (1994): 44–63.

Mill, John Stuart. *On Liberty*. 1859. Edited by Currin Shields. New York: Liberal Arts Press, 1956.

Mills, Charles. *Blackness Visible*. Ithaca, N.Y.: Cornell University Press, 1997.

——. *The Racial Contract*. Ithaca, N.Y.: Cornell University Press, 1997.

Moruzzi, Norma Claire. "A Problem with Headscarves: Contemporary Complexities of Political and Social Identity." *Political Theory* 22 (1994): 653–672.

Mouffe, Chantal. "Democratic Citizenship and the Political Community." In *Community at Loose Ends*, ed. Miami Theory Collective. Minneapolis: University of Minnesota Press, 1991.

——. "Feminism, Citizenship, and Radical Democratic Politics." In *Feminist Social Thought*, ed. Diana Tietjens Meyers. New York: Routledge, 1997.

Myers, Diana Tietjens, ed. *Feminist Social Thought*. New York: Routledge, 1997.

Neuhouser, Frederick. "Freedom, Dependence, and the General Will." *Philosophical Review* 102 (1993): 363–395.

——. *The Foundations of Hegel's Social Theory: Actualizing Freedom*. Cambridge: Harvard University Press, 2000.

Okin, Susan. *Women in Western Political Thought*. Princeton, N.J.: Princeton University Press, 1979.

Pateman, Carole. *The Sexual Contract*. Oxford: Polity Press, 1988.

Pettit, Philip. *Republicanism: A Theory of Freedom and Government*. Oxford: Oxford University Press, 1999.

Pufendorf, Samuel. *On the Duty of Man and Citizen*. 1673. Translated by Michael Silverthorne. Edited by James Tully. Cambridge: Cambridge University Press, 1991.

Rawls, John. *A Theory of Justice*. Cambridge: Harvard University Press, 1971.

——. *Political Liberalism*. Paperback edition. New York: Columbia University Press, 1996.

——. *Collected Papers*. Edited by Samuel Freeman. Cambridge: Harvard University Press, 1999.

Raz, Joseph. *The Morality of Freedom*. Oxford: Clarendon Press, 1986.

Reath, Andrews. "The Categorical Imperative and Kant's Conception of Practical Rationality." *Monist* 72 (1989): 384–410.

——. "Legislating the Moral Law." *Noûs* 27 (1994): 435–464.

Rich, Adrienne. "Compulsory Heterosexuality and Lesbian Existence." *Signs* 5 (1980): 631–660.

Richardson, Henry. "Democratic Intentions." In *Deliberative Democracy*, eds. James Bohman and William Rehg. Cambridge: MIT Press, 1997.

Rousseau, Jean-Jacques. *Oeuvres complètes*. Edited by B. Gagnebin and M. Raymond. Paris: Pléiade, 1959–1995.

——. *Letter to D'Alembert*. 1758. Translated by Allan Bloom. Glencoe, Ill.: The Free Press, 1960.

——. *The Social Contract and Other Later Political Writings*. Translated and edited by Victor Gourevitch. Cambridge: Cambridge University Press, 1997.

——. *The Discourses and Other Early Political Writings*. Translated and edited by Victor Gourevitch. Cambridge: Cambridge University Press, 1997.

Sandel, Michael. *Liberalism and the Limits of Justice*. Cambridge: Cambridge University Press, 1982.

Scanlon, T. M. "Contractualism and Utilitarianism." In *Utilitarianism and beyond*, eds. Bernard Williams and Amartya Sen. Cambridge: Cambridge University Press, 1982.

Schmidtz, David. *Rational Choice and Moral Agency*. Princeton, N.J.: Princeton University Press, 1995.

Sen, Amartya. *Inequality Reexamined*. Cambridge: Harvard University Press, 1992.

Skinner, Quentin. "The Republican Ideal of Political Liberty." In *Machiavelli and Republicanism*, eds. Gisela Bock, Quentin Skinner, and Maurizio Viroli. Cambridge: Cambridge University Press, 1990.

——. *Liberty before Liberalism*. Cambridge: Cambridge University Press, 1998.

Spelman, Elizabeth. *Inessential Woman*. Boston: Beacon Press, 1988.

Stolzenberg, Nomi. "He Drew a Circle that Shut Me Out: Assimilation, Indoctrination, and the Paradox of Liberal Education." *Harvard Law Review* 106 (1993): 581–667.

Sunstein, Cass. *The Partial Constitution*. Cambridge: Harvard University Press, 1993.

Taylor, Charles. "Explanation and Practical Reason." In *The Quality of Life*, ed. Martha Nussbaum and Amartya Sen. Oxford: Oxford University Press, 1993.

——. *Reconciling the Solitudes*. Edited by Guy LaForest. Montréal: McGill-Queen's University Press, 1993.

Taylor, Charles, et al. *Multiculturalism and the Politics of Recognition*. Edited by Amy Guttman. Princeton, N.J.: Princeton University Press, 1992.

Tully, James. "Diversity's Gambit Declined." In *Constitutional Predicament: Canada after the 1992 Referendum*, ed. Curtis Cook. Montréal: McGill-Queen's University Press, 1994.

——. *Strange Multiplicity: Constitutionalism in an Age of Diversity*. Cambridge: Cambridge University Press, 1995.

——. "Democratic Constitutionalism in a Diverse Federation." In *Ideas in Action: Essays in Politics and Law in Honor of Peter Russell*, eds. Joseph Fletcher and Jennifer Nedelsky. Toronto: University of Toronto Press, 1999.

——. "Multicultural and Multinational Citizenship." In *The Demands of Citizenship*, eds. Iain Hampsher-Monk and Catriona McKinnon. London: Continuum International, 2000.

——. "Struggles over Recognition and Distribution." *Constellations* 7 (2000): 469–482.

——. "The Unattained Yet Attainable Democracy: Canada and Quebec Face the New Century." Programme d'études sur le Québec de l'Université McGill, 2000.

Velleman, J. David. "How to Share an Intention." *Philosophy and Phenomenological Research* 57 (1997): 29–50.

West, Cornel. *Keeping Faith*. New York: Routledge, 1993.

West, Robin. "Legitimating the Illegitimate." *Columbia Law Review* 93 (1993): 1442–1459.

Westphal, Kenneth. "The Structure and Context of Hegel's Philosophy of Right." In *The Cambridge Companion to Hegel*, ed. Fred Beiser. Cambridge: Cambridge University Press, 1993.

Williams, Wendy. "The Equality Crisis: Some Reflections on Culture, Courts, and Feminism." In *Feminist Social Thought*, ed. Diana Tietjens Myers. New York: Routledge, 1997.

Young, Iris Marion. *Justice and the Politics of Difference*. Princeton, N.J.: Princeton University Press, 1990.

——. "Asymmetrical Reciprocity: On Moral Respect, Wonder, and Enlarged Thought." *Constellations* 3 (1997): 340–363.

——. "Communication and the Other: Beyond Deliberative Democracy." In *Democracy and Difference*, ed. Seyla Benhabib. Princeton, N.J.: Princeton University Press, 1996.

——. "Difference as a Resource for Democratic Communication." In *Deliberative Democracy*, eds. James Bohman and William Rehg. Cambridge, Mass.: MIT Press, 1997.

Index

natural law strand in, 34–35, 39, 41–45; on needs, 36–38; political approach of, 16; project of, 25–26; on reason, 26–30, 78; *On the Social Contract*, 25, 31–47; on the social contract, 34–35, 40–44, 46; on stability, 44–47; *The State of War*, 28–29; Charles Taylor on, 206n25

Sandel, Michael, 10n22, 170n20
Savings and loan crisis, 127–28
Scanlon, Thomas, 78n9
Schapiro, Tamar, 6n14, 109n17
Schmidtz, David, 74n3
Secession, 115n21, 179–80
Self-conception, 59–63, 66–67, 113–16. *See also* Practical identity; Identity
Self-determination, 46–47, 50–55, 59, 87, 114, 153–54, 180–85. *See also* Freedom; Self-rule
Self-reproducing institutions, 53, 59–60, 65, 187, 194–95
Self-respect, 145–46, 204–7
Self-rule, 28–30, 167, 173–74. *See also* Self-determination; Freedom
Sen, Amartya, 12n25
Sexism, 135–36, 147–48, 205–6
Sexual harassment, 147, 206
Shared action, incapacity for, 28
Shared identity: via common institutions, 51–52, 60, 169; heterogeneity of, 154; and pluralism, 105, 169; and Quebec, 179–80; via reasonable deliberation, 12, 97, 150, 203; requires mutual respect, 146
Shared intentions, 95n29
Shared purposes, 204–6
Shared understanding, 79, 83, 85
Shared will: commitment to reasonable deliberation embodies, 96, 126–27; conditions for, 37–41, 68–69; described, 36; exclusion and assimilation undermine, 13–14; homogeneity not necessary for, 63; legitimate political institutions must embody, 12, 27, 48–49, 53–54, 57–58, 65, 126–27, 132, 158; marriage as, 60–64; nonpolitical institutions which embody, 58–59; reasonable deliberation produces, 76–77, 97; Rousseau's general will as, 33, 42–44, 46; transformative aspects of, 62–63
Sikhs, 102, 165
Silencing, 142–43
Silverglate, Harvey, 4n6
Skinner, Quentin, 47n42

Social contract: establishes conditions for legitimacy, 34–35, 43–44; and fundamental interests, 31; and general will, 34–35, 44–46; Hegel's criticism of, 55; as the state's reason, 29. *See also* Deliberative strand of the social contract tradition; Natural law strand of the social contract tradition
Spelman, Elizabeth, 149n27, 154n35;
Stability: is a by-product, 187; citizens' endorsement necessary for, 118; deliberative liberalism achieves, 201–3, 209; direct pursuit of, impossible, 187; Hegel on, 51–52, 55–58, 64–67, 200; and justice, 52, 200 and legitimacy, 52–53, 55–58, 187; of practical identities, 87–88; problem of, 14, 170n21, 185; Rawls on, 199–201; of relationships, 79, 85–86; for the right reasons, 199–203; Rousseau on, 44–47
State: can address exclusion, 156–58; as coercive, 104; Hegel on, 55, 64–69, 169, 200n15
State of nature: Hegel on, 59; inhabitants of, 25–28, 37
Status quo neutrality, 160
Stolzenberg, Nomi, 165n13
Strategic decisions, 76
Subperson, 80
Sunstein, Cass, 160

Taylor, Charles, 1n1, 3n5, 78n9, 204–7
Thompson, Dennis, 12n25, 127n41, 160
Transparency, 56–57, 69
Trudeau, Pierre, 165n11
Tully, James, 3n5, 8n18, 11n23, 16, 23, 107n15, 124–25, 150n29, 160n1, 163n9, 165n16, 173–74, 177n26, 195–99

Unanimity, 10–12
Uniformity, 10–13, 23, 57, 187
Unreasonable, 105, 177
Untouchables, 142

Velleman, J. David, 95n29
Violence, 140, 148, 189n2
Voting, 121–23

Warner, Stephen, 179n29
"We"-reasons, 96–98, 104
West, Cornel, 144–45
West, Robin, 92n24
Westphal, Kenneth, 24n3